Another Side of
Bob Dylan

Bob Dylan and Victor at "The Castle" in LA before the 1965 world tour. *(Credit: Lisa Law/The Archive Agency)*

Another Side of Bob Dylan

A Personal History on the Road
and off the Tracks

Victor Maymudes

Cowritten and edited by
Jacob Maymudes

ST. MARTIN'S PRESS

New York

www.thomasdunnebooks.com

www.stmartins.com

Designed by Kathryn Parise

LIBRARY OF CONGRESS CATALOGING-IN-PUBLICATION DATA

Maymudes, Victor, author.
    Another side of Bob Dylan : a personal history on the road and off the tracks / by Victor Maymudes, cowritten and edited by Jacob Maymudes.
        p. cm.
    ISBN 978-1-250-05530-9 (hardcover)
    ISBN 978-1-4668-5843-5 (e-book)
    1. Dylan, Bob, 1941–   2. Singers—United States—Biography.
I. Maymudes, Jacob, author, editor.   II. Title.
    ML420.D98M17 2014
    782.42164092—dc23
    [B]
                                                    2014016598

St. Martin's Press books may be purchased for educational, business, or promotional use. For information on bulk purchases, please contact Macmillan Corporate and Premium Sales Department at 1-800-221-7945, extension 5442, or write specialmarkets@macmillan.com.

First Edition: September 2014

10 9 8 7 6 5 4 3 2 1

For my sister.

I know how much you miss him.

CONTENTS

~

ACKNOWLEDGMENTS

This memoir came to be through a series of unfortunate events that rocked me to my core. It was not a book I felt I could write—too painful a task, too emotionally jarring. My love and admiration for my father pulled me through the process. After the fire I was convinced that he was deserving of his moment in the spotlight, that his voice and all that was left was worthy of finally being heard. Throughout my journey I was inspired, loved, critiqued and encouraged by a few wonderful people—mavens to their industries, lifelong friends and family members: my mother, Linda Wylie; George Witte; Adam Gauntlett; Emily Schriber; Andy Greene; and Aaron Ungerleider and his family. With much love and respect, I thank you.

It felt like we were on the point of the arrow
that was going to pierce the dust.

—Victor Maymudes

Another Side of
Bob Dylan

INTRODUCTION

~

On the River's Edge

by Jacob Maymudes

My dad's ashes in the rubble of my mother's
burned stone house, January 2013. *(Courtesy: Jacob
Maymudes)*

I'm standing at the edge of the cliff looking down into the
canyon. I can see the winding river that was home to my
childhood. Snow covers the pine and cedar trees lining the river,
as it snakes around the New Mexican red clay and brown dirt
that is abundant in this part of the world. The dozen or so
frozen square miles before me were once my playground; some

of my fondest memories were found under rocks, in trees and splashing in the river of this magical place. "The Land of Enchantment" is the state motto and I believe it's solely because of this place—this secret place that only a small community of a hundred or so knows about.

My home is just below me, about five hundred feet down and half a mile ahead, centered in the middle of this majestic area. This house is our family home, my mother's home. It's a fortress of flagstone built by my mother Linda's hands over the course of fifteen years. She found the land while visiting Gary, her boyfriend at the time, now her ex and a man whom I consider my stepfather. He lives nearby on an adjacent ridge. Back then my mother decided to go to medical school for nursing in her mid-thirties; as a side project, with no money, while raising two kids on her own, she set out to design and fashion a two-story house using free flagstone she had access to from a rock quarry an hour south of here. The technique she employed was called "dry stacking," which is as simple and painful as it sounds. You take flagstone, you stack it. No mortar or cement between the pieces yet. She and Gary would stack two walls about six inches apart and then fill the gap between with cement and rebar. It took a small level of artistry, but not much. It mostly took hard work. It's the kind of long-term plan your friends would make fun of you for attempting, and chalk it up to wishful thinking. There was no time limit for construction and hardly a schedule. Many people have come to understand that my mother not only is unbreakable, but her interpretation of the impossible is merely an exercise in patience. She will achieve the impossible; it'll just take a while.

Fifteen years of construction with various helpers along the way. Bag of cement by bag of cement, and finally the house was finished. During this time she earned a master's degree in nursing and moved the family from Albuquerque to Las Vegas, New Mexico, then to Santa Fe, and finally to the house she had built stone by stone. From the start of construction to its completion, I'd gone from being a student in the fourth grade to college and living on my own in Boulder, Colorado.

My older sister, Aerie, and I would come and go from the house. Sometimes we'd make it our home while my mother was off exploring the world as a medical officer for the Peace Corps, which she did intermittently during the late 1990s. From her world travels the house became a museum of antiquities, shrines to lost loved ones and handpicked mementos placed in any worthy spot.

My tears have frozen to my cheeks. I've spent a mere ten minutes standing on this cliff this afternoon and I've been crying the whole time. It's not the home I remember visiting for my birthday in August five months ago. This is my first view of something I can't quite comprehend. That seemingly immutable fortress of stone with three-foot-thick walls had burned to an unrecognizable pile of rubble. We were wrong all those years for calling the house a bomb shelter, always eliciting a lighthearted laugh from my mother, for claiming it would be around longer than humans would occupy the planet. The house had succumbed to its one weakness, exploited by a singular design flaw. A lone wire buried deep in the wood ceiling of the bathroom sparked and ignited in the dead of winter. My mother awoke three days ago to black, billowing smoke in her bedroom. She sprang up and ran outside to fetch the hose.

It was a bitter and relentlessly cold night that only the high desert could provide. The hoses were frozen. With the house on fire, the nearest operating phone was a quarter mile up the dirt road at Gary's house. She sprinted up the road and took the shortcut through the forest, waking him and calling the fire department and local friends, who with trucks and shovels descended back down the canyon to the house. When they arrived the thick stone walls that were built to protect the house from every possible disaster became their own worst enemy by locking in the fire and encouraging hotter flames to engulf every last shred of our family history, a history marked by losses that my mother bore with stoic grace. By the early morning our family had sustained yet another catastrophic loss. Once again, my mother would be stripped down to the core and be required to start all over again with nothing. The shock would set in rapidly, and the pain would replace that shock in the days to come.

Three days have passed. One more deep breath and it's time to meet my mother in the house she's staying in. This house on the cliff was offered to her as an emergency refuge in the canyon. She could have picked a hotel or some other place that didn't have a perfect view of the charred remains of her collected life, but instead she chose to stay here. Her friend has similar style, so it was a less jarring change than a hotel. Friends of my mother would often receive unconditional gifts from her travels, so several of the items decorating the interior and exterior are actually things she had once owned and loved herself. It's the best possible transition considering the circumstances. Despite the painful view.

I walk in to find her spending time with her good friend, the local blacksmith. A soft, gentle man with an appearance hardened by heat and molten steel, his company is across the highway. My first job was with Christopher when I was thirteen, under the legal age for working and definitely too young to be cutting steel and grinding welds. For a thirteen-year-old boy it was a dream job.

I greet my mother with a long embrace, silent except for the occasional deep breath and sniffling nose. She's clearly in shock, her mind still processing the events that unfolded and the untried options that could have changed the course of the night. She smiles, but it's not an *everything is going to be fine* smile. It's a, *well, here we are again* smile. I, too, can't fathom the scale of this loss; it feels remarkably similar to losing a loved one.

There were of course the photos: my grandparents standing with my eleven-year-old mother at their farm in Macon, Georgia; my young parents and my sister, Aerie, as a baby, sitting between four-foot-high pot plants when they lived at Bob Dylan's house in Cerrillos, New Mexico. Or the photo of my dad, Victor: a typical pose sitting on the front porch of the same house, pondering the next steps in promoting concerts for a singer-songwriter named Eliza Gilkyson, who he was considering managing. Things were not going his way and it was in the midst of this realization that the photo was taken by a family friend, sixties chronicler Lisa Law.

I've read that people who suffer the loss of their home to fire say that losing the family photo albums is the hardest. I can now attest to this fact. The feeling it leaves you with is a twisting, everlasting knot in your stomach that twists more when you think of the wonderful moments in your life, knowing that the visual record has been erased. Moments that will never be repeated. In an email I sent to my mother the day I heard the news, I said simply: *All our family photos are gone, but don't worry, we'll make more.* I notice the printed letter sitting on the dining table. That's now the mantra.

The blacksmith heads home and says he'll be back in the morning to help. Gary and I have made plans to search the remains of the fire. It's been too toxic to visit in the first few days. The house was powered by twelve solar panels that stored their collected energy in eight closed-cell batteries. Needless to say, that corner of the house is covered in lead dust and highly toxic acids. We believe the rest of the house is relatively safe to explore, aside from the possibility of the rock walls collapsing.

My mother hands me a bowl of lentil soup she made and we sit at the little wood dining table and briefly talk about my journey home. I was in Reykjavik, Iceland, twenty-four hours ago. I took a four-month job there and was on the third month when Aerie called with the news. I flew nonstop to Denver and drove the five hours south. My mother and I avoid talking about the current state of the house.

I wake up jetlagged the next day. Since my mother has refused to take time off work as a nurse, I'll be searching the debris with Gary, with whom my mother is still good friends. Since he helped build the house, he's worried that something he might have done during the construction more than two decades ago helped to ignite the fire.

I head over to Gary's for a cup of coffee and some personal time. It's been months since we've last seen each other. I had commissioned several custom metal tables from him that didn't turn out exactly like I had planned, which left me feeling slighted, so we hadn't talked much on the phone. His house is a twenty-minute walk along dirt roads and through trees. Once I get there, it's as if no time has passed since the last time we'd been together. He tells me my mother's black cat is still missing, and that the insurance adjuster for the house is sending out a ballistics specialist to trace the cause of the fire.

We chat, drink coffee and wait for the fire investigator, who shows up within the hour towing a trailer that reads "Beasley Investigations & Fire Technology Inc., Expert Fire and Explosion Investigations." I guess the insurance adjuster is taking this more seriously than I had originally expected. Gary and I get into his truck and show him the way down to the house. He entertains us with recent stories of his investigations, describing a garage that belonged to a police officer that he suspected of burning down himself due to spill patterns in the concrete. Judging by his stories and the well-organized look of his monster truck, he's thorough.

We arrive. I can smell the charcoal in the air. The musk of

damp, burnt wood and plastic and metal. I see the house for the first time up close. The relentlessness of the fire is unexplainable. From a glance it looks like even the rocks burned. Entire walls of concrete and flagstone are missing, vanished into the gray dust piled on the floors. We all walk around to the front of the house and collectively notice a pile of black fur on a second-story archway that had not, at that point, collapsed. The fur is lifeless, not moving, not breathing. It's my mom's cat, the same cat that has been missing for four days. It probably starved to death or died of dehydration. More bad news that we don't want to contemplate. Since the cat was unreachable, I let out a loud meow as a last-ditch attempt to see if it has clung to one of its remaining nine lives. A minute goes by and the cat slowly lifts its head. It takes its time and eventually turns to look at us. We're all ecstatic, for this is the good news we definitely need to share with my mother. The cat slowly makes its way down and proceeds straight to Gary, a welcoming friendly face in its life. With the missing cat found and fed, we begin our inspection and search of the house.

Rocks have caved in on all sides, scattering debris and ash into piles and piles of destroyed memories. The fire inspector begins by chasing wires on the roof, looking closely and examining the frays and melted plastic casings of each. Gary and I start sifting in the bedroom for anything spared. Not much is left so we make our way to the living room. I climb the central heap of rocks, looking at one of the only standing walls. In the hallway between what was the office and the living room is where I find him. My father.

Victor Maymudes, my dad, is sitting nearly untouched in what was once supposed to be an air vent encased in quarter-inch steel but open on two sides—one side leading to the living room, the other into the shrine room. Both rooms are completely destroyed.

The shrine room was where my mother honored loved ones like Anatoli Boukreev, the world-renowned mountain climber, and Dr. Greg Gordon, an acclaimed oncologist. Both died climbing in the Himalayas; both changed my mother's life forever. They were her lovers, one after another and years apart.

At the time of his death in October 1993, Dr. Gregory Gordon was the director of the Cancer Treatment Center at St. Vincent Hospital in Santa Fe. He was a dedicated physician and an avid outdoorsman. Of all my mother's suitors he was the most practical, an educated man who was as tough as he was compassionate. His adventurous spirit influenced my life at a young age; it's from his encouragement that I took on white-water kayaking and rock climbing, personal favorites of his. Our relationship wasn't an easy one; he knew I was lacking fatherly guidance, which he provided in spades, but it came at the height of my childhood rebellion. He was compassionate, but he wasn't gentle. We would spar over most issues; the one that sticks out the most was his constant critique of how much reading I was doing. It was never enough for him. He would toss out brazen clichés like "useless as tits on a nun" when he was trying to rattle my cage into doing what he was asking for. To this day I can't remember the point he was trying to make with the nun cliché, but the comedy of it has been burned into my lexicon.

His intense attitude fueled his quest to be the best, the best doctor, the best kayaker, best mountain climber. In 1993 he decided to climb Mt. Pumori in the Everest Region of the Himalayas, a 7,161-meter (23,494-foot) mountain sometimes referred to as Everest's Daughter, mostly due to its translated name, "Unmarried Daughter" in the Sherpa language. Greg wanted to push himself physically as hard as he had pushed himself mentally; at forty-seven he had reached the top of the ladder professionally and climbing Pumori was a step away from climbing Mt. Everest.

In the days and weeks leading up to his expedition I would poke and prod him as hard as he would me, and on several occasions I would make the off-color remark, "If you die, I get your kayak!" He would push the idea aside as silliness. I have few regrets in my life, but repeatedly making that statement is one of them. Greg fell to his death descending after he summited. It is believed he was suffering from acute mountain sickness, either pulmonary edema or cerebral edema. Both cause dizziness, light-headedness, fatigue and headaches. These symptoms may have led him to forget to attach himself to the safety rope in a particularly treacherous section of the descent. When he slipped there was nothing to catch him before he fell over one thousand feet. I remember waking up the morning that news had traveled back home, the first time it snowed that year, October 31, 1993. It was my first real experience losing a loved one. Half the city of Santa Fe seemed to have attended his memorial service. The main newspaper of New Mexico, the *New Mexican*, put news about his death on its front page.

Greg's death brought the Himalayas to our front door in New Mexico. From that October forward the Himalayas became a common place for Mother to be found. She traveled there to pay her respects to where Greg was buried, she went back to trek on her own and was repeatedly invited back by elite mountain climbers she met along the way. I was fifteen in 1996 when she brought me along on an expedition led by Henry Todd, a Scotsman, to climb Mt. Everest. She was invited on the team as the group's medical professional. Her intention wasn't to climb but to run the basecamp medical tent. This expedition also provided her another great opportunity; she would get to spend a couple months with the only man she had fallen in love with since Greg's death, Anatoli Boukreev, a quiet, thoughtful and incredibly fit man who spoke a few words in English and the rest in Russian. I have many fond and slightly odd memories of them together. I would wake up for school in Santa Fe, New Mexico, in the dead of winter and be caught off guard by Anatoli butt naked with my mother, standing outside in the snow, bathing with buckets of cold water. Baffling, I suppose, but knowing who he was and what he had accomplished, his discipline was not something to question.

Anatoli Nikolaevich Boukreev was a Kazakhstani mountaineer who successfully climbed seven of the fourteen eight-thousander peaks, peaks above eight thousand meters (twenty-six thousand feet), all without supplemental oxygen. Between 1989 and 1997 Anatoli summited eighteen times on peaks above eight thousand meters. He was known as a world-class mountaineer among the international climbing groups for summiting K2 in

1993 and Mt. Everest from the North Ridge route in 1995, but it wasn't until he saved several climbers during the deadly 1996 climbing season on Everest that he became more widely known. He was criticized by Jon Krakauer in his book *Into Thin Air* regarding his actions and felt so unjustly characterized that he penned his own public response titled *The Climb*, which became a *New York Times* bestseller. After its publication in 1997 Boukreev departed on a fateful expedition to Annapurna in Nepal with mountaineering friends Simone Moro, an accomplished mountaineer, and Dimitri Sobolev, a cinematographer from Kazakhstan. Anatoli and Dimitri were killed in an avalanche in the first few weeks of the expedition. In the days that followed my mother flew to Nepal and led rescue efforts by helicopter, with the assistance of teams of rescuers equipped with dogs. She was unable to locate the bodies of Anatoli or Dimitri. The following year she mounted a plaque as a memorial at Annapurna base camp, inscribed with Anatoli's personal mantra, "Mountains are not stadiums where I satisfy my ambition to achieve, they are the cathedrals where I practice my religion." In 2002 my mother edited his memoirs and published them under the title *Above the Clouds: The Diaries of a High-Altitude Mountaineer*. The original manuscript and the thousands of photos Anatoli took along his travels were consumed by the fire.

My father, Victor, died twelve years prior to the fire. His ashes were put in a decorative cardboard box that was placed in the metal enclosure attached to the shrine room and living room. A fitting place. The box was eight inches square, veiled in gold leaf and blue paint and designed by Norma Cross, my mother's closest friend, who met my father in 1963 while working as a cocktail waitress at the Gaslight Cafe in New York. During that time Norma had an intimate off-and-on relationship with a promising young musician named Robert Zimmerman. The fire had incinerated the box and left behind a perfectly cubic Victor Maymudes. My beloved father had been baked for the second time since death. For a lifelong marijuana smoker it was a fitting fate, and later I would make this joke often; finding humor in whatever I could was a long-standing coping mechanism. It saw me through the deaths of Greg and Anatoli, and helped me negotiate life with Victor. Now with the loss of the family home, I would once again turn to humor to soften the pain.

The image of my father neatly packed as a cube of ashes, the only thing left relatively untouched, shatters me like a pane of glass. No number of jokes will help me for the time being.

My father died in front of me from an aneurysm in 2001, and that day twelve years ago is still on my list of things I need to process. So for the time being I'm going to leave him where I found him, a cube of ash in a vent, which is a typical action in dealing with the loss of my father. For twelve years I have avoided confronting his death, removing myself from discussions of him and steering clear of his friends and colleagues. It was all too painful. It is, however, extremely comforting that his ashes magically survived such a destructive fire.

The fire inspector concludes that faulty wires were the primary cause, with built-up residue in the upstairs fireplace also contributing. There was no foul play and the insurance claim can proceed. Given the circumstances, today was a good day. The black cat and I meet my mother for dinner in the house overlooking the canyon and we talk briefly about the next steps. She is wary of making any decisions and still needs plenty of space.

A few days later, I head back to Denver for my flight to the land of ice and fire to see out my contract.

My time in Reykjavik passes with ease and I speak to my mom often. At the end of the month I hop on my returning flight to Los Angeles, where my little bungalow in Venice and my lovely girlfriend of two years awaits me. My bungalow is a small two-bedroom house two miles from the beach. It was built in the 1930s and has had some remodeling but still retains its vintage charm. I've turned one bedroom into an office where I work on visual-effects projects for feature films, commercials and the occasional music video. After my father's death I picked up some of his rugs and various bits of furniture, including his favorite toaster oven, a twenty-year-old Black & Decker that still works perfectly. Some things are just made to last.

A few days into being back I settle in quickly. I have a free moment and decide to digitally process some photos of my Icelandic trip. I sit in my chair, turn on my computer and monitor and notice a box that my Aunt Zicel had given me the year before, a box she was going to ship to my mother but decided to give to me instead, because we both lived in Los Angeles and I could deliver it by hand to my mother on my next visit to New Mexico.

My heart sinks and tears pool in my eyes. This box, which

I've never opened, contains a Sony microcassette player that my father had purchased thirteen years ago. It also contains a dozen or so tapes on which he recorded his memoirs. These tapes are the last remaining hint of my father's existence, his voice and some of the wildest stories of his time and travels with his friend, Bob Dylan, with whom he worked in many different roles for forty years. These tapes were part of his writing process for an autobiography he was writing when he unexpectedly passed away; the book promised a peek into the inner circle of his legendary friend. The secrecy that surrounds Bob is well known and part of his mystique. He's one of the few living icons who never has faced a public scandal.

Now, twelve years after Victor's death, I finally have the urge to listen to the tapes. I'm afraid that if I don't listen to them they'll suffer the same fate as everything else our family has held on to. I'll wake up one day and they'll be gone forever.

CHAPTER 1

~

A Brief History

Hand-drawn poster for the Unicorn Cafe.
When the artist presented it to Victor, he
loved it for its eclectic hand-drawn style;
Victor's partner Herb Cohen denounced
it as amateurish for the same reasons.
(Courtesy: Jacob Maymudes)

Altogether my father recorded twenty-four hours of audio chronicling his relationship with Bob Dylan, Dennis Hopper, Joan Baez, Ramblin' Jack Elliott, Wavy Gravy, David Crosby, Tom Petty, the rest of the Traveling Wilburys and a few others who made up his inner circle of friends.

It's interesting and fortunate, in my opinion, that he chose this process for writing rather than something more traditional. If he only wrote what he was thinking, I believe there would be less of a chance of those pages being preserved over a decade later. Everything in this box in front of me seems brand new, aside from the deteriorating foam attached to the microphone.

There are several reasons he chose to record his voice rather than write. The simplest reason: My father always claimed he wasn't a writer and said on occasion it wasn't his preferred method of communicating. He was a conversationalist, an intelligent man with street smarts and a firm grasp of politics and current events. In his teens and twenties his education took place in coffee shops and music venues, not in the classroom. Nowhere is this more evident than in the opening paragraph of his term paper, dated 1956:

> In the following paper you will find that I have just about broken all the rules of proper grammar. For this I apologize. I realize I could do without doing this, but I do not feel that I can express myself to my satisfaction unless I write the way I talk.

Victor grew up with a sense of rebellion, most likely influenced by his parents' leadership of unions, social groups and religious fraternal orders. He was witness to them standing up for what they believed in, even when those beliefs ran contrary to the law. He adopted a mentality that he expressed to me when I was a child by saying, "We're a family of outlaws, not criminals, and that's a very important distinction. In order to do what's right, sometimes you have to live outside the law." As a nine-year-old child my interpretation of this was empowering, though sometimes in a way my mother surely regretted.

How his parents, my grandparents, indoctrinated him is complex and extends back hundreds of years. Both died from old age before I was a teenager, so with extensive research I've been able to piece together their history and plausible explanations for their ability to lead and protest.

Abe and Goldie Maymudes moved to New York City in 1920 from Brock, Poland, a small town located on the Bug River. The river was used heavily in the early 1900s to ship lumber from Poland to Germany. Both of Victor's parents lived in the same town as kids, but were only acquaintances. As teenagers they belonged to a Jewish organization for young boys and girls called Maccabee by the Germans and Herzliya by the Jews. Abe was the leader of the boys' section, Goldie the leader of the girls. Herzliya was a political and social club, embodying the spirit of the Russian Revolution at the time. Goldie and Abe were fifteen and sixteen respectively. The club was ultimately dissolved when Poland went to war against Russia in 1920. Goldie said in an interview in 1989:

The First World War really shook up the society. The youngsters went out from the yeshivas and from the *chedorim* [religious schools], and they went on to more worldly things. They went to learn; Maymudes [Abe] went to a German school for boys. We all went into regular government city schools to learn the language and to become more worldly people. This was a great change in our life. We stepped outside of the boundaries of our parents keeping us in their religious form.

Both Goldie and Abe came from extremely religious families. Goldie's grandfather on her father's side, my great-great-grandfather, was a *dayen*, a student of law and a rabbi. As the *dayen* he was the leader of the village, Brock. As for Abe, his lineage has been traced back thirteen generations to the Spanish Middle Ages, when the family name supposedly changed from Maimonides to Maymudes. This name change vaguely suggests the Maymudes lineage is connected to Moses Maimonides, the preeminent medieval Sephardic Jewish philosopher, astronomer and one of the most prolific and influential Torah scholars of the Middle Ages.

I've personally had a hard time believing this connection through our bloodline, but I admit the possibility despite lacking any hard proof. Maimonides's only son, Avraham, continued his father's legacy as a great scholar. As the history is written, the office of Nagid, the Jewish governing power, was presided over by the Maimonides family for four consecutive generations until the end of the fourteenth century.

Abe and Goldie's parents, my great-grandparents, fell on hard times after World War One. Work with decent-paying wages was hard to come by, so separately the families decided to move to New York City on the same day on the same ship in

1920. Abe's family, having less money, bought tickets in second class, while Goldie's family traveled in first class. Abe remembered seeing her once on the ship in passing. They were still only friends.

Once in New York the families both joined a left-wing Jewish organization. One afternoon during a boat outing on the Hudson River, Abe finally approached Goldie for a date. Within the next five years they would be married, and by 1930 Goldie had given birth to August, Victor's older brother.

During this time in the early 1920s, they both taught classes for the Workmen's Circle, a Yiddish language–oriented Jewish-American fraternal organization committed to social justice. In 1922 there was a contentious political rift in the organization's top brass, which led to the creation of the leftist International Workers Order (IWO). The IWO was established in 1930, promoting leftist, progressive values and operating as a fraternal mutual aid organization and insurance provider. Members were provided with low-cost health and life insurance, as well as medical and dental clinics. The organization also supported foreign-language newspapers, cultural and educational activities and operated a summer camp and cemeteries for its members. The Jewish Section of the IWO was one of thirteen other sections, including Italian, Ukrainian, Greek, Portuguese, Spanish, English and other language branches. The Jewish/Yiddish branch was the largest and, in Los Angeles, one of the most important Jewish organizations in the first half of the twentieth century. The IWO at its peak had over two hundred thousand

members, of which one third were Jewish. The Jewish section
of the International Workers Order was also referred to as the
Jewish People's Fraternal Order (JPFO).

In 1934, over a decade into their employment with the JPFO/
IWO, Abe and Goldie moved across the country and transferred to teaching in the Los Angeles branch. In 1935, Goldie
gave birth to Victor at the Los Angeles County Hospital.

The following year Abe was promoted from teaching to the
president of the Los Angeles chapter of the JPFO. His organizational and political role as a teen was resurrected there. After
the promotion they bought their first home in Rosemead,
California, about twenty-five miles east of Los Angeles. On
May 31, 1946, Goldie gave birth to Victor's younger sister, Zicel
Maymudes.

When Victor was fifteen, Abe was transferred back to New
York to become president of the entire organization. At the
same time the Special Committee on Un-American Activities
of the U.S. House of Representatives investigated the JPFO for
what they declared was a "huge patronage machine furnishing
positions for a host of Communist functionaries, who serve as
the party's controlling commissars within the organization."

The Los Angeles developments followed the pattern of the
nationwide McCarthy-era witch-hunt. The IWO was placed
on the U.S. Attorney General's list of "subversive" organizations on December 5, 1947, and on December 14, 1950, the New
York State Insurance Department moved to liquidate the
Order on grounds that its significant cash reserves, far beyond
what commercial insurers were required to maintain, would be

turned over to the enemy in the event of war with the Soviet Union.

This happened despite Abe using his influence to raise over four hundred thousand dollars from the sale of war bonds to his organization's members, an act that he was congratulated for in a letter from Major Prayski, chairman of the War Savings Staff of the Treasury Department. He was informed that the army was naming a heavy bomber "the Spirit of Boyle Heights" to honor the JPFO/IWO, which maintained its Los Angeles offices in Boyle Heights. I assume naming a heavy bomber after a group that has secular and Communist ideology is a rare occasion for the United States military.

After a four-year heated struggle, the Jewish Community Council (which became the Jewish Federation of Los Angeles in 1959) ostracized the JPFO from the Jewish community, froze the JPFO's assets and worked toward its dissolution. The Los Angeles Community Council also began a process of halting support for the other Jewish community centers in Los Angeles— the Soto-Michigan Community Center and the City Terrace Cultural Center. Within a few years, not only was the JPFO destroyed, but so too were the other most important Jewish cultural institutions in Los Angeles.

Abe left the organization in 1950 and moved the family to Pacoima near Los Angeles. As the former president of a suspected Communist front, finding new employment was tricky for Abe during the McCarthy era. With the family in a desperate spot financially, Goldie took to raising chickens and selling eggs to keep the family afloat.

From Victor's birth to age sixteen, he was witness to a committed social and political philosophy. His parents cared about their community and actively protected it by educating others, leading demonstrations and offering social services. What the government labeled as illegal was actually a peaceful organization, patriotic to the United States and nourishing positive growth in their communities. They were defined as outlaws while doing what they felt was morally right and just.

In 1951 the family moved to Canoga Park to start a larger chicken farm. Sixteen-year-old Victor took an interest in carpentry and helped construct a large-scale chicken coop for the family. This type of construction and carpentry intrigued him and, upon his mother's suggestion, he decided to make it his trade. In a college essay, Victor recounted that he was able to find construction work nearby at the rate of three fifty per hour and felt on top of the world. After a few weeks of work, he claimed to have more money than he knew what to do with.

When Victor turned eighteen in 1953, he was sent a draft letter and was required to attend an evaluation. His political and social ideology was heavily influenced by his parents' role as community organizers, and the idea of war or fighting for causes that contradicted his beliefs was something he would rail against. He attended the evaluation stoned and when asked if he was willing to shoot the enemy, he responded with, "If you give me a gun, I'll shoot everyone around me. Including you." His aggressive response wasn't born of inherent madness; it was a calculated statement targeted at failing the psych profile. He was deemed unfit for the draft and let go.

By 1955 a twenty-year-old Victor was entering the new culture of beatniks, music, art and drugs that Jack Kerouac would capture in *On the Road*, which was published in 1956. He and his friend Herb Cohen decided to open a coffee shop. They would become partners in the traditional sense; Herb would manage the business, and Victor would design and build the look and feel of the cafe. That year, in all of the city, there wasn't a single counterculture hangout or coffee shop. What they were planning was the first of its kind for Los Angeles: a home for live music and poetry; a reading room with a collection of hip books and ample space to play chess. It would quickly become a place where rebellion could thrive.

They found a perfect location in the heart of Hollywood at 8907 Sunset Blvd, the center of the Sunset Strip. Together they named the cafe: the Unicorn. For marketing they put posters up in liberal bookstores, music venues and any place that had a sense of hipness and a taste for folk music. Their posters were hand drawn with large hippie-looking characters playing guitars and sipping espressos. Swirling lines intertwined with slogans such as, "Where casual craznicks climb circular charcoal curbs for cool calculated confabulations" and "Espresso espression sessions on the patio." The cafe was painted entirely black inside and pictures of nude women hung upside down on the walls. They were defining what hip was and they nailed it. Once the place was built, Victor would reach out to musician friends and poets to book performances at the cafe.

When they opened the doors, the Unicorn was instantly a hit. Queues would stretch down the street and around the block. They had tapped right into something bigger than themselves, a cultural divide precipitated by the strict mentality of the 1950s. What they created didn't happen by chance, it was built by the entropy of a jaded youth reaching out for something to identify with. My father told me on many occasions about the feeling in the air at this time, as if everyone was waiting for something to happen. Some change of consciousness, like a giant wave that starts way out in the middle of the ocean. You know it's coming, you just don't know when it'll arrive or how big it's going to be. The venues for this revolution were being built, like the Unicorn; Victor would say they just needed a figurehead, a voice. They were waiting for someone to show up on the scene, someone who could reach across the oceans and connect people.

Marlon Brando, Dennis Hopper, Odetta, Peter Fonda and many other Hollywood A-listers would come to the Unicorn and hang out. Victor came up with a novel idea of putting brandy extract in lattes, which then became the must-have trendy drink of 1958. Worried parents would call in, asking why their teenage daughters and sons smelled like whiskey after an evening at the cafe. Police would routinely stop in and check for alcohol in the drinks but to their dismay couldn't find any, despite the strong odor of whiskey.

In the evenings Lenny Bruce would come by after working at Duffy's Gaieties and stage his own special comedy shows. Bruce's rise to the status of cultural icon began in the mid-1950s.

The iconoclastic edginess that would be his trademark was developed at the Unicorn and other clubs on the Sunset Strip. In his autobiography, *How to Talk Dirty and Influence People*, Bruce describes the importance of the freedom that came from venues like this:

> Four years working in clubs—that's what really made it for me—every night: doing it, doing it, doing it, getting bored and doing different ways, no pressure on you, and all the other comedians are drunken bums who don't show up, so I could try anything.

Police were troubled by Bruce's use of the word "cocksucker," and his use of the phrase "to come" (in a sexual sense) to the point that he was arrested for a performance at the Unicorn.

Herb and Victor also hired the "hippest" waitresses. They were referred to as being as mean as snakes, women fallen from grace. Waitresses would stare you down with menacing glares and have little appetite for wasting their time with your service. Departing from the chivalry of the 1950s, when service was king, these unruly waitresses were trend-setters in their own right. Once, Steve McQueen was accidentally denied entry due to overcrowding, when the hostess tending the door didn't recognize him and didn't care. It was the hottest spot in Hollywood, which put Victor in the center of the counterculture movement in Los Angeles. The following year, people trying to replicate the success of the Unicorn would open clones all around Los Angeles.

Paul Butterfield was an American blues vocalist and harmonica player who founded the Paul Butterfield Blues Band in the early 1960s and performed at the original Woodstock Festival. In 1966 Paul used the Unicorn to record his band's album *The Butterfield Blues Band Live at Unicorn Coffee House.*

During the time of the Unicorn Cafe, Victor moved to Topanga Canyon, a hippie community on the outskirts of Los Angeles in the Santa Monica Mountains. There he settled in with his friend Will Geer, who had a large estate. The same A-list attendees of the Unicorn would also take refuge at Will Geer's place with Victor. Woody Guthrie, Dennis Hopper, Peter Fonda, the group Peter, Paul and Mary and the singer Odetta were just a few of the people Victor became close friends with while living there.

Victor and his business partner started having issues with each other. Money and greed caused conflict in their relationship. Herb had a reputation for being abrasive and tough. The American folk rock musician, record producer and arranger Jerry Yester is quoted as saying:

Herbie was a lot scarier than people would think. They'd think he was a kind of pudgy Jewish guy, but he was absolutely terrifying in conflict. I mean, he had a box of hand grenades in the trunk of his car.

Herb Cohen started managing bands in the early 1960s. The first band was the Modern Folk Quartet, followed by the Mothers of Invention with Frank Zappa. Later Cohen and Zappa created several record labels, DiscReet, Straight and Bizarre. Alice Cooper, Captain Beefheart, Lenny Bruce, Ted Nugent's band the Amboy Dukes all released albums through Cohen and Zappa's record labels. Linda Ronstadt once said that Cohen "wasn't one to coddle his artists, he didn't let me get caught up with my reflection in the mirror." Herb Cohen signed Linda Ronstadt after hearing her perform at the Troubadour in Los Angeles during an open mic night. Victor wasn't the only one who found it difficult to maintain a relationship with Herb Cohen; one by one his business ventures with Frank Zappa, Linda Ronstadt and even Tom Waits ended in lawsuits. Jac Holzman, founder of Elektra Records, says that "something always went wrong at the end" regarding Cohen's business relationships.

After a falling out with Herb Cohen on the business side of the Unicorn, in the late 1950s Victor moved on to promoting concerts and getting deeper into the music scene. He partnered with Dan Gordon, Odetta's husband, to form a production company. They named themselves Dandetta Productions and started putting on shows with Miles Davis, Hugh Romney (Wavy Gravy), the Clancy Brothers, Joan Baez, Peter, Paul and Mary, Lenny Bruce, Ramblin' Jack Elliott and most importantly Odetta herself. Their main venue was the Santa Monica Civic Auditorium. In addition to promoting concerts, Victor took on trying to manage Wavy Gravy and Ramblin' Jack Elliott and began booking shows for them at cafes and little clubs around the country.

Wavy Gravy, born Hugh Nanton Romney, was a clown in the literal sense and used his talents in comedy to become a political pundit. Romney's clown persona actually resulted from his political activism. The police at demonstrations frequently apprehended him, so he decided he would be less likely to be arrested if he dressed as a clown. "Clowns are safe," he would say.

Ramblin' Jack, on the other hand, was a folky country singer who Victor met in 1952. Ramblin' Jack was born as Elliot Charles Adnopoz in Brooklyn to Jewish parents in 1931. He acquired his fascination with cowboy culture as a boy from attending rodeos at Madison Square Garden. His fascination led him to run away from home at age fifteen and join a touring rodeo founded by Colonel Jim Eskew. His rebellion was fueled by his father's relentless pressure on him to become a surgeon. Young Ramblin' Jack lasted three months on the tour before his parents tracked him down and had him sent home. His parents physically removed him from the cowboy lifestyle but the impression left by a singing rodeo clown on the tour named Brahmer Rogers imprinted options for a new identity that he would later adopt in life. Back home, rather than taking up medical school, Elliott taught himself guitar and started busking for a living. Through the years, his love of music took him on a path straight to Woody Guthrie, with whom he stayed and worked as an apprentice. In 1952 Ramblin' Jack introduced Victor to numerous provocative people, including Ralph Bellamy, then president of the Screen Actors Guild, Woody Guthrie and his close friend Cisco Houston, an American folksinger who lived over the hill from Los Angeles in the San Bernardino Valley. It was Ramblin' Jack who originally brought Victor to Will Geer's in Topanga Canyon.

Victor would continue to work with Wavy and Ramblin' Jack throughout the fifties and early sixties.

Then in 1961, Ramblin' Jack and Wavy, on separate occasions, told my father that he needed to go to the Gaslight in New York City and meet a promising new kid on the folk scene by the name of Bob Dylan.

CHAPTER 2

~

Tapes One and Two

There but for the Grace of a Falling Rock

Bob and Victor share a smoke, 1964. *(Copyright © 2014 Edward A. Chavez/The Archive Agency. Courtesy: Maia Chavez Larkin)*

A ll the audiotapes sitting on my desk are simply labeled one through thirteen, except for Tape One. It's also labeled 1961, which is when Victor met Bob Dylan for the first time. I'm on the verge of listening to Tape One, and it's a moment I've been dreading. I can't understand why it's so hard for me to take this step. It feels like I'm opening a wound that didn't heal correctly. When I was seventeen I took a month-long wilderness EMT class, studied the ins and outs of advanced emergency medicine. I know that sometimes you must reopen wounds to clean them, reset bones and restitch correctly. I'm aware of the potential benefits of such an act despite the chance of excruciating pain. For some reason—my own bizarre, twisted logic—I'd rather endure the emotional damage than confront this box with the remote chance of coming to peace with my father's death.

I'm looking at these tapes with fond memories. I see him playing Go, the ancient Chinese board game. He's sitting at his homemade office desk in the living room of his Pacific Palisades shack. This is where I saw my father eighty percent of the time in the last few years of his life, relentlessly playing Go right at the desk.

He had, for the most part, given up playing chess, which by my reckoning was his and Dylan's favorite pastime together. When I search online for "Dylan playing chess," every picture of Dylan shows him playing with my dad and only with my dad. Maybe he stopped playing because of where his relationship stood with Dylan at that moment. In 1999 there had been a huge fight between them that centered on my sister, Aerie, and her employment at a coffee shop Victor built in 1998 and operated, which Bob financed. My dad named it the 18th Street Coffee House due to its geographical location on 18th Street and Broadway in Santa Monica. The fight was so monumental that a couple years later, Bob wrote Victor out of his life in his own book, *Chronicles*. He didn't mention him once.

Maybe I'm digging too far into why he stopped playing chess; perhaps he just liked playing Go more these days. Or maybe the answer to this is recorded on the tapes in front of me. Maybe the answer to a lot of questions about their relationship is recorded on these tapes.

I take a deep breath. I put Tape One into the machine, clench my jaw and hit play. White noise and little pops and crackles are coming through the speakers, and then there he is! My father's booming, deep voice has taken over the room.

Well, I just can't believe it. All you have to do is push those two buttons down, and it's recording! It's a beautiful thing.

I hear my father take a deep breath.

It's the kind of voice that can command an audience. The roadies on tour used to call him "Victator" in jest. With a voice like his, you wouldn't want to be on the receiving end of a scolding. I know this from personal experience.

~

Tape One

So this is it. I'm going to try and give a little rundown of my life and times with Bob, which started around 1961. I'll start with my first encounter with him with the aid of Ramb-

lin' Jack Elliot and work my way to this very moment, and it's
neither my intention nor my desire to dwell on the negative. If I
could erase from my mind all the negative memories from my
life, I would. Not just the negative stuff between Bob and me,
but all of it—Hitler, Stalin, bankruptcy, all of it. I want to remember the great stuff; the stuff that really moved people;
the stuff that gave them comfort in their own struggle. All over
the planet Bob made people feel better, and I got to be a part
of that. People tell me about it, teachers tell me about it: how
they taught their kids in Russia, Israel and Spain and beyond;
how they used Bob's lyrics to teach their kids, and they empha-
size how significant words can be. Even when the words they're
focusing on are not the correct use of the language, the words
can still be emotionally powerful. They give Bob a lot of credit,
like a modern-day Shakespeare. And who knows . . . Shakespeare could have been a terrible guy, even Einstein had skeletons in his closet and collectively we recall only the good. I hope
this book is an assent on the beautiful, not the dumb. I want to
help people remember the great, the magic that was those early
days. The miserable shit that took place can be forgotten, for it
won't help anybody.

I have so much to say in respect of how amazing it was for me;
how much of a positive force he was for me and how truly wonderful our great adventure was. It was my own magical mystery
tour. I lived many people's dreams on the road with Bob; because of that I have more memories than I could fit into any one
book.

This book will be about a phenomenon that started in the late fifties and sixties, and in a way I saw it coming. I saw the winds blowin' and I rode that initial wave of change. I feel it chose me out of circumstance. There but for the grace of a falling rock.

~

The audiotape stops. I'm in tears but I'm smiling. My father is alive and well. I hear excitement in his voice. It's been twelve years since I've heard him and this excitement and tone is a welcome change from the last time we spoke on the phone, a mere ten hours before his death.

~

The cultural energy that created a need for the Unicorn Cafe in Los Angeles was present everywhere in America at the turn of the sixties. Every major city needed a gathering spot for people who were dissatisfied with the status quo and felt the impending change. Europe has had places for centuries where similar crowds collected. We were beat poets and writers, blues and folk musicians, painters and artists, actors and directors; we were scientists, philosophers, entrepreneurs and humorists looking for new ways to express what we felt but could hardly articulate about our times.

In the United States, the idea of the coffeehouse as the locus of all this activity had its roots in New York's Greenwich Village, where the original gathering spots from the twenties and thirties still stood: Caffe Reggio, the Rienzi, and the White Horse Tavern. There were clubs uptown in Harlem and all kinds of places spread around the city. But alternative clubs for

white, educated, middle-class Americans was a new idea; the
Village was the center. People came from around the world to
open new studios and theaters, to read poetry and make music
on its bare coffeehouse stages. It was a platform for young
singers from all over the world; a broad range of people, from
American Indians like Buffy Sainte-Marie, who toured and
raised awareness of Native Americans and also performed with
Joni Mitchell, Pete Seeger, Leonard Cohen, to African, Carib-
bean and European singers. They were all on the scene in the
Village.

The original idea to open the Unicorn Cafe had come to me
on a visit to Greenwich Village, and my trips back to the Village
were regular opportunities for me to stay in touch with what
was happening everywhere.

It would be one of these regular trips that changed the
course of my life. In the spring of 1961 Ramblin' Jack mentioned to me I should meet a singer-songwriter in New York;
Jack wanted to introduce me because he felt I was the right kind
of producer-manager type. He thought maybe I could help this
new guy out. Jack gave me the impression that he felt this guy
was doing what *he* was doing, but better; that this kid possibly
had an ability that could go further and touch more people than
what he had. This was a delicate thing for him to express to me.
He found something deeply profound in this person.

An opportunity to head east arose that July, so I flew into La
Guardia Airport and Ramblin' Jack picked me up on the curb
and took me to Odetta's apartment complex, which is where I
was going to be staying over the course of the next few weeks.

Odetta was touring in Europe and offered her place to me. Her duet single with Harry Belafonte, "There's a Hole in My Bucket," which landed her at number 32 on the UK Singles Chart, was paving her way for a financially successful tour. Back in New York she was amassing much notoriety, having recently been dubbed "the Queen of American folk music" by Martin Luther King Jr.

Later that evening, Jack picked me up and we headed toward MacDougal Street in Greenwich Village. We arrived and walked down into the Gaslight Cafe. The performers that night were Dave Van Ronk, who we called the Mayor of MacDougal Street, Fred Neil and Phil Ochs—all folksingers. Dave was the master of ceremonies and was introducing everyone on stage.

I had a little episode of déjà vu as I walked in: A few years before that night I was actually living in the inner courtyard of this very same building, and while I was there I dug dirt out of what was to become the Gaslight Cafe. I stayed in a little apartment in the middle of the rear building; my only view out the windows was fire escapes. It was one of the only buildings located in the center of the block, so it was a stand-alone structure behind the main building that was on the street. It was a historical building and one of the first to have lit gas available in the city. It was built before electricity was available in New York City. Another first for the building was that it had a bathroom on each floor that was available to be shared by the two apartments on each floor. My apartment consisted of three rooms, remodeled to include its own bathroom, a bedroom and a small kitchen and living room.

The owners of the building were the guys from the Florida Orange Growers. They tricked a wealthy kid named John Mitchell into investing so they could remodel. There was some funny business with money and John Mitchell eventually sued with the help of his dad, who hired big-time lawyers. They won, and John took over the building and opened the Gaslight in the basement just below a restaurant called the Kettle of Fish. The basement was filled all the way up to street level with dirt. It was buried on purpose a long time ago. This was my first time back seeing it in action.

Nearby were places I spent a lot of time, like Izze Young's Folklore Center, the Bitter End, Village Vanguard, Cafe Wha? and Cafe Bizarre. I helped to open the latter in August 1957, and even produced their first show with Odetta and Dave Van Ronk. I considered this *my* area, and the Gaslight was the new hip spot that I had yet to experience in its glory.

We walked downstairs and it's this dark place, wood tables and chairs in the center and booths on the sides. Only amber-colored candles lighting the room and it's much darker than what would be legal. Dave Van Ronk is onstage singing, "Cocaine, cocaine, all around my weary brain." I instantly felt like it was a fantastic spot.

There's a stage at the end of the room with the kitchen sitting behind it. Dressing rooms are upstairs. I noticed Bill Cosby walking around. He wasn't performing that particular night, but he was a regular figure in the Village.

And there was Bob.

He was sitting at a table on the right side with a couple of guys. He wore big clunky boots, a corduroy seaman's cap and a fall weather jacket. He was twirling a cigarette in one hand and clasping a cup of coffee in the other. There was no bar, so everyone was just drinking coffee. He and I got introduced and we didn't say much right away. Ramblin' Jack shot off a list of my accomplishments while I just nodded and tried to be unassuming. We smoked some cigarettes together and I rolled a joint that we smoked with the group. Bob was just sitting and writing in a little spiral notebook; his penmanship was unreadable, which I believe he never improved on purpose so it would be harder to decipher.

Looking very preppy in a collar and tie under his Temple University sweater, Bill Cosby came up to us while we were lighting up again, and started telling us that we shouldn't smoke pot. "You can't do this," he said to us as he shook his head with the very same voice and long face that would warn Fat Albert and raise the Huxtable kids, as well as an entire generation of television viewers. "You'll waste your lives. You'll grow hair on your hands and lose your sex drive. You'll grow breasts!" he said. We had a good laugh about it and just kept on smoking.

Bob wasn't performing like everyone else was at this time; he would wait till closing, then ask if he could do a song or two, which is what he did this night as well. He sat on the stool and sang "Corrina, Corrina," "House of the Rising Sun" and "Buffalo Skinners." None of his own, just those three. He did, however, do his own take on "Corrina, Corrina," a bluesy version that contains the original lyrics, but his melody was closer to what Robert Johnson was doing. As he started playing the cafe staff were working, cleaning up the place. But one by one they stopped, and their work came to a halt as they all fell under the spell of Bob's magic. Twelve people stood and listened until he was done and then applauded. His intensity and simplicity was fabulous, and his use of the harmonica was an instant hit for me. It should be said that at this moment, I had zero inclination that in the future he was going to write incredible songs, songs that would move mountains. The first time I saw him perform I knew he had something special, but it took me a few months to really understand the depth of his genius.

Our first real conversation started when he finished playing those couple of tunes and sat back down with me. We talked about Woody Guthrie, Lead Belly, folk music, delta blues, Cisco Houston—music he was interested in and music I knew a lot about. It was actually a cosmic connection. I was really into the music, the social and political stuff, and he was right there with me on that. Except I was more into the political stuff than he was. Bob wasn't politically wired up like me, or musicians like Phil Ochs. My upbringing made me very aware of the political stuff: what was going on in the world, the wars, various governments and the demand for social justice was my thing.

We continued to sit and get high—laughing, talking about the world. He was twenty and I was twenty-five, and between those five years everyone grows and learns a lot. I'd traveled and he hadn't really yet. We bonded heavily that first night, and it's because I'd learned things that he was interested in and he appreciated the way I expressed my knowledge. I never tried to have an ego about knowing something or experiencing something that he hadn't yet. In the decades to come I would make it my job to help him experience new things, I would continue this adopted duty well into Bob becoming a recognizable face around the world.

That night we talked about God; he said he believed in a heaven. I gave him the existential rap that I still give today. That I believe we're all moss on a rock searching for a meaning and the one grounding connection with every living thing on this rock is that we're stuck here and need to live in balance with one another, in harmony. I was happy to have an audience so I downloaded everything I had onto him. He didn't argue, just listened very carefully, and when he did respond it was calculated and well thought out.

He told me he didn't have any money and how he was eating by going to bars and ordering coffee and waiting till someone would buy him food, which is how he met Suze Rotolo, his girlfriend, who would be photographed with Dylan for the cover of his album *The Freewheelin' Bob Dylan*. We talked until the Gaslight closed, then I asked him if he liked playing chess. He said he did, and the gambler in me suggested the winner had to buy the coffee. We walked to Cafe Figaro and played chess till the sun came up. He was good at chess, and it stuck out to me how he took his time to make a move. I was immediately aware of his unique sense of rhythm and timing that spilled over into his persona, even his songs.

Very rarely in the history of our forty-year relationship has he ever reacted instantaneously. He was very comfortable in silence then and now, as am I. During our time together I learned how to master the art of silence, and in this area he was my teacher.

As we bonded that night our words connected and the feeling was a powerful one. As we smoked it felt like it had great future implications. It was a ceremonial smoke, a passing of the Indian peace pipe.

From this point on he saw me as someone who had been around, someone who knew people. I told him about Marlon Brando, who would come into the Unicorn Cafe and hang out with me, which impressed him. I think back now and wonder if he wanted to be more like Elvis and Brando back then—they could do movies and be social, kiss babies and shake hands, so to speak. Bob couldn't do that, he's not social like that. From the start he wouldn't talk to more than one person at a time. He would just listen and absorb information—always observing people, very aware of his surroundings. Not an extrovert, everything went inward to be processed later.

As the sun came up, we said our good-byes. We didn't make any plans to see each other again. We just figured we would be at the Gaslight or around the Village.

The very next day I was walking from Seventh Street to a friend's house, and I saw Bob on the sidewalk. He yelled over at me, so I walked up and asked what he was doing. He said he wasn't up to much and I mentioned we should hang out. Bob said he had a car nearby and we could go for a drive. I told him I was in, would love to. He called Suze on a phone in a booth and they got into a huge fight. He was yelling, "I'm going on a drive and you need to come with me." I was standing on the sidewalk, and I could clearly hear the argument. He kept yelling, "You need to come. When I go, you need to go." This was the beginning of the end of his relationship with her as far as I could tell, even if it was another year till it ended.

After the call we jumped in the car he had and drove around. We passed through Harlem, then headed up to the Cloisters Museum and went for a walk. We got back in the car and kept driving. We were smoking pot and having great conversations, everything was a subject. Bob was interested in knowing about everybody and everything. He was a sponge, soaking in the information. He was like an electrical condenser, a capacitor filling up with information and ultimately exploding on paper with songs. We could ramble about how barns were built one moment and be talking about Woody Guthrie lyrics the next.

He talked about trying to get a job in the past five years and the difficulties of growing up in Hibbing, Minnesota, an iron ore town that disintegrated. That kind of business went to South America around then, so it was a hard place to find work. He talked about working on a pig farm and the farmer asking him to feed the mother pig, and, while she's eating, to keep her from eating the baby nursing pigs. Bob explained, "He handed me a big stick and said, 'If she looks like she's going to bite one, you need to give her a whack so she stops.'" Well, the mother pig started eating and just didn't stop. She started biting the baby pigs, and Bob started whacking the crap out of her and she still didn't stop. She ate all her baby pigs right in front of him, and he kept beating the crap out of her. Well, I could tell in his voice that this messed him up a little bit. The farmer fired him on the spot.

He then tried to get a job as a ditch digger, but that didn't work out either. Bob's a small guy; he's just not built for digging ditches. So the other guys beat him up and gave him a hard time. He lasted two days.

He told me he was always running away from home. He first left when he was eleven but he went back shortly after. He mentioned going to juvenile hall and how he quickly realized there was a social structure inside and either you're going to get along or you really shouldn't be there. He talked about going with the carnival when they came to town. He told me deeply personal stuff like his dad leaving town and how he would have to stay with his dad's mother in Minneapolis; how she would tell him his mother was a whore, sleeping around with other men. It was the kind of thing that probably wasn't true about his mother, but his grandmother was sticking up for his father and trying to use her power to distance Bob from his own mother. Terrible things to deal with as a child.

We didn't go to Woodstock on that drive, but we did swing by Eastchester. We drove by the stables near Yonkers where I had worked when I was fifteen. I told Bob about my own life, what it was like living in this area we're driving through.

That evening we stopped by the Village Gate to see Lenny Bruce perform. After the show I introduced him to Lenny. Bob asked him why he was wearing his trench coat and hat onstage. Lenny explained to Bob that at any moment the police might arrest him and they usually do it when he's onstage. They never let him go back into the dressing room to get his stuff. So he was now performing while wearing his coat, hat and gloves. We laughed about it. The theater surrounding Lenny's life was fabulous back then.

Around two a.m. that second night Bob sang another Woody Guthrie tune at the Gaslight, and he did it in a very Woody Guthrie style. Afterwards I discussed with him how I felt he didn't need to spin it like Woody did, how he should just sing it like himself. I felt he didn't need to put anything on it. I talked to him about this in depth; that he's the guy and he didn't need to sing through somebody else. He didn't need an inflection to push it through.

Over the next week Bob and I ended up hanging out non-stop. We were together all the time. We would depart and ar-range to meet the following day. Eventually we even exchanged numbers. We had extensive conversations about everything. Dur-ing the days we would go see Fellini's movies and stop by all the happening clubs and cafes like the Bitter End. We would stay up till dawn each morning. I would introduce him to everyone I knew, like Richard Alderson, the guy you hear announcing bands at Woodstock. We went to Dave Von Ronk's house and played our guitars. John Hammond Sr. had a house on lower MacDougal Street and we would go there too. We played the new music, we played the old music; we showed each other the licks, the changes, how to play it in different keys. Bob was still learning musical structures. He could play all of Woody's tunes and did his best to sound like him too. Woody was an impor-tant person in Bob's life then, but what I found out that first

week is musically he had much more contact with Ramblin'
Jack Elliott. Jack was on top of his act, and Jack could do Woody
like nobody else could do Woody. Bob learned more about
Guthrie's music from Jack, who had spent years with Woody,
than he ever learned from Woody himself. Anyone who sees
Jack Elliott perform today should recognize how much of what
Bob does on a stage he learned from Jack.

While Bob and I were hanging out this first week, he was
writing bits of what would become "A Hard Rain's a-Gonna
Fall." He was showing it to me in pieces, just a couple of lines
here and there. Broken out like poetry. Way before it was a song
or even had a proper name. There were songs he was working
on that he would show me. There were others that he was writing that he wouldn't show me. He had a bunch of songs about
his loneliness that he wouldn't perform, songs about him hitchhiking, the loneliness of running away. But he didn't push these
songs in the beginning. These came out much later when he
started to become more comfortable. As the days and weeks
went by only then would he play them for me and turn me on
to what he was hiding. He wouldn't be rehearsing with the guitar either but he was always writing. He'd write in his spiral
notebook and then rewrite on his typewriter and show me.

I had my own typewriter at the time, and I was writing poetry as well. I'd bounce my stuff off him and we'd talk about it.
But where my vision would end with poetry his would keep
going. If I could see three feet, he could see to the horizon. His
ability was standing out amongst the crowd already and he
wasn't even performing his own stuff a whole lot at this time.

He mostly played his catalogue of Woody Guthrie songs, and he was still outstanding.

For the next thirty days I traveled through New England and down the East Coast, sometimes with Bob and sometimes without him. One trip we drove north with Jack Elliott to visit Manny Greenhill in Boston, where we saw Brownie McGee and Sonny Terry, and checked out the folk scene in Cambridge. We did a similar trip to Philadelphia around the same time.

After that month I went back to Los Angeles and focused on my production company with Dan Gordon, Dandetta Productions.

1962 started with a big show I was promoting for Joan Baez at the Santa Monica Civic Auditorium; it was her first major commercial concert. I had first come across her after hearing about a show she was going to do at Claremont College for about two hundred people. Her dad was a teacher at the college and he had a hand in putting it together. I drove out the evening of the show in a rainstorm to see her perform. She stood about five feet, seven inches tall, looking very skinny in a full-length tank dress with long sleeves. She was eighteen years old but looked fourteen, with long, black hair brushed straight back to her shoulders and no makeup or jewelry. She was beautiful. She had a tomboy's body and dark brown eyes in a Spanish face with the coloring of Madrid.

At a little after-party at a house on campus, I searched for her. I remember finding her off in a tiny bedroom, crying— from emotional exhaustion or relief, I suppose. I left without saying anything, but I already knew I wanted to put on shows with her.

The show I ended up producing with her was about a year before she did the Newport Folk Festival, the show that established Baez as a major star. The show was also around the same moment in time that her manager and Albert Grossman were trying to win Bob over for the management position.

The winter of 1961 I had booked a nationwide 1962 springtime tour for Wavy Gravy. This was my big push for Wavy. I called all the radio stations, publicists, agents, everybody. It was a make-or-break moment. The tour was set to start. I wasn't originally planning on going but I wanted to be back in New York. So I packed Wavy and his things into my Corvair sedan. After a show at the Unicorn in L.A. and a private show at the Playboy Mansion, we hit the road heading to San Francisco, followed by Denver and Chicago, ultimately ending in New York at the Village Gate.

Once I was back in town, I met Bob again. He was still living with Suze on Fourth Street; it was a little one-bedroom, one-bath place. He brought me over there and we hung out a little bit. He was still wearing the same clothes, boots and things. I showed up wearing a mohair suit with a scarf, wide-brimmed hat and carrying my briefcase. I was decked out and I felt on top of the world. I was producing shows and new, exciting things were starting to happen.

The Village felt like it was raging. You could see, feel, touch and taste it—everything was up for reevaluation. Social and political confrontations were spreading across the country. César Chávez was organizing grape pickers in California's Central Valley; Martin Luther King Jr. and a hundred and sixty civil rights activists were arrested during a demonstration in Georgia. The United States and Russia were testing nuclear bombs. Life itself felt on the line. It was easy for people to feel dominated by fear and phobias.

All the heavy hitters seemed to be in the Village now: Jack Kerouac, Allen Ginsberg, Peter Orlovsky, Jackson Pollock, Willem de Kooning, Truman Capote, Steve McQueen, Barbra Streisand and Woody Allen, all moving in and out of the clubs, perfecting their craft and listening to the new music coming of age.

During the time I was away, Bob went back to Minnesota for the winter and had just recently returned. He was playing at more clubs and venues. He was still going on at the end of the night though. No matter who was playing he would ask the venue and go on after.

He and I jumped right back into hanging out again. We'd tool around town, go to the clubs, play more chess and even head back to the Cloisters and walk around a few more times. We started a tradition of walking around, which we would do together for decades to come. It became our thing when we would arrive in cities around the world—we would get out and get lost.

Walking around the Village we would explore our minds while analyzing everything. We would talk about the socks and shoelaces and personality traits of people and how they fall into

categories—and there was enough human architecture walking around in New York City to make it interesting and funny.
Especially if you're getting high, and we were. . . . If we did
actually get into a conversation with someone, we would dismantle him or her, hitting them from all sides. Making them
explain themselves and tell us why they were the way they
were. This conversational tactic became a thing for us. We both
still do it to this day. Bob would famously use it in press confer-
ences. When asked any question, the asker had a seventy percent
chance of being asked the same question by Bob.

During our walks on this second trip to New York, Bob and
I talked about the future. He asked me about Manny Greenhill
and Albert Grossman; he was wondering who he should sign
with. Manny Greenhill was managing Joan Baez and her commercial success was increasing every day. At the same time
Dave Van Ronk's wife was managing Bob, but he was ready for
the next step. Flat out he asked me which one he should sign
with. I asked him how traditional he wanted to be and how far
he wanted to reach. Those questions appealed to him and he
expressed he wanted to go the distance, more commercial than
what Greenhill was doing. His day-to-day routine didn't paint
someone who wanted to go mainstream; he was more folky and
traditional at this point. But he knew what he wanted and where
he wanted to go from the start. So I said Albert was the logical
choice. He was much more aggressive and much more commercial. Bob signed with Grossman a few days later.

There was a big conflict between being commercial, accom-
modating the commercial sound and lyrics and being socially

conscientious. For musicians at that moment it was the biggest personal conflict. Our social group was conscientious and looking for change from the closed-minded mentality of the fifties. But if you wanted to pay rent playing music, you were better off not fighting the system. Bob's ability to bend and refashion words was like magic; he was the one that could break into the mainstream while still playing socially conscientious music. Bob believed in himself and so did I, and that's why Albert entering the picture made sense. Albert had the commercial connections and wouldn't ask Bob to change his tune to fit in. With Albert's help Bob could force his style in front of the broader public and ultimately make everyone else fit into what he was doing.

In the following weeks I was hanging out with Grossman more and more since I was hanging with Bob. Albert wasn't a new character in my life either. We had been in the same social circle for a while and we had talked on occasion. Now that he was managing Bob, I decided to approach him with some ideas.

I told Albert that Bob should stop playing clubs and he needed to go directly to concert halls. Albert wondered why I was making this suggestion. I told him that I knew it was the right way for Bob to grow, that his ability as a songwriter could reach beyond the folk scene and he needed help getting in front of those larger, more diverse audiences. I also told Albert that I wanted to be the one to put on the first concert show. Albert considered the risks but actually agreed with me. Albert had nothing to lose since I was willing to gamble my own money.

I put a deposit down on the six hundred-seat Carnegie Hall, and it was only after I put it all together that Albert changed his mind. Now he saw the genius in the idea and he wanted to produce the show after I'd set it up. Albert recruited his partner Harold Leventhal to take my spot. This was incredibly upsetting to me. I believed Albert was threatened by my friendship with Bob and that's why he pushed his way into doing my show. He did, however, present a peace offering. He invited me into his office and said he would give me a job. I could take on the marketing and coproduce. I thought about it and then I told him to fuck off and stormed out.

Later that day I saw Bob and we went for a walk down to Mott Street. He was on his way to buy aviator sunglasses, which wasn't a trend yet. I told him everything that happened and that I had decided to quit the scene and move to Yelapa, Mexico, to become a holy man.

Being bullied out of my concert with Bob turned me upside down. I was angry and dismayed. In addition to that, every show I put on with Lenny Bruce was ending with him getting arrested; Wavy Gravy wasn't growing as an artist like I had planned and my falling out with Herb Cohen and the Unicorn had left me at an all-time low.

I didn't ask Bob to intervene with Albert. I knew the gravity of his situation. This was a big show and it had to happen. Albert was taking a chance on Bob and he didn't want to put pressure on that new relationship, and I didn't expect him to either.

On the walk I told Bob about a premonition I'd had. It was about him and his future.

I told him Albert was ultimately going to screw him over like he had just screwed me. I didn't elaborate how because I didn't really know. I told him he was going to be a big success no matter who got involved. I told him when he records his own songs, it will make a huge splash and that he'll have to go on tour. He'll be bigger than the Village. I mentioned that if he needs someone he can trust, I can be that guy. But I'm leaving to Yelapa and if he wanted me, all he would have to do is tell whoever is standing next to him, doesn't matter who it is, "Get Victor" and I'll get the message. We were really into the magic at that time so that's exactly how I left it.

Financially, I was glad I didn't do the show. It ended up losing a bunch of money, but my feelings were still hurt and I was well on my way to being a holy man.

~

End of Tape One

The microcassette player clicks to an abrupt stop. I'm a cocktail of emotions after listening to both the A and B side of the first tape. For all the right reasons it's hard to listen to, remembering how much I miss him. What he sounds like. How funny he was.

I never knew how much of an impact the Unicorn Cafe had made on the local Los Angeles culture. My father's stories told to me and my sister usually stemmed from his fallout with Herb Cohen. He would say that after his experiences running the Unicorn, he never wanted to have another business partner. He felt bullied by Herb Cohen and money was never split evenly. He usually left it at that and omitted the fun parts regarding Steve McQueen, Lenny Bruce and others on the scene.

I remember my father telling me about his main interest in opening both the Unicorn and his follow-up cafe, Cosmo Alley, and also promoting concerts. He wanted to support the artists and protect them. He talked about being appalled by the racial segregation of the 1950s. On his trips to Las Vegas, Nevada, as a teenager, he would go to concerts where the performers couldn't walk through the lobby because they were Mexican or black. This drove him nuts, seeing incredibly talented people treated like a lower class, yet they were the ones with the magic. He would say that in those days, if you wanted to see the real talent, you had to visit the slums of Las Vegas.

Another interesting story left behind in Tape One is how my father became friends with Henry Miller, the prolific writer who penned *Tropic of Cancer*, *The Colossus of Maroussi*, *The Rosy Crucifixion* and many others. They met in the hot springs in Big Sur, California. From what I know about Miller, that seems like a fitting place to have met him. Unfortunately there's no mention of it on Tape One and my father didn't tell me enough

about it in person for me to write it now. And so, like many
other great stories, it's lost in a pile of ashes.

~

Tape Two

There are places in the world that are like diamonds
for the soul; Yelapa is one of them. Way before Dylan ever visited Yelapa, he would write and sing about it because of how I
talked about it. Bob wasn't the adventurer I was, and in the
early years I felt that he lived vicariously through me. I opened
his mind to this place as I did with many others. I brought John
Hammond Sr., who was very influential with Bob's music early
on. He produced Dylan's early recordings such as "Blowin' in
the Wind" and "A Hard Rain's a-Gonna Fall." On occasion
Yelapa would be referenced in the liner notes of Bob's albums,
homage to the magical place in his mind where he could see rain-
bows and gardens and find solitude, his personal Valhalla. He
loved the idea that nobody was there. For Bob that was the best
vacation he could have—a place to be himself, to write unin-
terrupted without the constraints of time or schedule.

In Mexico I let everything grow, wore only white clothing,
mostly robes. I spent all day playing the guitar and writing poetry. There was nothing around to distract me. I let my thoughts
wander and my worries fade into the ether.

Yelapa was a village of three hundred Native Americans
and a few foreigners, fifteen in all. We lived along the water in

thatched huts called *palapas,* which were spread out in a semi-elliptical shape around the small bay. A river emptied into the ocean and impressed a freshwater lagoon with a sandbar at the ocean's edge. The village had grown on the lagoon. The beach was five hundred yards wide and situated at the foot of a mountain. There were no roads into the village; the entire community was cut off from the rest of the world, accessible only by boat.

My poetry flourished in this time; I wrote hundreds and hundreds of pages. Words flowed out of me as if I was cracked open and left to bleed emotion. My friendship with Bob inspired me creatively but also compounded my inability to share my work. I was in the shadow of greatness and I was happy to be there. I didn't have a lust to compete nor desire to be in the spotlight. I've never published nor shown my work to anyone other than Bob; he was always very gracious and shared his thoughts with thorough critiques.

One day, just before sundown, I was lying on the beach with Tom Law, one of my great friends, who would later become the road manager for Peter, Paul and Mary. But at that moment he was sitting up watching the Mexican sunset while I lay with my face in the warm glow of the sand. A stranger came walking down the beach toward us. There was nobody else in sight. If you saw anyone on that beach and didn't know them well, you always looked twice. The stranger stopped in front of us and asked, "You guys know of this guy, Victor Maimondez?" mispronouncing my last name.

Tom, who was always cautious and protective of me, squinted up. "Yeah, maybe. What do you want him for?"

The stranger said, "I have a message for him. From someone named Bob Dylan, in New York City. He wants Victor to
come back. They're going on tour."

I felt a sudden surge of energy through my body, like a call
to arms. It made me shake. I lifted my head. Tom said, "Okay,
I'll give him the message." And the stranger walked off down
the beach. I never saw him again, and I never knew who he was.

That evening I called Albert Grossman, who told me there
was a plane ticket waiting for me. We briefly discussed my role
and came to the conclusion that in nine days I would fly to New
York and start as Bob's tour manager. My base salary would be
sixty-five dollars a week. I was ecstatic.

~

I hit the pause button on the microcassette player. Hearing this
story reminded me of some old poetry I found in the plastic box
my sister brought over to my house recently. The plastic box is
one of four that vary in size; they're the last remaining belongings
of my father. Everything outside of these plastic boxes, aside from
the audiotapes, was burned in the fire. I did a quick search of the
boxes and found about a hundred size XL T-shirts from various
tours over the years and an entire box of hats. These were pre-
sumably all the crew shirts and hats my father received. In the
largest box there's a massive collection of tour itineraries, backstage passes, photos, Bob Dylan books, magazines, business cards
and notes. There are also dozens and dozens of binders—all my
father's business paperwork—and five hundred or so pages of poetry and stories he wrote but never shared. The pages have

browned with age and have a musty smell, indicative of decades
passed in a wood drawer of some dusty desk. The bulk of the
work is typed, and about half of the text is red and the other half
is black.

All the text looks similar to the way Bob types his text. When
I was working at the coffee shop in Santa Monica I would ven-
ture into Bob's office on occasion, where he kept his typewriter.
His pages were typed with no margins—edge to edge, top to
bottom. It appeared to be intentional, perhaps to save paper. It
wasn't easy to read because there were no spaces, just a brick of
words. Mixed in with my father's pages is a screenplay for a movie
he wrote, reams of poetry and what appears to be a tour diary.

For You

If I could pass the knowledge onto you
and let out the cause that's bothering you
and mend the web you've fallen through
I would have done it all for you. But then you wouldn't
be you.

LSD

Well I rolled out of bed
sat on my head
didn't know if I was alive or dead
staggered to the door but fell to the floor

Then a vision came to me
of a waving tree standing tall and free

smiling down on me from up below around the back and
     down above
trapped in the way
fingers play

Came across some funny looking moss
it was Hoss the pig fat son of the boss
with his weight down on me
I was floating fast and free
stumbling enlighteningly
came upon a door that felt of peace love and unity
so I looked in to see what I could see
and it said L.S.D.
my own reflection looking back at me

Lost on Goodbyes

Though the day fades away
continuing my struggle you can see me go my way
having waved all my goodbyes
I stumbled down the road
wiping the tears from my eyes
carrying my thoughts far out loud
my ghost of yesterday stands so proud

Fork in the Road

He stood in front of me and plainly stated that he knew for he
understood and saw the two directions placed before the stage
and as he spoke of the wrong road taken I began to speak of the

devils rage that had been broken. With that the talk was over leaving me wanting to talk but left alone with only my mind to stalk.

Reading these words, I understand how much of my father's soul went unexpressed to others. I hit the play button to resume his voice.

~

I watched everybody else, singers, songwriters and Bob. But as much as I wanted to be a folksinger and performer myself, I put it aside when I went to work for Odetta, Joan [Baez], Bob, Peter, Paul and Mary and Miles Davis. I really wanted to be that person in the beginning, a performer; I had the hunger for it. In some of the early biography books and articles about Bob, they said I was a frustrated folksinger. They were absolutely right. One hundred percent, and they'd have to be deaf, dumb and blind not to see that. So what? Who better to do the job of helping someone with real talent and genius than somebody who was really into it? I loved what my friends did and I wanted to support it. The biographers and magazine writers would pick on me for that; they called me everything, horrible things, called me subservient. They would give me a hard time because I picked up the dog shit, literally, which was my job at times. The other stuff was easy; being in charge, telling people what to do came naturally to me. Actually, picking up the dog shit came naturally too. I didn't mind at all, I've always had a "whatever had to be done" mentality. No ego attached, which is one reason Bob and I got along. If I had an ego, I would have thought what I provided was worth more. When everybody else was posturing, I was carrying the luggage. When everyone was jumping in the spotlight, I was jumping out of it to make sure we didn't miss our ride or to make sure we didn't lose anything. And I was having more fun than anybody and still doing the job right. I was eating the best, I was the most physical and I spent everything I had while having a great time. It also took everything to be there, it's a twenty-four-hour-a-day job. I think I'll live the longest because I didn't drink as much, or smoke as much, as others.

~

Well, you can't be right about everything.

~

End of Tapes One and Two

CHAPTER 3

~

On the Road

Victor during his stay in Bearsville, New York, with Bob Dylan
at Albert Grossman's home, 1965. *(Courtesy: Abe Maymudes)*

Tape Three

[Future Byrds producer and manager] Jim Dickson
picked me up at the airport in New York; it was bitter cold outside and the air was crisp. The cold air burned my throat as I
exited the plane, a world away from the soft, restorative air of

Yelapa. I greeted my friend Jim on the sidewalk and he immediately informed me that President Kennedy had been shot in
Dallas. It was November 22, 1963. We listened to the radio
broadcast the entire ride into the city. I was, along with the rest
of the country, in shock. Ripped out of my serene mental state
that I had earned during months of meditation and writing
poetry. I fell dead center into the communal shock and sadness
of the nation. What did it mean that murder was a political tool?
Plenty of civil rights activists had died anonymous deaths in the
Deep South, and miners were getting their heads cracked open
in Appalachia, but shooting down the president in broad daylight made the line in the sand pretty clear.

Since Kennedy's election in 1960, there had been no sub-
stantive change in the political course set by the Dulles brothers
and J. Edgar Hoover in the fifties, whether in foreign policy or
at home. Yet his youth and intelligence spoke to us, and we had
a sense that reason and humanism could prevail, that those issues of social justice that we stood for were on the table for discussion. Practically all the people I knew who were red baited
and blackballed out of artistic performance or jobs were back at
work—back onstage, singing before audiences that were wide
open to them.

Immediately with Kennedy's election it felt like the country
was out of the shadow of McCarthyism. His call to young people to give back, to experience the world as it was, captured the
imagination of many college kids. Racism was another story;
if you were not in college and you were brown or darker, you
were soon on the way to the draft office. Still, everyone I knew

felt there was at least an opening for free speech and activism that would allow us to present our case nonviolently. That day Jim and I felt the violence implicit in Kennedy's assassination. Personally, it felt like a declaration of war against the social causes we championed. Dallas was a southern city, and the South boiled with resistance and hate at that time. My memory of American history was pretty weak, Lincoln's and Garfield's assassinations seemed so far behind us, and the road the country had traveled toward social justice in the Roosevelt years, and even the antics of McCarthy, made assassination an inconceivable option in our democracy. Public humiliation and economic manipulation that rendered people powerless was familiar to me from my family's political experience, but shooting the president had not been on my list of possible political options. Of course, Jack Kennedy's death was the first of many public deaths: his brother Bob, Martin Luther King Jr. and the Kent State students. That string of murders would be the hard line drawn by the political right to check our rising voices against the war and against racial segregation. I felt bewildered by the event.

I was grateful to be in Jim Dickson's company with other things to talk about. Now, looking back, making sense of all these characters is important; I was part of a group of people in Los Angeles and New York that had a profound influence on popular music. Jim Dickson, though not many people have heard of him outside the business, was one of those people, and he remains a friend. Jim was a couple years older; in 1963 I was twenty-eight and he was in his early thirties. He had been in the army in the late forties and spent the fifties racing sailboats. He came into the music industry through his love of jazz. I knew him from the Unicorn and Cosmo Alley in the late fifties but more from my association with Herb Cohen, Ben Shapiro and artist management. Jim produced records at Pacific Studios and was a talent scout for Jac Holzman at Elektra, whose office around then was in the Village. Jim had a fine ear and was laid-back in the best way, and he would draw on the talent showcased at the coffeehouses on hootenanny nights in L.A. He would pull performers he liked off the stage and record them during night sessions at Pacific Studios. He had some financial success with a group doing folk music on twelve-string guitars; it sold well enough to keep Pacific Studios open, and that success earned him free access to a recording space where he could listen to and mix artists. He recorded the Modern Folk Quartet with Herb Cohen and was in New York to see Jac Holzman with ideas for a group he had influenced in L.A., which would later become the Byrds. That's a longer story, but Jim had a way of being with music and musicians that I understood. He saw the possibility in sound and knew what he liked and had the venue for experiment. His taste for Hawaiian instrumental and harmonics influenced the evolution and sound of David Crosby, Roger McGuinn, Michael Clarke and Chris Hillman. The Byrds were not a long-lasting group, but they hit it big with "Mr. Tambourine Man" the following year and became the signature sound of L.A. rock. It was great to see him, catch up with what and who was happening in L.A. It was a soft reentry to the U.S. and let me sidestep the Kennedy news.

I settled back in the Village and soon after I saw Hamish Sinclair speaking at Columbia. Hamish was a big player in the miners strike going on in and around Hazard, Kentucky. He was in town to raise awareness and lobby support. At Columbia he described the conditions in Hazard and what the families were going through. Men had been out of work a couple years and started striking for better conditions. The situation there was complicated though. The United Mine Workers Union efforts had been so successful that big mines were actually paying taxes to them, and there were newly created mining hospitals and much better wages for people working for big companies. Small mines could not fit into the scheme; the big producers like Peabody had switched to strip mining and big machines and fewer employees. Small mines could not stay open and run with a union crew. Yet, at that moment in 1963, workers were supposed to hand deliver coal out of four-foot-tall tunnels for nonunion wages, below twenty dollars a day. The mines were not on rail lines in that county and so the cost of production was too high to pay good wages and the union tax, according to the companies. Basically the industry was dying, and the folks in those hollows and hills in West Virginia and Kentucky were in a squeeze they could not win, working or not. Hearing about folks hungry and cold with nothing and approaching Christmas led Suze, Bob's then-girlfriend, to collect a bundle of clothes for relief. It also piqued our interest in Hazard, Kentucky. Hamish wanted to mix it up with working people and the student activists on campuses at that time. I heard that, and Bob was listening too.

The same thing was happening in civil rights. Martin Luther King Jr. and the Southern Christian Leadership Conference (SCLC) had pushed their luck successfully in Birmingham, Alabama, with a peaceful march that summer. Passive resistance, big white cops hammering black men and women with clubs, was a revelation and game changer for the rest of the country. The march on Washington in late August had been an inspiring success. Medgar Evers's death and the killing of four young black girls in a church bombing made the South seem foreign and crazy. In retrospect, I guess it makes no sense that I was surprised Kennedy was shot—change was pressing and the South was a polarized and threatening place. Bob had been successful in colleges on the East Coast, but New York and Boston were the head and heart of progressive America. The Village was bohemia, in a milieu of folksingers, poets and radical political students at Columbia that fed off each other's great talent and activism, but Bob was far from the front lines.

Taken with social and political imperatives of that moment, I wanted, and Bob wanted, to see and hear and feel America firsthand. Bob absorbed the experience, listening hard and watching, and he worked it into song. Actually being there, I felt he was painfully honest in his lyrics, and the response was totally personal. He did feed off of what was around him. Interviewers and fans wanted more, but there was nothing more. His abstraction moved people viscerally and yet they wanted, literally, "What are you thinking?" Art is not that. Poetry is really not that; rather, the words have to move beyond the literal.

Jack Kerouac had promoted odyssey—the great American

road trip. We decided to hit the road, and Albert booked a couple gigs in the South, one at Emory in Atlanta on the seventh of February 1964, and another at a black college in Mississippi. We were scheduled to be in Denver on the fifteenth and Berkeley on the twenty-second. We wanted to swing through Hazard, Kentucky, to see Hamish and also stop in North Carolina to connect with Carl Sandburg. I was in charge of getting us there and handling the business details on the road for Albert. Our transport was a nondescript Ford station wagon. Bob asked Paul Clayton to join us.

Paul Clayton could have his own book here, so fine and formal a gentleman was he. I had seen him rise above the legal row his publishing company had set up with Bob's over the similarity in lyrics between Paul's song "Who's Going to Buy You Ribbons" released in 1960 and Bob's "Don't Think Twice." Paul let it go; he was a folklorist and had been cataloging songs since he was a teenager in the mid-fifties. He had recorded many albums that are classic documents now. He traveled the backwoods of North Carolina, Kentucky and Virginia, interviewing people up dead-end roads and recording their songs. He hung with June Carter and her family, had hitchhiked around Europe and America singing, all this while working on graduate and postgraduate degrees in musicology at the University of Virginia.

He wrote his own stuff too, but he drew on the songs he knew, like everyone did then. Real folk music was public domain, and the "singer of songs" could use it all and call it his own, in Paul's view. He could tell you the difference between a sea shanty and a mining shanty and could sing you a thousand songs or detail how one song changed by continent and time, knowing when, where and why the words had changed. Paul was about thirty-five then, I think, ten years older than Bob and likely in love with Bob in a personal way, though no one went there. His career was petering out. He was the perfect companion on the trip through the South. A tall, blue-eyed guy, soft-spoken and he liked to get stoned. A couple years later Paul would kill himself in a lonely, horrifying way.

Untimely death cast a long shadow on the bright promise of people of talent we knew in the early sixties. Clayton died in '67, Peter La Farge in '65, and Phil Ochs in '76. There would be others later: Rick Danko and Richard Manuel are two that mattered to me; drugs and possibly a depressing lack of financial success in the face of extraordinary talent caused those early exits. In my estimation, being broke is depressing if you have lived your talent earnestly.

People say all kinds of stupid things about those deaths and their relation to Bob. I have to say, the music scene in New York City was so full of talent and boiling with energy, there was no clear correlation I could make. Bob came, experienced, and when he sang what he wrote, it was like the air went out of the room. Simply, no one did it better. He would give people credit if he could, and later in *Self Portrait* he paid some musical tribute to Clayton recording "Gotta Travel On." As a scholar of our genre of music and a historian, Bob was not competition to Paul Clayton; he was the heir apparent to what bards and troubadours were in all human history. He lived the tradition, original interpretations of his moment laid over the musical influence of the past. Bob put himself to school in the Village in New York and Paul Clayton had definitely been one of his teachers.

At Suze Rotolo's behest, there also was a reporter named Pete Karman in the car. He was there to record the journey south into the dark and dangerous country of America. Albert Grossman made arrangements in late January, and we picked up clothes for donation to the striking miners in Hazard, Kentucky, and Albert bought a station wagon for the trip. We hit the road in early February 1964, and passed through D.C. toward Paul Clayton's house in Charlottesville, Virginia. Paul had a house and cabin near there. He kept vast volumes of self-collected folk songs. He had collected these songs the old way—from lips to ear—and in the fifties and sixties he had made records documenting the music of that part of the country and of his home in New England. Paul played the guitar but introduced us all to the dulcimer, until then a little-used instrument in popular folk music. He had a good stash of marijuana too and some connections for getting more. I rolled all the joints that night at his place, and we got very little rest. We woke early the next day and headed to the town of Hazard in Perry County.

Winding through those winter-stripped hills, we passed side roads—hollows with a few houses and shacks: the shanties of song. It was bleak, though beautiful, country. Mining was no new thing for Bob, but this county was. Hazard was actually an old town, established before the American Revolution like the rest of Appalachia by people from Scotland and Wales who

were trying to outlive their various defeats and subjugation
by the English. They brought fully developed folk culture in
poetry, music and a memory of battles lost and highwaymen.
The main industry in those places had been moonshine and
small farming and hunting until the whiskey tax, and much
later Prohibition, made them all hate the U.S. government.
Mining began in the 1800s to fuel the industrial development
of the East Coast. The coal was dug out and hauled up and
transported by rail and steam to where it was needed. It was
cruel and short-lived work until John L. Lewis took over the
miners union in the 1920s, and, like Hamish said, that day in
this country was as important as the birth of Jesus. A second
coming.

We picked up a hitchhiking miner on the way. He gave us
some firsthand ideas of what was going on up ahead. It wasn't a
pretty scene in Harlan County. Miners were protesting below-
living wages and the failure of operators to contribute to the
United Mine Workers' welfare fund. They forced most of the
mines in eastern Kentucky to close. I remember somebody shout-
ing, "There will be blood coming from the mines!" They were
fighting to receive a minimum wage of $24.25 for an eight-hour
shift and a forty cents-per-ton royalty payment to the union welfare fund. If that's what they were fighting for, then what they
were actually receiving was far less.

We were in town to meet up with Hamish Sinclair, who we
found bouncing off the walls. He was the secretary for the National Committee for Miners; he was, for the most part, the
strike leader and in neck deep with the local law authorities.

He really had no time to talk, and it didn't matter to us, we were there to see and feel it, and it ended up being a little too much for us to handle. Three whiteneck Jewish boys and a Virginia scholar in a depressing situation for everyone involved, and an angry miner is not someone you want to get in the way of, even if you're there to support them. The slightest bit of confusion about what you're up to could end with you getting punched in the mouth. We did feel and see that change was coming and the answer was not easy; deep coal mining was a way of life, and no one was prepared for what was next. The people were presented with no other option than to leave. There were plenty of scrawny kids and hard-eyed, worn-out women in these isolated communities. There was no real chance for education or information; it was obvious we were watching the slow end of an old, isolated civilization. We did our bit; Bob dropped off clothes and I drove us south out of town to Pineville, Kentucky, for the night.

In the morning we piled into the station wagon and I drove through the Blue Ridge Mountains to Asheville, North Carolina. I had a couple puffs of my joint, Clayton was mellow and talking about the blue-collar history of the small towns we were passing. Bob was in the back writing; he had taken the newfound space the clothes had occupied as a place to pour his thoughts onto paper. We were in harmony; the feeling of adventure was flowing through the car and being inhaled with every breath. We only spent the night in Asheville. To pass the time we trawled the few bars in town, we played pool and went bowling. The town was still segregated, which basically meant two types of everything divided by color: one for white men and women, one for coloreds. Water fountains: two of each. Toilets: two of each. Places to eat: two of each. We were strangers in a strange land.

Bob and Paul wanted to make a pilgrimage of sorts to pay respect to Pulitzer Prize winner Carl Sandburg. Bob had made a big deal about dropping in on him. Paul was known to Sandburg, who had made an important collection of American folk music in the twenties. We didn't really know how to find him, just knew we could. The mountains gave way to rolling hills and hardwood forest and big fields, leftover plantation country. His place was called Connemara, a tribute to Galway in Ireland. We thought with that name and goodwill, we could just tap into the energy of the moment and the path would present itself to us. This of course didn't happen, and I ended up driving in circles for hours. But the excitement stayed the same. The adventure continued after receiving directions from a farmer who shared the same name as Sandburg. In general, people were suspicious and held back in the South; Paul and some charm were our only hope of breaking through the divide.

We rolled up to his house to find his wife, Lillian, sitting on the porch; we all got out and greeted her. She was very welcoming and asked that we wait outside while she fetched her husband. We were jazzed to have found the right place; it was as if we found a treasure without looking once at the map. Bob and Sandburg talked for a little while, touching on poetry and how his farm came about. I spent the hour walking around the front yard and admiring the low-key estate they had built for them-

selves. Carl was in his late eighties and tired easily. Bob was
hoping he was going to be more spry and eager to indulge us.
After about an hour, Carl said his good-byes and politely ges-
tured that he planned to retire inside. For the most part we
were all happy that he took the time to say hello. I know Bob
wanted to spend some significant time with him, maybe befriend him on a deeper level. But this wasn't the time for that.

We left the Sandburgs' home for Georgia. On the way, Pete
Karman and Bob started to bicker about poetry. I think this
rift was created while Pete and Bob were talking to Carl, since
Bob was holding court and Pete was just the eager buddy trying to win the spotlight in their conversation. I heard Pete shout
in the station wagon, "How do you write the stuff you do when
you don't even understand what it means?" Bob looked up and
caught my eyes in the rearview mirror; we were on the same
page. Pete just didn't get it. Bob didn't say a word and went back
to writing. He was punching in words to "Chimes of Freedom."
I smoked the last of my joint. Bob would soon need more paper,
and I would soon need more pot. I had made arrangements
with a friend to mail me a bag of marijuana. He shipped it to a
post office in Atlanta and had them hold it for me. In those days
most people didn't know what weed was, so it was easy to slip it
under the radar.

Atlanta provided us with a place to stay, more drugs and a
venue for Bob at Emory University, which proved to be a magical moment. It was the heart of the local civil rights action, and
many of those folks showed up. Emory was a bastion of light in
that place and Bob was on point with the locals; there was a

deep connection in the air. "The Times They Are a-Changin'"
was an anthem. It was home ground for Martin Luther King
Jr. and the Southern Christian Leadership Conference. The in-
justice and indignity of segregation had people on both sides at
boiling points throughout the South. In my eyes, it was King's
mastery of the moment—his poetry and earthiness that, like
Gandi, kept everyone's eye on the prize and the violence off
of the streets. The giant Heart of Atlanta Motel with its two
hundred-plus rooms was still enforcing its strict whites-only
policy. Within a few short months of our passing, the Supreme
Court would declare the "separate but equal" methodology unjust and level the playing field for how private businesses could
treat whites over blacks. These were the ideas our greater group
was fighting for. Bob may not have been at the head of the picket
lines like Hamish Sinclair, but he was still the adopted voice of
those who were.

Waking up with a hangover in Georgia, I took Route 80 out
of town, and we headed deeper south through the Delta and
through the bayou country—Talbotton, Columbus, Tuskegee,
Montgomery, Selma, Meridian. I list these names and they do
not convey the muddy rivers, the shacks on the side roads, the
gray, damp southern cold or what we felt and saw in the black
and white faces we passed. There was really no time to stop, to
know anything about anybody, but the geography sure was
something. We absorbed what we saw and heard in those slow
and incomprehensible cadences of English. We soaked in as
much of the culture as we could, and that ride was plenty for
Bob to hear and see what he needed to finish writing "Chimes

of Freedom." Our next stop was New Orleans, where Mardi
Gras loomed like a safe haven and proper stomping ground for
stoned whitenecks on tour. Bob, Paul, Pete and I found a place
to stay, dropped our bags off and quickly headed out to the Seven
Seas Bar in the French Quarter.

Mardi Gras was in full swing. The guy at the front desk said
there was a Ping-Pong table at the bar; Ping-Pong was a favorite of mine. I took up playing games against a nice fellow we
met named Joe B. Stuart, who called himself the "white southern poet." I took him for a couple of bucks. Between games Bob
and I played some chess.

Bob was in the habit of responding with, "Victor speaks for
me!" when asked questions by Paul and Pete. I thought that
was funny, but I took it seriously and I did speak for him. Bob
and I were tight and like-minded so it was easy for us to communicate without even opening our mouths.

After a few more drinks we headed out of the bar and Bob
ran into a girl who told him, "You sure do have long hair." Bob
replied, "Yes, I am going to let my hair grow down to the street
and write my poems from the tops of these buildings!" We
were rowdy and ready to pounce on anyone who wasn't on the
same level as us. We walked up Bourbon Street and I noticed
a young man with a guitar singing "Don't Think Twice."
We stopped and listened to the young fellow. Bob told him,
"You sing that very well." The guitar player looked at Bob
and said, "You . . . you. No, it couldn't be. You aren't Bob
Dylan, are you?" Dylan replied, "No, I'm not," in a dry, matter-
of-fact tone. We laughed about it as we walked on.

We arrived at a bar called Baby Greens only to be denied entrance by the bouncer; it was a blacks-only bar located on Burgundy Street. Back then, Dylan and I both felt very strongly about the notion that if you wanted to listen to good music, you had to go to where the blacks and Hispanics hung out. I had learned this many years before in Las Vegas and in Los Angeles. The segregated white clubs were not the place to be for groundbreaking music—in those places you'd find only groundbreaking assholes.

Bob was trying to get the bouncer, who also ran the place, to let us in. He kept saying, "Why, man?" "Why not?" The bouncer told us to "beat it" or he would have the cops come and lock us all up. The bouncer repeated, "Son, go on home. Somewhere your mother is on her knees praying for you." Dylan shot back, "I don't have a mother, and if I did she wouldn't be praying for *me*." It was clear that there was nothing we could say to gain entrance to Baby Greens.

Walking away, we ran into an acquaintance, high as a kite and standing atop a parked car. As he started walking over it from front to back, we all yelled, "No! Get off!" Amidst the chaos, this guy asked Bob if he'd ever read Jean-Paul Sartre. Dylan replied that he had and then asked the guy, "Have you ever read Jean Genet?" The young man answered, "Yes." Dylan shot back at him, "Yes. Yes. But have you *really* read Genet?" It was literary one-upmanship at its drunken finest.

While walking around Jackson Square, the still-present White Southern Poet asked Bob when he was going to go into the military. Bob replied, "I tried to join. But they wouldn't take me."

Around three a.m. we settled in at the Athenian Room, one of the Greek bars on Decatur Street. We were all getting a kick out of a drag queen dancing with a drunken sailor from the USS *Lexington,* which was in port. The sailor thought he was dancing with a woman; he would bend her over and give her a big kiss right out of that famous Alfred Eisenstaedt photo of the sailor kissing the nurse. Except this nurse was packing more than a stethoscope . . .

After a good laugh, we left and were walking along in front of the Hotel Monteleone and Dylan saw two young girls. He asked them if they wanted to go to a house party on Madison and Decatur Street, but the girls said no. Bob chased them a little way down the street saying, "Come on, we are going to a party." They, of course, had no idea who he was because in 1964 Bob was still unknown outside of the folk music circles. Bob gave up his relentless pursuit when he tripped and fell on the street; I helped him back up to his feet as we found the house party. As we were climbing the four flights of stairs to the party I heard Bob say, "We are all just steps."

The party guests were all wearing suits and evening gowns; we were in blue jeans and scruffy clothes. Nevertheless, we made our way in, grabbed drinks and struck up some conversations. Bob started telling the girl whose apartment it was about our trip down South and how we had stopped in North Carolina to see Carl Sandburg. I was busy talking with another girl who struck my fancy, although it was fast approaching five a.m., and we all were unintelligible.

We had a show the next day. I drove us three hours north to Jackson, where Bob played at Tougaloo College, a black teachers college. Mississippi in 1964 was a foreign country. We would pass a church and hear a choir and see the pickup trucks parked with sullen, thick white men inside. Watching, just watching. Our clothes, our demeanor . . . I think back on how we looked, and I'm glad I insisted we keep moving.

Denver was a long haul and we stopped in Ludlow, southern Colorado, for the night before the concert on February 15. We cleaned up a little bit, walked around to stretch our legs and made our way to the venue. While Bob was onstage at the Denver Folklore Center, he debuted "Chimes of Freedom" and the crowd was very responsive. Hal Neustadt, the promoter in town, loved the show. We spent a little time at the local coffee shops before Bob offered to show us around Central City. The last time he had been there was in his teens. We were all fairly unimpressed, but it was a good excuse to get out into the trees a little bit. It was on our way to the San Francisco Bay Area by way of Interstate 70, Grand Junction and Reno.

Heading out of town we found ourselves in severe traffic, slow-moving bumper-to-bumper traffic along a stretch of road that ran along the Colorado River. I was all the way in the back of the station wagon when I realized what was going on. Paul Clayton was driving at the time, and I yelled out to him to speed up and pass the endless amount of cars. He declined since it would have been quite dangerous, and I didn't push him too hard since I didn't really trust anyone else's driving over mine.

Bob was sitting on the second bench seat, Pete was sitting on the first bench seat and we were traveling at a turtle's pace. We had a million miles to go the Bay Area so I got real antsy. I proceeded to bully my way up to the driver's seat while the car was in motion; the last thing I wanted to happen was to fall behind even more cars by pulling over. I asked Bob to climb over the bench seat to my bench; once I was on his, I asked Pete to climb over onto Bob's bench and I switched with him. Once there I was arm's length to the steering wheel, so I grabbed it and told Paul Clayton to slide out of the way, and I'd quickly jump into the driver seat, before we crashed into the car in front of us. The dialogue we were having was absurd but I wasn't giving up. Everyone in the car was pushing back on my request except Bob. He didn't seem to mind I was asking Paul to jump out of the driver seat in a moving car; however, he was questioning my ability over Paul's to pass cars on blind corners. After a minute or two of figuring out the logistics, Paul and I made a plan and we executed it by simultaneously sliding in and out of the driver position. We nailed it and didn't even jerk the car around.

Once in the captain's seat I began to pass the first batch of cars, five at first. Then ten. It was a winding road in the mountains, so finding a safe moment was tricky and fairly dangerous. Pete Karman was the least sympathetic to my plan. Another opportunity to pass presented itself and I stepped on the gas, getting the station wagon up to seventy or so as I entered a blind corner in the oncoming traffic lane. We were passing car after car for what seemed like forever. Then out of the blue we saw the cause of the holdup. It was a funeral procession for a local mayor! I had the station wagon floored, so slowing down by the time we passed the police cars that were in front of the hearse was impossible. Instantly the lead police officer turned on his lights and began to chase us. I had to keep going long enough for the gang to hide all the drugs, which was much longer than any normal person would have taken to pull over. I figured I was going to jail at this point.

Once I got the okay from everyone in the car that all the drugs had been hidden, I pulled over to be berated by the policeman. I did my best to offer an excuse, stating that we were a travelling singing group with a show booked in Reno that started in a few hours, and if we missed it we were not going to get paid. The cop looked around, noticed Bob's guitar and eased up on us, letting us off with a warning.

On February 22, we arrived in Berkeley, the stomping ground of North Beach poets, Joan and Mimi Baez and Richard Fariña. Paul was tight with Richard. Bob's reception was warm. The venue was packed to a sold-out crowd at the Berkeley Community Theatre. Bob hammered out new tunes like "Walls of Redwing," "Who Killed Davey Moore," "Eternal Circle" and "Chimes of Freedom." Pete Karman asked me for two tickets for his friends, which further illustrated his cluelessness to our scene. Bob and Pete were already at each other's throats in recent days, and him asking me for tickets to a sold-out packed show left me with one response: "Fuck off." Pete was out, Bob and I had already agreed. It was time for his departure; I had him book a flight back to New York the next day.

After Pete's exit we picked up Bobby Neuwirth, a kid from Akron, Ohio, a songwriter who would ultimately be my replacement as tour manager after my second exit from traveling with Dylan. There was only one person who could partake in Bob's and my existential conversations and really contribute to the way we spoke and maintain our style of dialogue, and that was Bob Neuwirth. Our talks would expand the boundaries of our philosophy; we would push the limits of the meaning of words and bend ideas around new phrases.

There were lots of people who would try to get close to Bob, to communicate with him on a deeper level; the most aggressive attempts would be from people using their power in the entertainment business to get access to him. All of these people failed. When I was on tour Bob would ask me to stand between him and them—this happened many times—and was the case with an Italian promoter, a German promoter and even Bill Graham. They would try and draw Bob into conversations as if they were friends and not just business partners for a day or a tour. Bob wasn't interested. He would even tell me, "Make sure he doesn't get me alone," when dealing with these situations. Bob Neuwirth, on the other hand, was on our level from day one. My only concern with him was his drinking. Since Bob was a drinker, I knew the two of them wouldn't be a good influence on each other in the aspect of excess. At the time Neuwirth thought I was silly for even bringing up the idea that he needed to tone down the drinking. I didn't bring it up much, but I did bring it up.

Bobby, Bob, Paul and I headed to Joan Baez's house in Carmel, California. We rolled in with some of the backstage food we took with us from the show the night before as gifts to the Baez family. Joan's mother made us dinner and afterward we all went to a coffee shop in nearby Monterey's Cannery Row district, named in honor of John Steinbeck and his novel that described a lively past of cannery culture. Joan's father, Alfred Baez, and Bob butted heads; Bob's anti-authority vibe was contentious for him. Bob's lyrics for "The Times They Are a-Changin'" were a talking point for Alfred.

The next morning we hit the road to Los Angeles; Joan followed us in her Jaguar XKE. Los Angeles would be our triumphant end to the sedan station wagon tour of 1964.

Flash forward fifty years, and the Ford station wagon is not only still around, it has become an art installation in the front yard of Garth Hudson, a member of The Band. It's now growing grass and trees out of the trunk and windows. It's truly taken on a life of its own.

When we got back to New York City, Albert Grossman came to me and said, "You forgot to do one of the shows?!" I said he was crazy and we ended up in a big argument. Albert launched into me, saying it was my fault that we didn't do one of the concerts he planned along the way. I showed him what paperwork I had regarding the tour and told him that I had no idea what show he was talking about and that the office had never called me to inform me of a new show in the schedule.

He tried to dump this debacle on me but it was really his fault. At the end of our argument I told Albert to shove it up his ass and I stormed out of his office. Mind you, this was only a few months into my employment with Bob. But it wasn't Albert's idea to hire me, it was Bob's. Albert didn't like that I was closer to Bob than he was.

After I stormed out of the office, Bob came up to me and said I shouldn't have played my final card with Albert, referring to me telling him to shove it. I looked Bob in the eyes and said that Albert was trying to blame something on me that wasn't my fault and I wouldn't roll over that easily. Bob was already leaning toward believing Albert, but in the end Albert admitted messing up the tour schedule and the situation resolved itself.

This was an especially sticky situation since I was living at Albert's house in Bearsville, New York, with Bob at this time. My room was the old kitchen in the back of the house, a section constructed of old bricks and solid wood beams. There was a massive fireplace and a brick floor. There were a couple of studios on the property as well, and a pool. The entire property was about thirty or forty acres. Albert bought the place with his Peter, Paul and Mary money.

When I first lived with Bob, I would be out in the street in the middle of winter. He would be in his room typing or writing, drinking coffee and smoking cigarettes. In the evening he'd start drinking liqueur, while continuing the coffee and smoking. He would take breaks and go to the store and see me with people, having fun and communicating. I remember hanging out with a buddy, Tony Price, in an abandoned mill. It was an old waterwheel-type place but run down with a lot of crap lying around. Bob saw me and said, "You're having fun?" This was curious for me and equally curious for him. His driving force isn't to have fun, it's to think and internalize things in his life. What drives Bob is looking for compassion, understanding and sympathy from others. I believe it's three things he has a hard time giving to anybody.

Bob would torture me; on occasion he was very hard on me. I drove him over to visit his parents at a house on Sixty-first Street in New York and he gets out and says, "You stay in the car. Don't get out of the car." So that's what I did, I just sat there. But a few minutes went by and his mother came outside and noticed me sitting there, so she yelled at me, "Victor! You gotta come in! We have birthday cake, it's Bob's birthday." She pulled me out of the car and dragged me into the house. Once inside, she put her arm around me and said very quietly, "I know, if not for you, he might not be living." She said it like a mother would say such a thing, as if the meaning behind the words was more important than the statement as a fact. But I didn't think much about it. I sat for a moment, had a piece of cake, used the restroom and then excused myself and went back to the car.

I was expecting Bob to come freaking out at me any moment, and sure enough, he barreled out of the front door yelling at me. "You were in the house! I said stay in the car!" Just completely nuts in broad daylight in New York City. Now, you have to understand this type of chemistry because it happens to all of us at certain times in our life. He could lose control more than other people and go off like that. He was on the edge, I think, because he had, and still has, a narrow social view for his personal relationships. But where he has a narrow view in one area, personal relationships, he has a view of poetry that reaches further and sees more than anyone else, which he's able to write down. So the dynamics of his personality balance out, if you're willing to accept his shortcomings and be in awe of his brilliance. He's not perfect; he can be an asshole just like the rest of us.

I walked off while he was yelling at me. I just got out of the car and walked away. He kept flipping out and yelled for a bit, then went back inside.

Over the decades I spent much time at the house on Sixty-first Street. Katharine Hepburn lived next door, and Bob's dog Brutus would shit in her flowerbed all the time. Katharine, however, loved Brutus. Brutus never lay down in her flowerbed, which was her fear since he was a 160-pound dog, and he covered a big area. She would spend her time out gardening every day in the summertime. Brutus seemed to love taking a crap there, and I think it was due to the fertilizer that she was using. Maybe, he wanted to help out or just thought that the flowerbed was the spot for his poop since there was already poop there. He was actually a very conscientious dog. I want to write a children's book about Brutus since he was so fantastic.

Katharine would come over, looking very well put together, and say, "Victor?" in a sweet voice, and I would instantly know to grab a plastic bag, because Brutus probably left a five-pound

turd in her flowers. The dog could really lay some logs. I think
if it was a small dog, she wouldn't have cared. But with Brutus
it was truly a landmine.

People would run across the street to talk to this dog! But
for the many people who would run towards Brutus, there were
just as many running away from him. He had eyes like silver
dollars, had a head bigger than a human's resting on top of
massive jaws. These types of dogs, British bullmastiffs, were
the dogs of the Roman legions. They traveled along with the
soldiers and ate the carnage left behind from the battles.

In May of 1964, Bob and I flew to England, our first trip to
Europe together. The plan was fairly simple: Bob was going
to do some press and perform one show. In the mix was a plan to
visit Paris and Athens. Our time in London went by quickly.
After an interview with the BBC, a few local TV appearances
and a press conference, we set up for the Royal Festival Hall
show on the seventeenth. Bob was scheduled to perform in
the early afternoon to a sold-out crowd of two thousand five
hundred fans. I was baffled by this; I didn't understand how
the show was sold out. In the United States we were still on the
edge of filling venues this big. When we arrived we didn't expect
much, and we definitely didn't know the Royal Hall was such
an important venue.

When we loaded into the venue, I could see it was being remodeled and wasn't surprised to see the entire dressing room
area under construction. They provided us with a temporary
dressing room, deep down in the building at the end of a long,
narrow hallway. Bob went onstage and completely captivated

and bewildered the entire audience. He had them in the palm
of his hand. He played straight for two hours with magic in
the air; if they weren't singing along, they were screaming.
Bob surprised everyone with "It Ain't Me, Babe"; it was the first
time he had ever played it for an audience. He also played
"Chimes of Freedom," "Who Killed Davey Moore," "Walls
of Redwing," "Masters of War" and "A Hard Rain's a-Gonna
Fall." It was hit after hit, and the audience couldn't handle it.
When Bob finished the show I rushed him back to the dressing
room, but the crowd was so worked up they weren't leaving. It
seemed like they all wanted more—which became a concern of
mine, since we didn't have any security. I was the security.
When we got to the dressing room, deep in the basement of the
building, crowds and crowds of people followed us back. There
was nobody telling anyone that any place was off limits!

I closed the door, and behind me in the hallway were hundreds of people, shoulder to shoulder. It was evident that we
were not going anywhere for the time being. Inside the dressing
room was also a small crowd: Albert Grossman, the local
promoter, the local public relations guy and others from the
production staff in London. Knowing the gauntlet of people that
awaited us outside the door, I told Bob and Albert that we
weren't going anywhere; that we needed to wait them out and
relax, or else we would have to fight our way out. Bob agreed,
so I did what I did best when it was time to relax: I pulled out a
few joints and Bob and I sat and smoked and filled up the entire little room with smoke and laughter.

We really made the best of it and ended up having a great

time. Bob felt comfortable enough and talked with the few people in the room. I didn't allow the door to open or people to exit or enter, so the vibe stayed the same. Albert, on the other hand, wasn't as relaxed as Bob and I were; he was quite uneasy at the thought of the overzealous crowd lining the hallway all the way to the street. We carried on for two hours talking, smoking joints and hanging out with our new British friends.

When Bob was ready for the action, he asked me, "What do you think, Victor?" I looked out the door, but not much had changed. I responded, "If you're ready, we'll push our way out." Bob agreed and jumped up. I opened the door and when the crowd noticed him they all went nuts screaming and trying to grab him. I pulled Bob between my arms, put both my hands on the wall and slid down the hallway slowly pushing people out of the way. I could feel pressure on my entire body from people pushing into us. There wasn't an inch of space. I was afraid of Bob being crushed by the weight of the crowd!

I was covered in sweat, pushing and forcing people out of the way. In the middle of this chaos, I noticed Bob's expression. He was in a trance, in thrall to the moment, and it was at that time that he first felt the true essence of the rock star; he knew from that moment forward that his life would never be the same. His trajectory into the stratosphere of fame had started and there was no stopping it. This really was also the first time Bob was introduced to the crazed fan, something that he would have to endure for the rest of his life. It ultimately would have a significant impact on his personality in the years to come. We noticed those personalities emerge with the growth of his fame.

Four days after the show we traveled to Athens, Greece. Bob and I had no plan in mind, nowhere to go. We just showed up. We received many suggestions from people, mostly saying that we should go to the islands. But what Bob wanted was a quiet place where he could write, so I suggested that we just drive out into the country without knowing where we'll end up. He agreed and I pointed the rental car south and drove us outside of Athens. A small village called Vouliagmeni sparked our interest and we decided it was the spot for our vacation.

We found a small, comfortable place to stay in a bunker left over from the First World War, situated on a rocky beach at the edge of the Aegean Sea. Two elderly ladies had turned the bunker into a five-room hotel. From their sun-splashed appearance they could have been a hundred and fifty years old and they took us in with motherly care; with open arms they took care of Bob day and night. They took care of me too, but I needed less since I was out exploring most of the day. Bob on the other hand buried himself in his writing; his focus was sharper than ever.

The older ladies didn't speak English and we didn't speak any Greek so we only communicated by hand gestures. It was a charming experience and we benefited from being their only guests for the entirety of our stay. They made us feel right at home.

During our first real day at the hotel, Bob and I drove back to Athens to get some hash to smoke, which we were able to score in the old part of town. After we smoked a few tobacco and hash cigarettes, our hunger implored us to find a restaurant on the way back out of town. We stopped at a fancy place on the sea, got a table and ordered some food. Bob got up to use the restroom and I sat at the table waiting for what seemed like an hour.

After the food had arrived and I'd eaten most of what I had ordered, I started to think that either Bob had left, or that he was dead. Granted, we were very high from the hash. I resolved to find him and went straight to the restrooms around the back of the hotel; when I approached I heard banging coming from the toilet and it was Bob going nuts from being locked in the stall for almost an hour. The door had jammed, and since it was all mortar and concrete, you couldn't hear anything once you stepped out of the restroom. For the entire time nobody came to his rescue. He was irate but we had a good laugh afterward. However, our laughter proved short-lived—we ran out of gas immediately after getting back in the car and ended up pushing the car a block to a gas station.

Once back at the hotel it was obvious that Bob had had enough excitement for a while. The days that followed were simple and relaxing. I explored the coast and swam in the sea; Bob stayed at the hotel writing with unbridled access to coffee and cigarettes. I didn't put any pressure on Bob to hang out or ask anything of him; as his friend I was sympathetic to his needs, as he was to mine. He needed a quiet place to think and write; I wanted a place to swim and explore the scenery. Together we found it in this hotel in Vouliagmeni and took from it as we needed. In addition to being a sympathetic friend I was also the tour manager—not that we were on tour, but that mentality carries over into our general time together. My feeling about being tour manager is fairly simple; my number one job is to figure out how to make Bob's personal space as comfortable and organized as possible. The days rolled by while Bob wrote and I swam. We both had a wonderful, relaxing time.

When we got back to New York in August 1964, we dove straight into the recording studio and Bob played a bunch of new songs: all lyrics he had written while in Vouliagmeni. He played them all one after another without rehearsing. Out of the eleven songs on the album I had heard maybe one or two on our trip. It was amazing to me. He practiced all by himself, wrote by himself and never sang them in front of anybody until this moment, and when we got to the studio he just blurted it out, like electricity building up in a capacitor and then shooting out: He had packed it all inside himself and let it explode. I was on the floor; it knocked the air out of me. I was in a daze; some of those songs are the best, ever. They're not a promise, they're not a dream, it's not bullshit, he's laying it down so accurately, so clean, he could have been talking about toilet paper and it would have still pulled you up. You had to listen to it. This recording session became the album *Another Side of Bob Dylan*. I'll never forget it, while I was swimming in the Aegean Sea he was making history and that's how our friendship was. No pressure, you do your thing and I'll do mine.

Bob wasn't making a massive amount of money at the time; the crowds were just starting to show up. The fact that the Royal Hall show had drawn two thousand five hundred people was a big deal. Realizing that you're going to be rich and very successful is a heavy thing to consider; you don't just start out that way, it's a fantasy. A fantasy that, as a musician, all your friends share with you—the idea that one day you'll be rich and famous. It's very much a group fantasy for all artists. And suddenly in those months in 1964 Bob started to notice it was different for him than it was for the other folksingers in the Village scene. He noticed he was being separated from the group, elevated in popularity. When this happens to musicians, or to anyone who's seeking notoriety for that matter, they become uncomfortable with their original group, because it seems unfair they were singled out.

As the months rolled by after the Royal Hall show, Bob became closer with people on the same level of success as him, because they could identify with what he was starting to deal with and the social implications that came along with it. When you become a celebrity, any idiosyncrasies that are peculiar are amplified by fame and fortune. But that also works in a positive way, because if someone is a health nut or clean from drugs, that new power can push them to be even stronger with their ideals and convictions. For Bob, it was both ways. His quirky social norms were amplified because his celebrity power kept people's ability to control him at bay. He could sleep in his clothes and on couches if he wanted to. This may not sound so great to you and me but it's something Bob became very comfortable with early in his life. Being broke and without a home will force you into personality traits that are hard to erase. On the other hand, he developed the financial means to create better environments for his writing; writing is what Bob loves to do above all else. In my opinion, he's a writer/poet first, a musician second and a singer third.

In these early years his magic was manifested in the words he spliced together and the phrases he bent the meaning to; through this he got everybody's attention. Although not everyone enjoyed Bob's opinion; as a matter of fact, there were many that didn't like what he had to say. Some of those people turned around later when they realized what he was really doing. The remaining few who didn't like his message became increasingly emphatic, usually putting him down for his quality of singing and not for what he was singing about. This was a personal conflict for me because there were guys out there, other folksingers, who I looked up to that fell into this camp. Like Erik Darling, whose first comment to me about Bob was that he was a "guttersnipe." Erik went off to me about Bob, which isn't something most people do when talking about somebody they know you're close with. These days Erik has come around and says that he was wrong all those years. But there are still those who will never change and appreciate what Bob has to offer. I call them the right wing of folk music. Bob was thoroughly accepted by the left-wing folksingers and industry people; they gave him all the awards right away, acknowledged him and his ideas early on. They accepted him much faster than the greater public.

When we got back to the United States, there were a few months in late 1964 and early 1965 when Bob and I would drive around a lot to explore. We were driving around the East Coast, through the Midwest and randomly made it to the University of

Wisconsin at Madison. On these trips we would just show up at colleges and talk to people. We would find someone walking around with a guitar and start a conversation. One thing would lead to another, and we'd be someplace with all the local musicians playing music.

In Madison, we ended up on the second floor of a guitar shop with about thirty people playing music and hanging out. We had a great time, and later in the evening Bob and I left with two gorgeous women.

As we walked back to the sedan, I jumped into the driver's seat with my girl and Bob got in back with his girl. I started thinking, Well, this sucks, he's always in back and I'm chauffeuring him around. I want to be in the back kissing the girl I'm with, but instead I'm forced to drive! Granted, I didn't mind most of the time, since we had our new Ford station wagon and what felt like boundless money. But this moment was different. I remember thinking this was fucked, that he always got to be in the back. About eleven minutes into driving, Bob said, "Victor, stop the car, I want to drive." I said, "What do you mean?" He was adamant about it, so I pulled over.

It was unbelievable, like a lightning bolt hit the car! I got in the back with my girl and Bob and his girl climbed in front. We started driving, and I noticed the girl was all over Bob, kissing his neck and grabbing on him. After a few minutes Bob said, "Victor, can you jump up front with me, I don't know where I'm going." I shot back, "What?!?!?" I'm kissing the girl I'm with, feeling her up and having a great time. Bob kept going and said, "Yeah, I want you to sit up here and help me figure out where we're going." He pulled over and made his girl get in the back.

The fact of the matter is, he couldn't handle the girl being so forward, he's never been able to. He's only attracted to the passive and mellow women who don't ask too much of him. It was a funny situation with this very forward girl who wanted to get in Bob's pants; he just didn't want anything to do with it. So I got in front and we dropped the girls off somewhere and hit the road laughing about it while smoking some joints. Bob just wasn't a sexual guy like I was. It didn't matter to me, I was still having fun.

The first time Bob took acid I offered it to him in Albert's house. Sally Grossman was there. Sara Lownds was there and possibly Patti Elam, my lady. Albert wasn't around that night. Tom Law had the acid and gave it to me. At that time Bob and I were kicking around a movie idea—it was based on the sense of alienation that couples with fame. He would write some ideas down and hand it to me, and I'd type some stuff and hand it back. We never ended up writing a whole lot about it, just a little bit here and there. That night he wrote several pages, it could have been about the movie concept but I'm not really sure. I was enjoying my own acid trip.

To write, Bob would retreat to his room and only come out when he was taking a break or getting more coffee and cigarettes. Three, four hours later he would walk out as if only two minutes had passed. He would walk out and ask me what I thought, but he wasn't looking for help with it. It was more like a, *This is finished, how does it make you feel* kind of thing. In the time that he was hidden away writing I had been up a tree, in the pool and around the block exploring my surroundings. In a way there was a parallel to our experience, I explored the physical world and when I found something worth sharing, be that a beach or cafe or whatever, I would show it to him and he explored the existential, the emotional, the inspirational, and when he had something special he would share it with me and then the world.

We also drew a lot that night, the whole gang. We had a four-foot endless roll of paper that we unfurled and filled with miles and miles of illustrations.

When the sun came up, we all crawled into bed like bats, vampires.

~

End of Tape Three

CHAPTER 4

~

Bob and I Make Some
New Friends

Bob Dylan near the Brooklyn Bridge, 1965. *(Courtesy Victor Maymudes)*

Tape Four

♩♫ August 28, 1964, was a gray day in Bearsville.

Summertime in New York State is usually lush and green
but this day seemed to have had the saturation drawn out of
it. As we drove the half mile down the driveway through the
woods from Albert Grossman's house, Bob lit a Marlboro and

I lit a joint. Our tires crunched the gravel and a sweet, loamy smell rushed in, carried on the damp wind. A light rain created a pensive mood as we bumped onto a two-lane country road outside Woodstock, headed for the thruway into New York City to keep our date with the Beatles.

While I drove, the two of us talked over what we knew about them. The first time I ever read about the Beatles was in my office on Sunset Boulevard. I used to get all the trade papers every day and read them cover to cover. One day, the *Weekly Billboard* had an article about a group who were creating a buzz in Hamburg, Germany, and I felt a connection. The article said that this English rock 'n' roll band was packing in the audience in big numbers. Thanks to them, the club at which they were performing had become a hot spot in Hamburg. They were writing their own tunes that were becoming major hits like "Love Me Do." I actually cut the article out of the paper.

In the early sixties, those of us who felt the winds of change and welcomed that change as a necessary corrective to life in the United States and the world felt a particular camaraderie. We sought each other out. One clue was the length of your hair. When I started growing long hair, people would stop me on the street to ask, "Why don't you get a haircut?" The length of my hair was a statement, they were feeling the force, but I had no interest in articulating my rationale. I didn't want anybody to know that there was a private club. Bob started to grow his hair longer, too. And then, lo and behold, we saw a picture of the

Beatles in the paper with long hair. So we already knew that they were with us, before we ever exchanged a word.

Bob could feel the magic in their music. As we listened to their songs on the drive, we analyzed their words; we focused on the architecture of their sentences. They used phrases in their songs we didn't understand: "Birds" we knew were girls, but what exactly did "gear" mean? We had heard them use Liverpool slang in interviews and we knew the lyrics from their songs, which were playing continuously on the radio, but it wasn't always easy to understand what they were saying or what they meant. Bob understood why their rock 'n' roll songs crossed over into mainstream culture. It was a boundary he very much wanted to cross.

We had read about them, and seen their pictures, and couldn't believe the kind of public adulation they attracted. They even had a word for it: Beatlemania. Bob had made a name for himself by 1964, although it was still within a rather limited group of people in the know. The Dylan phenomenon had not yet moved from counterculture to the mainstream. Bob's model, like John Lennon's, was Elvis Presley. The Beatles had conquered the hearts of the world by singing very simple songs, and frankly we wanted to know how they did it.

"Do you think they really get high?" Bob asked me.

We thought they might, because of the line in their song "I Wanna Hold Your Hand," which actually ran: "And when I touch you, I feel happy inside. It's such a feeling that my love I can't hide, I can't hide, I can't hide!" But because of their accents, we thought they were singing, "I get high, I get high, I get high!"

Al Aronowitz was a reporter on the scene from the earliest days in the Village. He had introduced the Beat Poets to the mainstream press, writing about Jack Kerouac and Allen Ginsberg when no one outside of a tiny circle of aficionados knew their names. Billie Holiday, and a generation of black singers, might not have achieved crossover status had it not been for Al Aronowitz. Aronowitz wrote for the *New York Post,* where his first article about the Beatles had been so successful that the paper had sent him to Europe. He met the Beatles in England and told them about Bob Dylan.

Al Aronowitz had called us from Europe to tell us that they would be coming to New York. In his usual way, Bob had at first been indifferent to the idea of meeting them but eventually had allowed himself to be talked into the idea, despite their "bubblegum" music, as he called it. Al had talked to John Lennon about meeting Bob. John had told Aronowitz that he wanted to wait until he considered himself Bob's ego equal. The Beatles' first American tour began in the early months of 1964, and by that summer, both sides were ready.

That night of August 28 was the big night. The Beatles were in town staying at the Delmonico Hotel. On our way to Manhattan, we stopped by Al Aronowitz's house in Berkeley Heights, New Jersey. He was hosting Allen Ginsberg and his boyfriend, Peter Orlovsky, for dinner when we arrived. Al wrapped up his dinner party and jumped in the car with us, and we all headed for the Delmonico. On the way, Al told us of

his plan to turn the Beatles on to pot. Al was a great believer
in the enlightening power of marijuana. He considered pot a
wonder drug, nourishment for the brain, the consummate head
food. He had the zeal of a convert and wanted to share what
had transformed his own psychic experience. The Beatles had
been wary of it in Europe, but Al had convinced them to open
up their minds. He believed that our influence would make it
happen.

We parked three blocks away on this quiet street and Al
jumped out and left us all sitting in the car. He walked off to
the hotel and we waited close to an hour. He returned with the
Beatles' public relations guy, Derek Taylor, who turned out to
be a fabulous guy—a truly great guy who was with the Beatles
from the beginning. We all got out and started walking.

New York City seemed serene and beautiful that night; we
were surrounded by huge, towering buildings all around. You
could see shadows from the streetlights dancing off the windows in an endless, dizzying display of reflections. It was also
very quiet, so quiet you could hear a pin drop. As we got closer,
we started to hear what sounded like an ocean. Continuous
noise. Like white noise from a television. We turned a corner
onto Park Avenue and there was this *huge* crowd. We couldn't
believe it. It was like a crisis had happened. There were people
behind barricades on both sides of the street and cops on horses
walking up and down Park Avenue. People were everywhere; I
had never witnessed such madness.

Nobody recognized Bob Dylan either, which is an interesting thing to note considering he was surrounded by a sea of

people, most of whom knew who he was. I can explain it like this: Bob can walk and look *unlike* Bob. He hunches over, he softens his body, curls his shoulders and walks so innocuously that you don't pay attention to him. I walk in front of him, so I block a lot of what people can see of his face and his body. He gets in step with me so we're real close, like synchronized military walking. Later on, in the venues around the world where you have to exit out the front of the venue, we would use this same technique. And it worked! Even when we were walking through a crowd of people that had just watched him onstage. Nobody would ever recognize him.

Derek Taylor led the way to the Delmonico Hotel; he had all the credentials and papers. We made it through the first barricade and approached the second one, where cops and security guards were stationed ten feet apart. There must have been a hundred cops there. We got to the second barricade and Derek showed the credentials again. I didn't have any documents; neither did Bob or Al Aronowitz. Derek yells at the top of his lungs, "These guys are with me!" He repeats this over and over. "These guys are with me!" I don't think the cops actually heard him over the noise of the crowd but they seemed to understand and let us pass.

We walked up to the hotel, which we had to enter one at a time through a revolving door. Derek went through, Al went through, Bob went through and then I went through. We had just gotten inside the lobby, when suddenly I felt a hand on the back of my jacket, on my shoulder like someone was going to ask me a question. I went through the regular door over the

first barricade headfirst on my back and was *thrown* into the
crowd! Before I could blink an eye, I was back outside in the
middle of the braying masses. It happened in an instant. I was
thinking, Oh, fuck! I'm going to get arrested; I'm holding all
the pot! People were staring down at me and the scene was a
mess. I heard someone yelling over me, I looked up and it was
Derek Taylor, screaming, "He's with me! He's with me!" They
helped me up and dragged me back inside. I was extremely
shaken up, my heart pounding at the walls of my chest. I was
hurting a little bit, but luckily I still had all the pot in my pocket.

We proceeded to the elevator and headed up to the top floor.
There was a cop in front of every door going down the hallway,
all sitting in chairs in front of the doors. It was like the president was staying on the floor—totally locked down. We got to
the suite where the Beatles were; everyone else was at the other
end of the hallway, in another suite. Every celebrity you could
imagine was down the hallway, including friends of mine—
Peter, Paul and Mary and their road manager, Tom Law.

Derek, Al, Bob and I entered the amber-painted suite. Pitched
against one wall was an overstuffed couch upholstered in navy
blue. Against the opposite wall was a dining room table covered
with stemware and ice and every kind of liquor. In the center of
the room stood a glass coffee table and a few more plain wooden
chairs. Brian Epstein and the four of them were waiting for
us. They looked just like the pictures. Their hair was not long
but neatly trimmed, combed down in their mop-top cuts. They
were extremely clean and youthful looking, without a trace of
facial hair. They dressed in gray collarless suits and skinny

black ties, white shirts and black leather boots with a seam that ran down the middle to the pointy toes. They looked sharp, like perfect mod gentlemen. We were in jeans, T-shirts and leather jackets, looking scraggly and relaxed, the image of laid-back American youth in every James Dean movie. Bob was still wearing his motorcycle boots. Of course, they were on tour and we weren't, but the different styles went beyond that. At that time, Bob wouldn't have worn a suit like theirs, even if he played for the Queen of England. An ocean yawned between us, but it didn't take us long to cross it.

Al Aronowitz introduced me. They didn't need to be introduced to Bob, nor he to them. Bob extended his traditional limp handshake and each shook it in turn. Then they shook mine. John lit a cigarette and as they always did afterwards, offered another to everyone in the room. They were smoking American cigarettes; Bob and I accepted one to be polite even though we had our own. Al told them what had happened to me in front of the hotel, and they could see I was still a little rattled from it. They were very kind to me, asking if I was feeling all right. I checked again to make sure the pot was still in my pocket and told them I was fine.

At first Bob said very little. He cannot talk to a group of people except from the stage, and that's hardly a conversation. It's a monologue. John Lennon was the same way, both wordsmiths who got tongue-tied speaking to small groups. But Bob turned his smile on them, and the Beatles answered with their own happy charisma, the five of them eyeing each other like bashful kids at a dance. Bob made an effort to talk to them, answering their questions. We talked about guitars and about music, but only superficially. Their banter was very funny as they talked about people at the party down the hall and exchanged cryptic lines about New York.

Aronowitz saw his chance to spread the psychedelic gospel and asked the Beatles, "You wanna get high?"

They did. Bob took the marijuana from me and pulled up a wooden chair next to the glass coffee table in the middle of the room. He wanted to show them he knew his stuff—he tried to roll a joint and it fell to pieces in his hands, scattering pot over a bowl of fruit sitting on the table. I sat down next to him and took the pot away from him so that I could roll joints, as I usually did. The four Beatles were walking around the room, very animated, and excited about what was about to happen. They were wired, running on coffee and adrenaline from touring.

Bob grabbed a drink while I rolled a joint. When he came back to the coffee table, I lit it with a match and passed it to him. Bob took a hit and passed it to John, who then handed it to Ringo without putting it to his lips. "You try it," John told Ringo. Ringo hesitated. John called him his "royal pot taster" and then Ringo did as John commanded. He held it like a cigarette between his fingers, taking one deep drag after another. He didn't know the proper etiquette of pot: to pass it on to John, who was sitting next to him, patiently awaiting his turn.

I wasn't going to tell him to pass it because we just met, so I just rolled one for John. He lit up the joint and didn't pass it either! So I rolled another one for Paul and then again for George. I kept rolling joints till everyone had their own except

Bob. He just had alcohol and took a few hits here and there but not a whole joint like the rest of us. Bob had a couple of drinks and within an hour, he passed out on the floor! By this time, Paul was laughing so hard that tears were streaming out of his eyes. This was their very first encounter and Bob passed out! This wasn't entirely because of the booze either. We were up all the time; he was exhausted. He might have been up nonstop the three days beforehand. But the booze didn't help; it shoots you up and then crashes you down.

With Bob sleeping on the floor, one by one John, Paul, George and Ringo talked to me. We discussed life and politics. They wanted to know about everyone and everything: who was in our scene, what it was like in New York. I couldn't believe how sensitive and aware of everybody they were. How concerned they were, whether I was okay. I was never made to feel inferior to them.

A little side note about the Beatles smoking pot: That first night wasn't actually their first time trying it, like everyone believes. They had tried it before but they didn't get high. The stuff they had was cheap and low quality. They knew about hash, that kind of stuff was more popular in Europe. But until that night, they never had the rush. They'd never laughed till tears rolled down their faces.

The following morning, Paul came up to me and hugged me for ten minutes and said, "It was so great, and it's all your fault! It's all your fault because I love this pot!" He went into his thoughts on music while on it and how it made him feel. "It was just magical," he said. Ringo also came to me and said, "Is this the thing I have to be smoking now for the rest of my life, to enjoy a feeling like that?" I responded with, "Yeah, unfortunately it doesn't stay with you. You have to keep doing it."

Later that morning John talked to me about the other Americans he had met so far. Before Bob and I met him, he was in Texas, where he met a rancher who owned two million acres of land. He said to me, "What does a guy want with two million acres? The gentleman was so proud too!" We talked about the stupidity of excess, how accumulating wealth can be an addiction of its own. You see, John's social-political awareness was in its infancy. I was very in tune with progressive politics at the time, due to my upbringing and my parents' political activity. This was the beginning of many conversations with John about U.S. and world politics. We also touched on the relationship between politics and music.

We discussed black singers and black music; he was very interested in the blues. The blues were really coming into the scene. Even Bob played the blues. That was no secret. Bob basically played simple twelve-bar blues, and some people thought at this time that he only knew one song mechanically. He insisted, however, that he only knew the structure and chords of five songs and all else was a spin-off or continuation. Our conversation continued in this vein; we talked about everything, flitting from subject to subject.

John explained how the doctors had already got to him. How they had given him and the other guys open access to pills and various pharmaceuticals. Every type, you name it. They had handfuls of pills in their room—uppers and downers. I mean, *handfuls* that the doctors had downloaded on them. I instantly put the doctors down and proceed to explain my philosophy on the medical industry. To me they were the enemy, overmedicating and pushing pills as the only course of remedy. And in these situations they can be overzealous from the celebrity interaction, going beyond what's necessary to impress or befriend. Just like drug dealers would hand out drugs to artists backstage, doctors played the same role for the same reasons. I watched it happen and on a few occasions, I took advantage of it too. But I believed they were the enemy then, and I do to this day. Not all doctors, but that mentality—always enabling patients to take pills, especially celebrities, giving them unbridled access to shit they don't need. John said this was the first time he had ever heard someone talk like that about doctors. It opened him up to the idea that what they were prescribing could be excessive.

Around midday I was walking around the suite and I went to the window to check out the scene, to see the madness below. The room was six floors up and I looked over the window's edge down at Park Avenue. I saw the crowd below, and all of a sudden, the roar of them knocked me back. The noise was so great, it forced me away from the window. It felt like the crowd could come right in! And we were six floors up! It was a surreal experience because they all thought I was one of the Beatles. I looked at Bob and told him to try it out. He walked up to the window and, sure enough, the same thing happened: huge screams, a tidal wave of noise. We were laughing and carrying on with it, one by one we all did it. All the guys, each one of us, kept going back. We could control the level of noise; it was like we were making a song. Roaring cheers then subtle cheers, then roaring cheers, then subtle cheers. At the end we all went up together and the people went bananas! I thought the glass was going to shatter, it was so loud.

At one point after our window gag, George came to me and mentioned that none of his roadies knew what to do when things got a little out of hand, when things started to fall apart. He started this conversation because he saw me check it all out. I'm a restless guy and my nature was to check it all out—the whole scene, wherever we were, whatever we were doing. I was good at being aware of my environment, avoiding problems and solving them should they arise. George saw this in me and mentioned that his guys were not professional, they were new guys, and that level of fame and touring was new to them. The thing is, I'd already had years of experience with this, years of experience promoting concerts. This was my world. George noticed that and appreciated it. This was the foundation of our friendship, this sort of respect for how we each operated. Over the years George and I would grow closer and remain good friends.

A few weeks later, the Beatles were playing a benefit concert for United Cerebral Palsy and the Retarded Infant Services, the only benefit concert of their first American tour. The venue was the Paramount Theatre at Broadway and Forty-third Street. Over thirty-six hundred people were in the audience. Bob and I met them in their dressing room and watched the show from the side of the stage behind the curtain. Again, the audience was so loud, you could not hear the band.

There were so many flashbulbs, billions of flashbulbs, a

blinding amount of flashes from cameras. This was the moment Bob decided he didn't want flashbulbs at his shows. Just like that, we couldn't tell people not to scream, but we tried to keep cameras and flashbulbs from concerts. All because of that Beatles show.

The whole thing was truly silly. The Beatles could have put a record on; they didn't have to try and sing! It would have even been better for the audience, because in those days bands didn't have speaker monitors, so they couldn't hear what they were doing over the screaming. Not to mention, the Beatles didn't have the right equipment to handle such a show in the first place, the PA wasn't enough. At that very moment, the PA systems and monitors that could handle it were still being invented, so not everyone had them. Even road cases, proper road cases, didn't exist. We had to use military cases on our tour to Australia. That Beatles show was a perfect example of the evolution of the massive rock show and the demand for new and better technology.

Later on that week, Bob and I were at a hotel with the Beatles by the airport in Brooklyn. Brian Epstein was hanging out with us now, mainly because the schmoozing was over and it was just the guys, Bob and me. All the other celebrities and industry people had left. John and Paul talked Brian into getting stoned, so he had a couple of hits and then went bananas! He was instantly in the corner freaking out and telling people to leave him alone. He went nuts; he was an extremely insecure guy and the pot exposed that.

Pot is a curious thing like that; it can either help you or expose your inner demons. I couldn't imagine the pressure he had at the time, being gay in the sixties. At that point being gay in England and Wales was a criminal offense! It was things like that that drove him to coping mechanisms like prescription drugs, which he had open access to. Ultimately he died from an overdose of sleeping pills. It was an incredibly sad moment for everyone in our circle.

After Brian calmed down that night, we gathered our things and headed out to the limousines to drive to dinner. After we ate we were packing back into the two limousines we had: Albert, Brian and Al were in one; Bob, John, Paul, George, Ringo and I were in the other. I opened the car door and they all jumped in, then I got in and closed the door. Well . . . somebody farted . . . I instantly thought it was Bob. But John looked right at me, like I did it, and said in that brilliant British accent, "The secret is to jump up and down before getting in the car to shake the farts out." I thought that was hilarious—words of wisdom from one of the world's greatest songwriters. I still laugh about that to this day.

~~~

End of Tape Four

I'm a bit embarrassed that my father's legacy will largely consist of having a hand in turning the Beatles on to pot, rather than something a little more creative or academic.

This story about meeting the Beatles was so common during

story time when I was a teenager; I'd heard the ins and outs of it many times. It usually elicited a response from me to the tune of, "Dad . . . I've heard this before. Tell me something *new*."

It was also the first chapter that my father wrote when he started his book-writing process. It was used in his book proposal, which won the affinity of Kathleen Anderson, my mother's literary agent, and George Witte, my mother's publisher for *Above the Clouds*. My father was offered an advance to write his memoirs: He would receive one half to start writing, one quarter upon delivery of the manuscript and the remaining one quarter when it was published. This was a huge deal for my father, and he was thrilled by the offer.

He signed the publishing contract on July 24, 2000, for a book tentatively called *The Joker and the Thief: My Life with Dylan,* and started recording as much audio as he could. The manuscript was due to St. Martin's Press on or before December 1, 2001. One day before my father's sixty-fifth birthday.

Our stone house on Pecos River, Cerrito Amarillo Canyon, New Mexico, before and after the January 2013 fire. *Credit: Janelle Croshaw*

My father composed and played guitar all his adult life. Victor in Los Angeles in the mid-1950s. *Credit: Abe Maymudes*

Victor in Washington Square, Greenwich Village, New York early 1950s. *Credit: Abe Maymudes*

Bob Dylan enjoying some downtime after releasing his tenth studio album, *Self Portrait*. *Credit: Victor Maymudes*

Joan Baez holding her son Gabriel Harris while Bob Dylan waves to the camera. *Credit: Victor Maymudes*

Victor, lost in thought while writing poetry on the beach in Yelapa, an idyllic Mexican coast village that was my dad's refuge, 1963. *Credit: John Phillip Law. Courtesy: Pilar Law/The Archive Agency*

Victor and one of his closest friends, John Phillip Law, sharing a smoke in Truchas, New Mexico, 1969. *Credit: Lisa Law/The Archive Agency*

Napalm protest: my dad and his burnt baby mandala making a statement at the Monterey International Pop Music Festival, 1967.
Credit: Lisa Law/The Archive Agency

My parents Linda and Victor with my sister and our cousin, Michael Cord, relaxing in the yard of my grandparents' home on my mother's side, El Paso, Texas, 1973. *Credit: Maymudes Family Archive*

My grandparents Abe and Goldie with my father, sister and me (in the center) during my birthday party at the La Posada in Santa Fe, New Mexico, 1984. *Credit: Linda Wylie*

My mother, Linda Wylie, at a reunion with Dennis Hopper in Santa Fe, New Mexico, 1987. *Credit: Lisa Law/The Archive Agency*

Victor stands behind David Crosby on stage during setup for the Peace Sunday: We Have A Dream concert at the Rose Bowl in Los Angeles, 1982. *Credit: Lisa Law/The Archive Agency*

MOTEZUMA E 9/12
MASTERS Bm
TOMORROW IS E
LONG BLACK F#m
RIVER FLOW E
SIMPLE TWIST D
SERVE G

JOHN BROWN D
WOODY G.
TAMBOURINE D
BOOTS G

SILVIO G
TEARS OF RAGE C
WATCHTOWER Bm
WILL IN G
GARDEN B/MAGGIE G
ROLLING STONE C

To keep concerts fresh and unique for the audience, Bob Dylan individually selects each song to be performed from his catalog of over 450 songs with his band before every show. They are always handwritten and then photocopied for the production assistant to spread around the venue to all the roadies and sound engineers. *Credit: Maymudes Family Archive*

MONTE ZUMA 10/30
YOU GO YOUR WAY E
BE YOUR BABY G
MAN IN ME F
WHAT WAS IT Bm
SERVE SOME BODY G

HARD RAIN D
BOSTON BOY C
DESOLATION D
BOOTS G

JOEY C
PILLBOX HAT B
I BELIEVE IN YOU. E
WIGGLE WIGGLE F#
TV SONG A
RELEASED B♭

CHAPTER 5

~

Rock 'n' Roll Royalty

Bob and Victor pose for a publicity shot for Edward Chavez, 1964.
*(Copyright © 2014 Edward A. Chavez/The Archive Agency. Photo
Courtesy: Maia Chavez Larkin)*

Tape 5

In the early days we grew our hair long as an act of
defiance, but I took that further and rebelled inside of our own
group. When everyone around Bob and me started wearing suits,
I started wearing railroad conductor outfits with open-toe

sandals. Sometimes I'd mix it up with a naval captain's hat as well. It would fry the minds of Albert Grossman and the accountants because it was obvious I was rebelling against them. *À rebours.*

Bob and I searched for an identity in the clothes we bought; granted, it was only after Bob started to have an income that we really dove into fashion. He and I would go shopping at thrift stores together, searching for new identities when the one we were using started to get picked up by those around us. This cat-and-mouse game pushed us to wear increasingly outré clothes. We would try on every oddball outfit we could find, trying to stay one step ahead of our social group. On tours around the country, we would seek out the salvage clothing stores and pick out the wild stuff. I found polka-dot shirts with Bob, and I made that a big deal. Polka dots would become our contribution to the fashion of the sixties. I look back on it now and I think it's pretty funny how ridiculous we looked and how everyone around us took it so seriously. Bob and I shared this together, but I didn't have the spotlight on me the whole time as he did.

I did get to watch our taste in clothes influence a generation of kids. I was able to have fun with that. I would make jokes to Bob like, "What else can we make trendy?" At the end of the day, we were just clowning around, but the repercussions were tremendous; if we wore it, two weeks later everyone was wearing it. The kids copying us would take it even further, they would come to our shows in our style but times ten. Punk rock culture and that style seemed like the result of an evolution from us to our fans and, ten years down the road, to the punk music and that style. In the 1960s we created a platform of self-expression that opened up the next step, not only in music but fashion and all forms of creativity.

The only difference between then and now is that we didn't have a generation that did it before us. Our departure from the fifties was huge, like an explosion. Since then, fashion has been building on top of itself, deconstructing and rebuilding itself. But since the sixties fashion hasn't completely started over like it did then. It felt as if we hit the reset button and actively tried to piss off our parents, or any authority figure, for that matter. Now the larger youth buying market has easier access to music, making the ebb and flow of style more transparent and fluid.

The guys in suits around us didn't like my style or sense of freedom when I was on the job as tour manager, but Bob did. It's not like he ever said anything specific, but my take is that he liked the fact that I wasn't "one of them." Instead, I was "with him." My dress and my character showed that I didn't care about "them." I showed it through my sandals and conductor outfits and my polka-dot shirts. I was more like the musicians than anyone else. I supported their independence; the music and the poetry were alive in our identity. We all just wanted to be heard, that's why we looked the way we did. There's a human need to be heard and have an identity. Our culture in the United States tries to melt us together. This pushes the young to try even harder to be heard, to show their unique identity; it's like this with every generation.

We'd get derisive looks traveling through airports. We

would shake people up just by how we dressed. People wouldn't know what was happening because our looks were so different. That's where Bob's lyric "will soon shake your windows and rattle your walls" came from: our ability to cause a scene without even trying to cause a scene. Just walking in public disturbed people, and we were nothing compared to what was to follow! The old guard of the fifties hadn't seen people with dreadlocks or facial piercings or tattoos all over the body before! The Sex Pistols, and other cutting-edge bands like that, were still a decade away.

We saw the weird stuff coming from around the corner. We saw it, we ate it and we loved it. We looked for people who had the vision of what was next, the ones with a clue. Those were the types of people that we gravitated toward—the people with new and exciting ideas in style and music. We knew there was a Woody Guthrie or Paul Robeson or Will Rogers of our time and we were constantly on the search for who that was. Bob Dylan never assumed it was him. I could see his impact all around us, but we still felt like players in the orchestra, rather than the conductors. We wanted to find those who could speak better than us, those who had a clearer vision. Our banter in coffee shops was just that, exercises in who was smarter on the subject, who had the clearer connection to the pulse of our emerging culture.

We were into the competition of who could orate the best; we would speak one at a time and listen to each other. We would focus on the intention behind the words. We would go around the room debating one at a time, yearning to be the best at communicating our ideology. If you don't care about what you're saying, then everybody babbles, like at a bar. Nobody cares what's said at a bar, it's loud and everyone just speaks over each other. That wasn't us, that wasn't our group. We were intent; we were the children of the bushwa. We were the working class that gave up status quo to be liberated.

In the sixties, there wasn't an earlier generation that had guitars like there is now. There wasn't a level of organization for being liberated and creative that there is now. The television and radio enabled us to communicate in an unprecedented way, much as the Internet is doing now. But, fifty years prior, not every one had a phone! There weren't televisions or cars, so to speak. You had horse-drawn carriages on the streets of San Francisco and New York in the early 1900s; newspapers were the big things then. We were riding the tidal wave that brought in instantaneous information; now we float in the ocean of its aftermath.

Our group digested current events as if they were our only meal. We tore into every piece of information from around the world we could get our hands on. The more remote the story, the more incredible. We were eager to learn what was happening over "there." Was it similar to what we were experiencing, or were we missing out on something new? We wanted to talk about physics one minute and whatever was fascinating about Bhutan the next. You didn't need to be a physicist or world traveler either, just be interested and well read enough to carry on a conversation about it.

Bob was a sponge for it all. He read everything, every book, every newspaper he could lay his hands on. In the early days he and I would have deep philosophical conversations. He and I would exploit the mechanics of individual words and the philosophy behind them when we talked. Bob's genius stemmed from his insatiable appetite for knowledge, which fed into his identity as a prolific writer and extremely hard worker. To this day, I don't know anyone else who works harder than he does for his craft. He puts in a lot of energy and unlimited amounts of time. But it's not like he's hammering nails, it's more like he's thinking over coffee while at his desk with his guitar. Typing and handwriting between smoking cigarettes, and he can do that for longer than anybody I know. All the writers I know don't spend as much time as he does in the chair—he can do days and days sitting in a chair working. It's not just duration, he can work on a single thought or phrase longer than anyone as well. Fine-tuning something simple is incredibly hard to do. I don't think Bob ever truly understood the power that his songs had, even now.

His original aspirations and what happened to him are not even in the same ballpark. I think he would have liked to be someone with more social ability, closer to an Elvis. His persona fell together with the grace of a falling rock—like it does for all of us. We all have our own rising-to-the-top moments, and that's when we show our true colors. His fears and phobias are certainly his masters and his success and power have only manifested more fears and phobias. On the other hand, you and I get to enjoy and appreciate his struggle, because that is where his magic comes from. His best songs come from his sadness, loneliness and desperation to be accepted. We're lucky he cares enough to share his feelings because they're so powerfully universal.

When it came to writing songs, Bob never asked anyone's advice. He never talked to me about having a problem with his songs, ever. He never consulted me for a word in his songs. On the other hand, we would have these magical conversations where the subject matter leaned in the direction of song lyrics. But I would only remember the connection to our conversations and the lyrics he was singing after the fact. I would get annoyed when Bob's songs would leave the existential, which is what really appealed to me. He had so many more ideas than anybody else who was playing at that time.

Bob's vision is bad but he doesn't mind. He doesn't wear glasses because the world he inhabits is an internal one. His thoughts and his ability to process ideas is how he relates to and views the world in a practical sense, and this is what makes what he says so important to the rest of us. Our vision isn't the same as his, nobody's is. His enjoyment doesn't come from watching people or generally seeing the world. Most of the people on the planet are the opposite, they enjoy seeing people perform, and they enjoy seeing the beauty the world has to offer in extraordinarily exotic places. Bob does not; he doesn't travel much outside of work. He doesn't climb mountains or go rafting. He's not sitting on a beach on a private island enjoying the view. He's internalizing the world around him and creating beauty out of his perceived ideas of the world and relationships. The beautiful sunset is rendered in his mind and it's probably more beautiful than any sunset anyone of us has ever seen.

Bob always wrote about himself, all his songs are about his struggle. There's something to be said even for the fantasy songs, like "Mozambique." He was never there, nor does he dance. He put together a lovely melody and fantastic lyrics, but it was an escape from himself. And that's a wonderful thing. If he couldn't create these fantasies for himself he would be locked into the moaning and groaning of being left behind, being cut off and lonesome.

He's only had a few women in his life and all of his songs about relationships relate to those women. A part of a song might be about his mother and the next line might be about his last girlfriend.

What I needed from Bob, I was more than willing to pay the price for, to have front-row access to his brilliance. For me it was a good deal: I gave him all my attention and took his friendship seriously and tried to keep him aware of what was going on around him. For a lot of other people his friendship wasn't such a good deal. He never really hurt anybody along the way other than denying people empathy. But just that alone is a hard thing to leave out of a friendship. He didn't know how to deal with Paul Clayton; he respected him, but couldn't relate and definitely couldn't empathize with his struggle. He didn't know how to deal with any of the jerks that came wanting more energy and demanding more attention. There's a limit to what Bob can offer as a friend, and there's nothing wrong with that. I could meet him halfway and accept this shortcoming in his personality; many others couldn't.

In those years between 1964 and 1967, we met what felt like everybody, we traveled to foreign lands and everyplace we visited here or there we met the local intellectuals, the artists, the writers, everyone who was creating something. Brilliant people, people who could really communicate, people who could articulate without an "uh" or "um" between their sentences. I was meeting fabulous people, and in those years I met more of them than ever. It wasn't a new playing field for me either. I was already in the scene before I met Bob, but after meeting Bob everything was tenfold. My social group was bigger and better because of Bob and I loved it. I wallowed in it, I appreciated it, I rubbed it in my face I was so fucking into it. I was having the greatest life in the world.

We could meet interesting people with ease since we were always traveling. On tours around the country we would pull into towns early in the morning and drop into pool halls. They typically opened early and because of the way we were, I guess we looked like guys who wanted attention. You know, we were hipsters. So every oddball character would come and talk to us. Everybody had a story and we loved to rap about it, it was our way of investigating the local hip scene. We wanted to know where the local guitar players were and asked questions like who was playing what and where. We collected friendships, but at the same time were fairly critical of who we really let in. The guys we brought on the road all tended to have something to offer, some quirky behavior that we could appreciate.

On an overseas tour, we had a roadie named Cory who had an amazing ability to get laid. I'm going to call him Cory for this story, but that wasn't really his name, I don't want to call him out publicly and offend him and there wasn't anything overly bizarre about the guy; he just had a personality that attracted women, and lots of them. This guy could go out into the audience and come back with girls for the guys backstage to sleep with that night. He was amazing at it. I've never met someone who loved to have sex more than this guy—he even had problems with masturbating too often; it was something he would do all the time, whenever he had the chance. I know this because he would joke about it. That was his way of making it acceptable, bringing it out in the open and getting everyone laughing about it.

Every night on this particular tour he would rope in women for everyone, and we would have an instant party back at the hotel. Night after night he would repeat the process. Most musicians are not capable of being as persuasive with women as Cory was, and if they become savvy in that regard, it's because they've learned it from guys like Cory.

One morning, Cory's excessive behavior caught up with him. I heard knocking at my hotel door at five a.m. I knew instantly something was up. I walked to the door in my underwear and there he was in handcuffs, surrounded by police officers. The sergeant snapped at me, "Are you the tour manager? We want to see everybody's room, right now. We have a warrant to do so. We want to search your room first and Bob Dylan's room next."

There wasn't much I could do at this point; their paperwork

was in order. I responded, "Okay, let me put some clothes on, and you can come right in." I was all too aware of a large vial of liquid LSD in my right pants pocket and an even larger ball of hash in my front luggage pocket. A surge of nervousness rippled through my body

I was very into LSD at the time. I carried a small glass jar that had previously been used to hold over-the-counter pain meds, and I replaced the contents with pure liquid LSD. I would hold my finger to the top of it, turn it upside down and then lick my finger to get a single dose. I'd also do this for anybody on the crew that wanted some. Only a few were doing it with me on a daily basis. Bob, on the other hand, was not. It wasn't his thing. At this time, Bob preferred stimulants, like coffee, and various other things that lift you up. My love affair with LSD was a powerful one; it was the gateway into the unknown. I couldn't take enough mushrooms or peyote to ever really depart into the ether, but I could with acid.

As I walked back into the room to fetch my pants, the police followed, scanning the room for details. Luckily, I was very clean and well organized. All of my things were put away, so the room looked normal. I could feel right away that they thought I wasn't a threat; they didn't search my pockets or my luggage. Bob was really the prize catch—if they could snag a huge celebrity on drug charges, they would be local heroes.

After they searched my room, we all headed out to Bob's. I had no chance to warn him. Cory followed me in handcuffs held by the sergeant and eight or so police officers behind them. We got to Bob's room, and I started pounding on the door.

After a minute or two Bob opened up. As he was trying to open the door to speak to me, I grabbed it and held it tight, as if he had just cracked the door to peek out without opening it all the way. The cop to the left of the door was trying to push it open, but I made it seem like Bob was keeping it shut with the chain lock. I spoke quickly. "Bob, look, Cory got busted with some hashish, and the police want to search your room. They have a warrant. There's nothing I can do about it. They've already searched my room and want to search everybody's in the band." I was doing my best to give him as much time as possible to react and prepare himself. God only knew what was in his room.

I noticed Albert had joined us and was at the back of the group, flanked by another policeman. I assumed they had already searched his room. Bob gave me a look and said, "All right, let me get dressed." He was already dressed enough, given the circumstances. The door was only slightly cracked, and I was the only one with a real view of what was going on inside. Bob turned around and walked to the side table. He grabbed something and dropped it into his hat, right as the cops pushed the door open and pressed in. Bob put the hat on his head just as the police began their search of the room. They didn't find anything. Not a single rolling paper or roach. Nothing.

As they were searching Bob's room, word got out to the rest of the crew, and everyone cleaned up before the police arrived. At the end of the whole debacle, Cory was taken to jail and not a single other person was arrested. This event could have derailed the whole tour but ended up as just another day on the road.

Albert Grossman wanted me to fire Cory and fly him home. I didn't agree, so I asked Bob what he wanted to do. He didn't take a position. He said that whatever had to be done was fine with him. Albert pulled the trigger, fired him and flew him home immediately. I was upset about it because I felt like it was an honest mistake. If Albert wasn't on the tour, I would have paid the bail, made sure Cory understood his fuckup and moved on. Albert wanted to punish him.

With Cory leaving, I had to pick up his tasks, which made me the roadie. Albert loved this because he didn't really want me on the road. I was there only because Bob demanded I come along.

I called Albert the "brain," based on the fact that he looked like a potato and the only muscle he ever used was his brain. For me, he was a very powerful person. I respected him like my big brother. But we had our issues because I would tell Bob the truth, about anything. Even if it was just my hunch that someone was trying to manipulate him I would make sure Bob was aware of what was going on. Albert felt threatened by my transparency, and my criticism of his management.

Albert was an asshole who bent over for quarters when thousands were flying by. He had his problems and he definitely was not perfect, but I considered him my older brother. I loved him and I respected him but he was an asshole to the core and I couldn't save him when I tried. My little intelligence and my inept way of expressing it wasn't enough to get him to see that he was killing himself. And because of him I've had some of the greatest times of my life and I do believe that I'm the one who put Bob and Albert together. It was my confidence in Albert that sealed the deal with Bob. Albert was important to me and he felt completely threatened by me. Like someone who is threatened by darkness, he had absolutely no reason to be afraid; I wanted him to teach me, to take me under his wing.

Albert knew that what was common knowledge in Albert's world was not common knowledge in and around Bob. Bob did not know that he was giving away the rights to his songs when he handed them over to Albert to publish. Bob was receiving all of the money from writing the songs but was splitting fifty-fifty the proceeds from the publishing of the songs, which is where the real money was. When the Byrds took over with their version of "Mr. Tambourine Man," Albert made a fortune. In addition, Albert had complete control over who could use the songs, commercially or otherwise. When Bob finally realized this, he couldn't believe it. He awakened to the idea that he could be manipulated by people he trusted. Incidentally, George Harrison told me the same thing: that the Beatles didn't know they were giving away the rights to their music when they signed the contracts, that nobody laid out what was really happening or what the terms really meant.

The tension between Albert and me escalated over the years. Nothing I did seemed to smooth over our relationship, so I moved out of Albert's house a few months prior to July 29th, 1966, the day Bob had his motorcycle accident. Bob and his wife,

Sara Lownds, were using the Ford station wagon to move some things over to their new place. The car was packed and Sara was at the wheel, Bob was in front on his motorcycle and, in slow motion, simply fell over. He was going about one mile an hour, not fast enough to sustain his balance. When he tipped over he tried to compensate by turning the wheel sharply into the direction he was falling, but that only amplified his descent to the ground. He hit his head, hurt his neck and was fairly banged up from such a simple accident.

~

End of Tape Five

I find the story of Bob's motorcycle crash fascinating, mainly the discrepancy between rumor, legend and my dad's memory of the events. He would always scoff at anyone recounting the history of that day. Even Bob on multiple occasions has had varying descriptions of the events. Biographers have fueled the debate and even at times categorized Bob's career as "preaccident" and "postaccident." My father's recollection of it was always very simple, it was merely a small incident that Bob was embarrassed by and his reluctance to talk about it fed everyone else's wild speculation.

CHAPTER 6

~

Taos, New Mexico

Our extended hippie family—a portrait taken by a traveling photographer in Santa Fe, New Mexico, June 1979. *Bottom row:* Aerie Maymudes (far left), Mary Kaufman, Chloe Goodwin, Sunday Peaches Law, Laina Reynolds, Dhana Pilar Law, Tom Law, Solar Law, Ethan Miller, Brahm Reynolds, and Linda Wylie (seven months pregnant with Jacob Maymudes). *Second row:* Steven Miller, Kathy Miller, John Phillip Law, Jesse Lee Rainbow Law (on shoulders), Seth Roffman, Harry Frishman, Libby Frishman, Jackson Frishman, and Victor Maymudes. *(Courtesy: Maymudes Family Archive)*

Tape Six

🎼 Bob's motorcycle accident and his decision to pull back from the public signaled an end of an era in my life. We both needed a timeout. In an interview in 1984, Bob said publicly, "When I had that motorcycle accident . . . I woke up and caught my senses; I realized that I was just workin' for all these leeches. And I really didn't want to do that." The year and a half prior is regarded as Bob's most prolific period, during which he produced what most people consider to be his best albums: *Bringing It All Back Home, Highway 61 Revisited* and *Blonde on Blonde*—all recorded back-to-back. Bob paid a price for that level of creativity and his energy and focus did not come from a bottomless well; we were touring nonstop and awake around the clock. Timeouts at Albert's house in Bearsville were the interludes which fed his fires of inspiration, though the drugs were still plentiful.

Bob married Sara Lownds in November of '65. Sara had been around the Bearsville house a while. She was a beautiful girl, tall, already a mother, which on Sara was becoming; it actually made her more attractive as a person.

Bob's desire to get married to Sara surprised me. I asked him about it. "Why Sara?! Why not Joan Baez?" He responded with, "Because Sara will be home when I want her to be home, she'll be there when I want her to be there, she'll do it when I want her to do it. Joan won't be there when I want her. She won't do it when I want to do it."

I personally would have gone with Joan in a minute, but Bob didn't want to compete with her. If Bob was a king, Joan was a queen, and Bob didn't want a queen. He wanted something simpler.

Sally Grossman invited Sara to her wedding to Albert, and that fateful day was her first introduction to Bob Dylan. She did not have a hard edge. She was beautiful, soft-spoken and simple. Her dark-haired, fair-skinned beauty would age well. At Bearsville, Bob would hole up writing for twenty-four hours at a time and collapse to sleep it off. Sara, bored, would come to me; we had a favorite hilltop outside Bearsville where we would drive to, smoke a joint and just talk. I wondered if she was in over her head with Bob, but she was patient and for anyone close to him, patience enough to be forgiving of genius was mandatory.

When Bob tipped over on his bike and hurt his neck, she was there, and the crazy schedule we had endured for years did not appeal to him anymore. The right moment to slow down had appeared. For Bob, family life was the next developmental milestone. But at that moment I did not understand that as well as he did, and not much in the previous years had made the quiet harbor of that notion an easy behavioral transition.

Albert and I had another blowout fight after the '66 tour with The Band; I was worn down and, at thirty-one, needed to understand if there was a future for me in his organization. The two hundred a week plus expenses I made secured nothing. I never took advantage of Bob financially but there were many others who did. Albert, for instance, took more than his share from Bob. I knew his arrangement regarding publishing and thought it was unjust from the start. In the beginning Albert made it seem like a great deal for Bob, because Albert had connections, experience and an organization; but watching what happened on the ground, Bob's phenomenal personal concentration and his consistent poetic productivity meant the money being made had more to do with Bob and less to do with Albert. By the late sixties Bob's success had a life of its own; he was making tremendous amounts of money from other people singing his songs.

I couldn't do anything about Bob's situation with Albert. I tried to make it as transparent as possible, but that was a thin line to walk. On one side I would become Albert's enemy, and on the other I would lose Bob's trust—I might appear to be furthering my own agenda, an agenda I did not have. I did feel like my vigilance, and Bobby Neuwirth's when I was not there, had held a space for Bob to operate, and literally kept him alive in some moments. In the end I couldn't help the relationship between Albert and Bob, and in time Bob figured it out on his own.

Looking back, I see Bob as Ulysses: tied to the mast, paying the price with whatever drug was available to hear the Sirens sing. I was in awe of his genius, just like Paul Clayton, but I was not a romantic. I knew plenty of talented people. I knew that I had done my job: kept the car on the road, checked the exits, the stage, watched the audience, the crowds, handled a thousand details and generally held a space for Bob to be himself. For those who bought into the personality cult, the payoff for me should have been just being there. But practically, even in that rarified air, when it was over it was over, and I would have appreciated a few grand to get started again.

After the stress of the tour, we had all seen enough of one

another. Albert said there was no place for me. So it was over. Naomi Schwartzman, Albert's accountant and later Bob's, gave me an extra week's salary as severance pay without Albert knowing, and I hit the road. Naomi and her husband would become Bob's main administrative support when he left Albert. Naomi knew exactly what was going on and was always sympathetic to my position.

The high-profile intensity of the era was imprinted on my psyche. We had truly been to the mountaintops on continents and performed before kings and queens; moving out of that orbit was necessary and disorienting.

The "tune in, turn on and drop out" mandate of the moment gave me a direction, but no road map. At that moment I had no real savings, so I retreated once again to Yelapa to recoup physically, write and figure out what I wanted to do next. Once rested, I moved back to Los Angeles.

My friend John Phillip Law, remembered as the blind angel in the film *Barbarella*, had a big house in L.A., which we called the Castle. Bob and I had used the house during the L.A. rehearsals for the '66 tour with The Band. Lisa Law, John's sister-in-law, took some iconic photos of Bob at the Castle during that time.

I rented a room from John and that was my home when I was in L.A. John's career had taken off after a good part in *The Russians Are Coming, the Russians Are Coming* and starring in three spaghetti westerns in one year had set him up financially.

Because of age, I guess, I was always closer to John than Tom, his brother.

The Castle passed for communal living in L.A., not a commune really, but a melting pot for an extended family that would be my social group and support for the next twenty years. Various artists and musicians moved through as tenants. Donovan became a good friend there. Yogi Bhajan, a Sikh immigrant from the Golden Temple in India, was sponsored and supported by our group. He became a central protagonist in our personal development. I stopped smoking cigarettes, became a strict vegetarian and practiced the discipline of concentrated yogic breathing. I would not consider myself a hippie, ever, although my kids would argue this, but I was tuning in and turning on. Tom Law and Lisa, his soon-to-be wife, lived in the house.

Lisa could annoy the hell out of you taking pictures, but she could have run the army. She moved us all toward a macrobiotic diet, she would be the archetypal mother and, in my opinion, she personally emancipated and demystified the experience of giving birth and motherhood. Lisa showed us it was a natural process, and the natural process was a higher and more profound spiritual moment than any of us had ever experienced. She and Tom would become "family-focused" icons in the hippie moment. In the years '66, '67 and '68, there were many extemporaneous communal groups that formed and morphed into recognized entities: the Diggers, the Merry Pranksters, the Hog Farm, the Motherfuckers (a small group of anarchists from New York). Their cooperation was functional, they could

set up a kitchen and run freak-out shelters at shows or demonstrations. They moved between L.A., San Francisco, New York
and northern New Mexico.

My old friend Hugh Romney had morphed into Wavy
Gravy, cutting his teeth on acid in San Francisco flower power.
Wavy was spot-on, he had a razor-sharp wit that could bust you
for all ego infractions and leave you loving him. He was charis-
matic and dependable in a crazy way. The potential for social
and cultural evolution in the cities seemed to burn out, and our
new insight or disappointment with the street inspired migra-
tions. The high end of all those demonstrations and New Age
philosophies piled into buses, learned how to set up tipis
and yurts and headed back to the land.

In 1967 New Mexico captured our imagination.

As I said, I was not a hippie, not a communalist. I had too
much history with socialism from my folks to think that was a
clear answer. Initially on my return to L.A. to make money, I
went back to construction. Remodeling a couple of commercial
buildings into recording studios, as after spending so much
time in them with Bob, I had a fair amount of insight into how
they should be laid out. My old music business contacts accepted and respected that. I soon had enough work to hire day
laborers and a few extra carpenters. I found a nice fellow who
did great work when he was available; the kid was bouncing
between acting and carpentry to stay afloat. Unfortunately for
me, he quit in the middle of a job, claiming he had just booked
a good role in a sci-fi film. In hindsight I think he made the

right choice. His name was Harrison Ford and I don't think he ever returned to carpentry.

By spring 1967, I started working for a cooperative of artists that produced the '67 Monterey Pop Festival. Politically and socially, our communities in L.A. and San Francisco were light-years apart. The planning and execution of the Monterey Pop Festival in June '67 was the coming together for those two musical schools of thought. In L.A., John Phillips of the Mamas and Papas was collaborating with Lou Adler, Derek Taylor and Alan Pariser for publicity and money to put on a show that was a benefit of sorts. In the end all artists got paid expenses, and the proceeds went to selected charities. On the board of directors were various musicians, including Donovan, who got me involved in production, mainly on the security side of things.

My friend David Wheeler was in charge of security. I worked for David doing ground work, traveling back and forth to Monterey. At one point we handed over a check for twenty-five grand to the local sheriff to look the other way while walking around the Monterey Fairgrounds. The police were still nervous but the "donation" helped. David Wheeler was the pot dealer of choice for all of Hollywood, and many suspected David had a second life as a CIA operative in Mexico and South America. He was impeccable during the festival. Even in his long-haired hippie garb, he was a suave interface with the police. The Monterey city and county government somehow went along with our plan. Various extended family groups,

Ken Kesey's Pranksters and Diggers, did support, freak-out tents, kitchens and first aid.

The bands were lined up by Lou Adler and John Phillips and represented the state of the art in pop music. Chip Monck was hired for staging and lighting. Chip had done that job with us on the '66 world tour. Chip could manage a stage under any conditions. The show came off flawlessly. The commitment of producers from top to bottom would create an atmosphere for creativity that would blow the top off what a folk/rock/pop music concert could be. The Byrds, Otis Redding, Hugh Masakela, Big Brother with Janice Joplin, Jimi Hendrix and Ravi Shankar were part of the show; every day was astounding. Monterey was a turning point for rock 'n' roll commercially, and music that weekend would endure, in my opinion, outshining everything produced for the next forty years.

Jimi Hendrix made himself a household name that weekend by his stage theatrics; smashing his guitar into pieces, lighting it on fire while praying to it and tossing the charred bits into the audience, all to a cover of the Chip Taylor song, "Wild Thing."

About eighty thousand people showed up at the fairgrounds in Monterey for that weekend in June, and logistically it was a flawless concert. The police were blown away, the organization and support we had on the ground worked. The event, in some ways, had been an attempt by the Los Angeles crowd to live down the criticism from the San Francisco artists. The movement down south was more sex and drugs than politics; the music in San Francisco was authentic. Who could argue with Country Joe?

The musicians there were the backdrop to the political activism at Berkeley that was leading the country's move out of the dark ages on every front: free speech, political organization, the Students for a Democratic Society and in Oakland the Black Panthers. Consciousness raising with bona fide scientific studies at Esalen and Berkeley on the usefulness of psychotropic drugs. That June weekend a hundred miles down the road, at the beginning of the Summer of Love, none of us could have imagined how well the spirit of the event at Monterey would come together.

It was a gathering of like minds from the world of art. It took place at a time of great social injustices. The festival itself was a monument to the protest against these injustices—the Vietnam War, for instance, and the social struggle at home.

Woodstock was another example of this very thing. But whereas Woodstock was the teenager, the Monterey Pop Festival was the birth of getting together like that.

Actually, remembering history, the love-ins and be-ins preceded the Monterey Pop Festival, which came out of the marches, which came out of the protests, the anguish of the population itself. All those people who couldn't handle it found themselves through song.

Throughout the festival, I carried a mandala of burnt plastic babies. Mandalas are usually symbols of life. But what could remind you more of how fucked up it was, how bad it really was, than a mandala of burnt babies. For me, it was the issue, the protest. We were dropping napalm at that very moment on Vietnam. We were burning babies, we—the United States—were burning babies.

Around the country the protest was in full swing, and we were demonstrating at the Dow Chemical Company. But Monterey Pop wasn't like the marches through the cities, which are more educational to the people who stand on the sidelines. It was a very political event in which nobody got on a soapbox to say the obvious. Instead it was a celebration. It was itself a major statement.

San Francisco was heading for the Summer of Love after Monterey; Los Angeles was on a different track. Clubs on Sunset Strip were being shut down and cops were busting my friends for smoking pot. One Sunday, guys who looked and acted like a SWAT team blew into our gathering at Barry McGuire's pool, and that was it for me. (Barry McGuire, who wrote and sang the hit song "Eve of Destruction," later pioneered contemporary Christian music after finding God.) I had a relationship with Maggie Ryan Denver at the time. Maggie had been a waitress at the Unicorn. She was recently divorced from Bob Denver, of *Gilligan's Island* fame. Maggie had three young kids: Megan, Ryan and Kim. To escape the oppressive atmosphere in L.A., in 1967 Maggie and I moved to New Mexico. We used local contacts in the community and learned of a house in El Rito, a Spanish village up on the Chama River Valley that sounded perfect. Jimmy Hopper, a local gone hip, rented us a log cabin built by his father, who had been a country doctor for the area. The cabin was across a log bridge on a creek nestled in dramatic red rock country. It needed work, which I undertook in exchange for rent. Up the road in Abiquiú was Georgia O'Keeffe's place, the painter who many hail as the Mother of American Modernism.

We heated our house with three wood stoves; I cut and chopped piñon and juniper from the plains on the west side of the Rio Grande Gorge from Taos. My skills as a handyman let me pick up work as a carpenter, plus Maggie's alimony allowed us to live comfortably. We were financially better off than most of the hippies, and certainly we had more disposable income than our neighbors. The per capita income in rural New Mexico was about fourteen hundred dollars a year at that time. I put in a garden, and we homeschooled the kids. It was a nice moment in time. I was there because I wanted a place that allowed me to cultivate consciousness that I experienced first in Yelapa. I had an instant family. The neighbors accepted Maggie and me. And I, a high-strung, cerebrally front-loaded guy, had the great opportunity to interact and learn from people who were still practicing an authentic spiritual life. We were not in a social vacuum—Tom and Lisa Law, the Jook Savages and Ken Kesey and the Pranksters all set up shop in Abiquiú, living in buses, tipis, vans and an old adobe house with a kitchen.

The hippie scene in New Mexico was flying high; it felt like all signs in our social development pointed away from the cities and toward the land, in particular Taos and northern New Mexico. In Taos communes like New Reality, New Buffalo, the Lama Foundation and Lorien were in the short flights of their heydays. It was a small, tight community in 1967. The social experiment was made possible by the commitment and financial largess of a few well-off kids. A kind, tenderhearted friend named Rick Klein was footing part of the bill for the New Buffalo commune and for a universal religious center up in San Cristóbal that became the Lama Foundation. Cynthia West, a local Santa Fe artist and a great woman, would also commit her fortune to Lama. The land was adjacent to the D. H. Lawrence ranch, at ten thousand feet with panoramic views of the Rio Grande Basin and the far-off mountains in southern Colorado.

Lama would be the home of Ram Dass, born Richard Alpert, and the ceremonies that happened there, and in all our many group gatherings in those years, was our synthesis of all religion. We would gather weekends and impromptu, spontaneous original music would flow. There was no gathering without dancing, a free-spirited exuberant physicality. We read the romantic Iranian poets, Rumi, Hafiz, built ceremonial sweat lodges for saunas, engaged in Buddhist meditation and Hindu yoga and ate rice and homegrown vegetables. Wonderful drugs, great LSD and pot, were on the menu, free association and making your own music was the order of the day. I stopped listening to what was popular, though in the wake of Monterey there was a quantum leap of great music.

Our New Mexico invasion was met with mixed feelings from the locals. New Mexico has a powerful and influential cultural fabric; the Pueblo Indians strung out along the Rio Grande had their traditions, which we aspired to emulate. Their values and rituals became our mantras: speak softly, carry no stick and respect the Earth. Their feasts and dances, the drumming and costumes attracted us. They were open to us in those early days, thanks largely to the relationship that had been built by three people I knew. Stewart Brand had been on Kesey's bus with the Pranksters; he was married to a Plains Indian and was accepted by the Hopi elders in Taos. In those days he was collecting Native American ceremonial music and pushing for collective activism against the Peabody Coal Company.

Peabody was after the contract to mine high-quality Black Mesa coal from the Navajos. Stewart was well educated and placed for that success by connections at Berkeley. In my opinion, just the *Whole Earth Catalogue* would have given him founding father status and lifetime achievement awards, but he was an activist then and continues to this day to speak relevantly for the loyal opposition to greed in America.

John Kimmy and Jack Loeffler were the other two, and already established in the New Mexico scene when I got there. They were our link to the Hopi and Taos Pueblo elders. Jack was a friend of writer Ed Abbey, and Monkey Wrench member John Kimmy, an ethnologist with a good hand at carpentry, had somehow managed to be adopted by Little Joe Gomez, the Peyote Church leader at Taos Pueblo and by David Monongye, the Hopi leader that befriended Stewart. Called on by Stewart and Jack, individuals such as Harvey Mudd, Andrew Ungerleider and Chick Lansdale put family fortunes on the line to fund and sponsor the first environmental defense lawyers, whole food restaurants with no smoking or alcohol, whole food cooperative markets, local alternative newspapers and communal living experiments in New Mexico.

Thanks to those connections, I would attend the last public

experience of the Hopi snake dance. David Monongye had observed during his teaching with John Kimmy that the Hopis sang and danced for those elements that were rare, water principally, and our music was all about love, maybe because for us that was rare. The snake dance was held on one of the mesas each summer in late June, before the monsoons. The Hopi were people of the first migration to this continent and lived on high-topped mesas, in the midst of what would later be the Navajo reservation.

By June the water was scarce, and if the Hopi were to have corn, it had to rain. They would go out in ceremony and collect snakes of all varieties and take them down into the kivas, their belowground ceremonial chambers, and there they would fast, chant and feed the snakes corn meal. On an appointed day, the dance would begin at dawn and all the snakes would be brought out of the kivas and released. First kept in piles in a circle, they would be lifted up by a masked, dressed member of a particular clan, prayed over, brushed again with corn meal and released to one of the four directions. The snake was a metaphor for lightning, lightning being a communicator between this world and the next, the caller of clouds and rain. We arrived in the early morning and watched, mesmerized by the snakes, rattlesnakes erecting themselves in the hands of dancers, harmlessly relaxing and crawling off when released. Even talking about it, I am in awe with the memory.

The Spanish villages in which we settled were harder to crack. New Mexicans were Catholic, and had settled in the valleys in the early 1600s, which is where we camped. I had my own theory, which years later would be validated by some historian at the University of New Mexico, that the men who came up from Mexico in the 1600s to marry local Pueblo Indian women were likely Jews who had converted during the Inquisition in Spain or Mexico and wanted to get as far away from the Catholic Church as possible. They had an interesting pseudo-church called the Penitentes, a social organization really, where the men met, chanted, sang and on Easter conducted a theater reenactment of the crucifixion. There was a windowless adobe church in El Rito, and the locals made sure we knew to leave it alone. Up the road from Abiquiú, the Spanish people in the area were not the same folks you met in Santa Fe, which has been the capital since the Spanish reconquest of the area in about 1700.

So many of the families we met had a son siphoned off into the military. New Mexico is a low-population state and the war no one was interested in fighting made these strong country boys natural selections. In time they came home damaged by the carnage, angry and strung-out on heroin. I understood these kids were going off to fight for a country that their folks felt was foreign and they had no way to connect those dots and re-sist. I know the locals felt the invasion of draft-dodging refu-gees from the cities was a mixed bag. There were some pretty blatant violations of sensitivities.

Maggie, the kids and I had a quiet scene in El Rito. The neighbors gave us tips on the garden and where the best wood to burn could be found. I thoroughly enjoyed my physical con-nection to my own survival: chopping wood, carpentry and working in a garden. I got a dog, a fantastic white husky/wolf that I named Nooky. Nooky lived until my son, Jacob, was born in 1979; I loved her and took her everywhere. Our greater group was a flamboyant tribe, to say the least, living in psyche-delic buses and extended families that were a world away from conventional nuclear setups. Wavy Gravy's Hog Farm was a happening place wherever it was—the Hog Farm finally ended up in Las Trampas, New Mexico—and the other Taos com-munes were making or not making it.

Tom and Lisa Law continued to be the proto-hippie family; they even had an arranged marriage by Yogi Bhajan. The Law family and the wider social group in L.A. helped the yogi found his 3HO Healthy, Happy, Holy approach to life. It was a relief raft in an ocean of drug excess. The summer solstice invi-tations to Tesuque reservation in '69 and '70 paved a road for him to move to New Mexico with his followers. He founded a communal organization that eschewed drugs, alcohol and mul-tiple partners as part of a spiritual reawakening. His guidance embraced yoga, meditation and chanting. The solstice celebra-tion in 1969 was remarkable; all our eyes opened when the yo-gi's powers of concentration caused a bus wreck in what he termed his protest of acid excess. I didn't question it; I was pretty high on acid.

John Law came out when he was not working, and he and I continued to have a close friendship. Tommy and Gloria Mas-ters arrived from Maryland that year. Years later, when I went back on the road with Bob, I hired Tommy as Bob's bus driver. They came out to see the guru and stayed. I first met Tommy one evening at the Faithway Street house, a place in Santa Fe where Maggie and I and the kids crashed if we came to town. My bridge to the house in El Rito washed away in a flash flood and Tommy, Gloria and I bonded when they came out and stayed at the house while helping me fix it. That relationship is another, like John Law, that has endured for me.

Tommy had been a racehorse trainer back east. He had first met Tom Law and Sally Anne Bueler, who were then dating, a couple years earlier in Puerto Vallarta and told them about Yelapa. I introduced Tom and Sally to Albert Grossman in 1963 and shortly after that introduction, Sally left Tom and married Albert and changed her name to Sally Grossman. Tommy Masters's friend Tom Neuman took Tom Law, and later all of us, under his wing and that's how we knew about Yelapa. There were often connections that seemed sort of impossible, inside the group. By that time, John Law had bought his brother Tom a beautiful place in Truchas. Tommy's horse-training skills would be turned to teaching Tom and his wife Lisa's big black horse, Prince, to pull a plow.

Dennis Hopper decided to use northern New Mexico and New Buffalo as a backdrop in his 1968 film *Easy Rider*. The film was a world-shattering success in 1969. From that success Dennis Hopper had been given an open checkbook by Universal Studios, as well as complete creative freedom for a new project. It was called *The Last Movie*. Dennis was a genius in ways the average person would not get. I knew him well in L.A. He asked me to travel to Peru and meet him before principal photography, to build sets and scout locations in the spring of 1970. Dennis also cast me as a gun-wielding, horse-riding cowboy who would meet his demise in the first ten minutes of the film.

I flew down to Lima, the capital and largest city of Peru. I was expecting to be met by someone on the production team when I arrived. Nobody was there. I was standing at the airport all alone after deboarding, wondering what to do or where to go. So I started asking around if anyone from the production was looking for me, and through a series of random events I find out I'm actually booked on another flight to the city of Cusco, near the Urubamba Valley of the Andes Mountain range at around eleven thousand feet. My flight was scheduled to leave in a few hours. With my mind at ease, I decided to go explore Lima since this was my first visit to Peru.

I hired a taxi for a few hours to drive me around and show me the city. The first car I can remember my father having was a black 1941 Plymouth with a purple cloth interior. The cab I rented was exactly that, in perfect condition. The cabdriver informed me that he was the only owner, he had bought it new three decades prior. The cabby had enormous pride for this Plymouth; he said he shined it every day. Made a living with it as a cab, it was his livelihood. He showed me everything in Lima, the rich, the poor and the Gypsies. He showed me the poor people and told me how they had moved down into the area and how the government was trying to deal with it. They were in these small valleys, thousands and thousands of people in little huts. It was a fascinating ride around the city;

the cabdriver would have been better fitted as a tour guide than a cabbie.

When I arrived in Cusco, Dennis met me at the airport and gave me the lowdown on the production. In the days that immediately followed, he and I drove around scouting locations for the film. There was a moment that stands out for me, one that he happens to remember quite vividly as well.

We were driving around in the production truck on a dirt road that narrowly made its way over the top of a small mountain. On both sides of the road you could see down into a small valley. We both needed to take a leak and agreed this random spot was just majestic enough for such a release. He was on the passenger side of the truck and I on the driver's side, and while we were in the middle of relieving ourselves, I saw lights, little tiny lights, far, far away and an instant later I was surrounded by them. All around me are these little fast-moving orbs of light, everywhere else is pitch-black, and the lights are bending around the entire truck and heading back down the side that Dennis Hopper is on. About three minutes later the lights disappear. Now, let me make something really clear: I've done a fair amount of acid. I get back in the truck and just look at Dennis without saying anything; I wanted to gauge if he had just witnessed the same thing I had or if that was a full-blown hallucination. Dennis didn't mention it. So I turned the truck back on and started driving down the road. If we had continued our dialogue from before we stopped, I would have chalked up the lights to a flashback and thought nothing more. But we drove for twenty minutes without saying anything to each other and that was my only indication that maybe I wasn't alone in my experience beneath the swarming lights. When I asked Dennis, he freaked out. "You saw it too! I thought I was losing my mind, man!" he shouted. We spent the next several weeks retelling this story; we have no conclusion to the event. It happened, it was amazing and we reminisce about the magic of it.

A month later the whole crew arrived and Dennis pulled in everyone from the old L.A. crowd: Michael Greene, Peter Fonda, Ted Markland, Kris Kristofferson, Dean Stockwell, John Phillip Law and Owen Orr. With the cast all together, the party was on at eleven thousand feet.

The larger-than-life L.A. crowd could be found at tables with mountains of cocaine. Coke literally formed the centerpiece on huge, dark Spanish Colonial tables; it was a new drug and wasn't readily available in the States until after that time. And those quantities were new for everyone. Luckily, I am a small player in all indulgence but sex and marijuana. I look back and think the shadow of excess haunted our lives. Longing for a simple life was one thing, but for me it wasn't just Bob Dylan, it was my whole social group that kept me on the crest of a cultural wave that was anything but mundane. Behind the spotlight was the shadow and sooner or later it would be dark.

The Last Movie was a longtime pet project of Hopper and writer Stewart Stern. (Stern had written *Rebel Without a Cause*, in which Hopper played a small role.) After developing the script in the early 1960s, Hopper tried for years to secure financing for the film, intending it to be his directorial debut. Due to the artistically challenging nature of the film, no studios were interested until Hopper's first film as a director, *Easy Rider*, became a massive hit in 1969. Given free rein and a budget of one million dollars from Universal, Hopper spent much of 1970 in Peru shooting the film under the working title *Chinchero*. He brought many of his actor and musician friends to Peru, including singer Kris Kristofferson and director Samuel Fuller. With hours and hours of footage, Hopper holed up in his home editing studio in Taos, New Mexico, but failed to deliver a cut by the end of 1970. Hopper was in a period of severe alcohol and drug abuse (as shown in an extremely rare and barely released documentary called *The American Dreamer*, which was directed by Lawrence Schiller), but managed to put together a fairly straightforward cut in terms of conventional storytelling. He was mocked over it by his friend, cult director Alejandro Jodorowsky, who urged him to edit the film unconventionally and attempt to break new cinematic ground. This caused Hopper to destroy that edit and craft the more disjointed narrative that is known today, and he finally completed that final edit in the spring of 1971.

Back home in New Mexico, Maggie's head turned towards a more happening scene; she wanted more action than our quiet, backwoods life could offer. Also the kids were older; they needed better and closer schools. We talked about kids of our own, but Maggie was my age, and at thirty-four the kid thing was done for her. I packed her up and Tommy Masters helped me move her to a house in Woodstock in the summer of 1970. I drove home to New Mexico, my last line to Maggie Ryan Denver—the frozen moment lasts forever—hung in the cab of my pickup truck. Parting is not sweet sorrow, and it is lousy with recrimination and failure. I wanted a family.

Dennis Hopper bought the Mable Dodge Luhan House in Taos that summer. Taos had long drawn the culturally savant. Mable Dodge Luhan, a New York heiress, moved out in the twenties; she was the center of left-wing and avant-garde culture. She financed journalist John Reed and novelist D. H. Lawrence and brought people like Mary Austin, Alfred Stieglitz and Isadora Duncan to her salon in Taos. She married one of the chiefs at the pueblo, gave him a big touring car for his cronies to drive around in and the pueblo let her have land right on their border with the town of Taos. The compound included a long, rambling fifteen-room adobe, three stories in the Pueblo style, with various guesthouses. The back door was so close to the Taos Pueblo that you were on their land when you stepped out the kitchen door. When Dennis bought it from Bonnie, Mable's niece, the old house was crumbling. Dennis was perfect for the place, a savant like Bob, and in the early days at the house Dennis joked that he was Mable's reincarnation. He moved in a world-class collection of art, his own work and others': Ray Lichtenstein, Tony Price, Ron Cooper, Ron Bell, Warhol, Bruce Conner. Bonnie left all Mable's furniture, some great stuff that had a faded glory. Dennis hired Taos Pueblo plasterers and local Spanish carpenters, and had an editing room set up for *The Last Movie*. He met a twenty-one-year-old woman named Linda Wylie at the El Patio restaurant that May; she was keeping the locals boozed up and entertained bartending, and the second time he saw her, he asked her to come and help keep the house organized as the property manager and resident chef. After a little bit of convincing, Linda Wylie was to become the mother of my children: Aerie and Jacob.

Disillusioned by the Vietnam War, Kent State, the Chicago convention and Bob Kennedy's death, Linda left college during her last semester and moved to Taos in June of 1970. Having marched in civil rights rallies and devoted time to teaching destitute families, she arrived eager to rethink her life.

Initially, she made a modest living teaching English literature in a New Age school and tending bar in the evenings at the El Patio restaurant off the plaza in Taos. It was a funky, authentic place that welcomed everyone, a two hundred-year-old adobe where Taos Pueblo Indians had murdered the governor of New Mexico for encroaching on their land in the mid-1800s. At twenty-one she was not really a hippie either. She liked working and was more into poetry, the Native Americans, and climbing the local mountains. She had made friends with some of the Taos old guard, including painters Andrew Dasburg and R. C. Gorman. She rented a little adobe that had belonged to John Collier, the Indian agent under Roosevelt, who brought the Native American cause to the table in the forties. This special cause was close to his heart and would finally culminate in 1971 when Spiro Agnew's daughter, a fourteen-year-old girl, officially gave the land and area around Blue Lake back to the pueblo that the Taos Indians considered their "coming-out place." The neighbors loved Linda, teaching her to mud finish the back room floor in the little adobe so she had a bedroom. The Morada, the Penitente church, was a hundred yards away and she lived all alone with her dog.

Linda's formal education was better than mine. She set to work digesting a two thousand-volume library of seminal work in sociology and anthropology and ethnography before Collier's family donated it all to Princeton.

Dennis drew her into his house and that world, and I met her there in the fall of 1970 when Larry Schiller was filming *The American Dreamer.* She was young, green-eyed, innocent, athletic and had a quick kind of intelligence and humor. She was intimidated by and suspicious of the carelessness of the scene. She was not comfortable playing the way we did but could relate to Dennis, despite his stream of women and marriage to Michelle Phillips, and he, like her, thought it was funny he had a college-educated cook.

Linda would work at the house all day, managing dinners, rooms and the special requests of Dennis's endless guests. When the afternoon was quiet, she saddled up one of his horses and rode off through the sagebrush to the Taos Pueblo to clear her head. At six p.m. she would pack up and drive back to her Talpa house. The social scene at Mable's was nonstop. At one point Dennis entertained senator and presidential candidate George McGovern at a fund-raising dinner and Linda orchestrated the whole evening for him. The regular drop-ins from the L.A. and New York elite were Jack Nicholson, Kris Kristofferson, Leonard Cohen, Henry Geldzahler, who was the director of the Museum of Modern Art, and a mix of avant-garde international artists. Dennis was the focus of a lot of well-deserved creative attention. *The Last Movie* editing crew lived and worked in the compound. I dropped into Mable's house more and more often to spend the weekend with Linda and for entertainment. There was always room for me at Dennis's table. We had been friends since the Unicorn Cafe days. Dennis scrambled to be a success for years and, like John Law, he worked at being an actor. But Dennis was much more; he was a very good photographer and all visual art was interesting to him. *Easy Rider* really was his project. Producers Peter Fonda and Bert Scheider got him the shot, but it was Dennis's vision that created that movie. Our time together in Peru was great, we were alone for a couple weeks getting the set together, and he had fun doing that movie. I was sorry to see his focus and clarity come apart. That really did not start until the spring of '71.

The scene at the house deteriorated—too much coke and too long doing it. Dennis couldn't make decisions that stuck for *The Last Movie*; he'd frequently change scenes that ran beautifully, which drove the editors crazy. He did not want to make a one-and-a-half-hour movie, he wanted to tell the story in two and a half hours, and the studio just would not let him do it. He railed against those kinds of restrictions; he was, after all, primarily an artist, and the commercial concern pressed on him by Universal heavies was not his main consideration. As his frustration mounted, the good vibe in the house evaporated.

I had an interesting job at the time. Bob Downey [Robert Downey Sr.] was coming to Santa Fe to film *Greaser's Palace,* and I was living onset while working as a carpenter on this fantastic frame house that was to be the main feature in the action. Linda gave up the Collier house and moved into my small travel trailer with me. We had agreed that we were going to try to stick it out, to create a life that would support kids. We both wanted a family.

Linda was suspicious of the high life; she had, and has, a Calvinist work ethic. We both had an aloof approach regarding traditional marriage. We did not see much point in getting the government involved in a personal decision. These ideas were fixed in early hippie philosophy and her quasifeminism and independence. We negotiated a partnership, not a marriage, though it would become that. She would remind me later that my existential rap was so off-putting to a woman in the early days that she thought that I would likely be alone forever if she had not decided to take me on and have kids. Her folks' only comment concerning our announcement that we were going to have a family was: "At least he's not black." Though they were pretty sure I was something.

The *Greaser's Palace* job allowed us to stockpile a winter's worth of cash. I owned part of a beautiful piece of property in Truchas, near Tom Law's place, with Tommy Masters at that time. Truchas was remote from a steady source of work but it is the most beautiful place in New Mexico. We spent the late fall getting used to one another. We made a couple of trips to L.A.; she met my folks, who loved her. We lived a classic alternative life at eighty-five hundred feet in the Sangre de Cristo Mountains. Our funky little trailer with a framed porch and hammock had a ditch running through the property, with a field of wildflowers out the door. The magnificent thirteen thousand-feet-high Truchas Mountains formed our eastern backdrop; we could see two hundred miles up the Chama River drainage as it cut through mesas in the west. Tom and Lisa Law had communal dinners and fired up the hot tub on a regular basis, John Law showed up often and we had many other friends who had chosen that idyllic spot to make a stand.

I wanted Linda to see Mexico and know Yelapa like I had, so in January we packed up my Suburban Travelall and the dogs and headed south, making our way slowly down to Maya country and the small town of San Cristóbal de las Casas to visit Richard and Flora Alderson. Richard was the soundman on the Dylan/Band '66 world tour; he married Flora and moved to Mexico to record indigenous music, raise a kid and grow organic vegetables. Their place was spectacular, a traditional Mexican adobe hacienda. The simple elegance of adobe construction and the beautiful details of hardwood in the house impressed both Linda and me, and we recorded that as an aesthetic we would try to reproduce when the time came to build our own place.

Moving on, we came back up to Oaxaca and took a mountain pass over to the Yucatán; we passed through jungles and overpasses in the Sierra Madres on treacherous roads. We fell asleep in a bed in the back of our Suburban van to the sound of monkeys howling. Stopping in village markets to buy tacos and tamales wrapped in banana leaves, we hiked through the awesome Mayan ruins at Palenque before they were open to the public and swam in emerald pools of water that were the bathing pools of the Mayans, made from giant black basalt rectangles covered in carved glyphs. The trip was amazing. Linda could drive the roads and speak enough Spanish to get by and was a better camper than I was.

Exhausted after three months and about ten thousand miles on the road, we crash-landed in Yelapa. In Yelapa we socialized with Ben and Micki Shapiro, who had bailed out of L.A. and in partnership with Bert Schneider, Dennis's *Easy Rider* producer, built a big swank palapa with guesthouses for L.A. drop-ins. Old friends, Benny had been Miles Davis's L.A. manager and Micki was one of the Unicorn waitresses. Tom Neuman—who had been with me in Yelapa years ago—was still alive and the place was just as I remembered it, though Benny and Micki's place was pretty deluxe for bush housing. Peggy Mundel, another old friend and one of the first folks to land in Yelapa, lent me her beautiful open palapa house. The house was strung out up the hillside, had a beautiful view of the bay from every separate room. Our bedroom had a birdcage that was actually a wall for Peggy, with about thirty canaries in a natural jungle of plants. Peggy collected textiles, pottery, carving, silverwork, you name it. The house was an open museum of quality indigenous art. In that enchanted atmosphere, our daughter, Aerie, was conceived. We came home with a world-class collection of Mayan and Mexican textiles, ideas for our new house and Linda pregnant with Aerie, who would arrive December 1 that year.

When we arrived back in New Mexico in April, we were broke. Tommy Masters contacted me with an offer from a couple of high-end pot smugglers who wanted to make a drug-smuggling road movie. Why not? I wrote a script called *All for the Good*, and called John Phillip Law and Michael Greene and got them onboard as actors. Tommy dropped off a paper bag with twenty thousand dollars in it and Linda and I flew to L.A. to buy a Travco motorhome to retrofit as a carryall to make the movie.

John Law drove back with us from L.A. and we swung south to Scottsdale to see Bob and Sara Dylan, and to meet their kids. Bob had gained some weight and seemed pretty relaxed. I think Sara was pregnant with Jakob or Sam at that time. We hung out by his pool and spoke of our family and what I was doing; Linda was pregnant, Bob and Sara had kids running around the pool. It was far-out to see Bob with a little weight on and kids crawling all over him. He was obviously into his family. Later, Bob drove out to his favorite spot on the Verde River with us. He liked the Travco private bus and said he was interested in one.

Sara and Bob drove to Santa Fe in May on their way back to New York City for the summer. Sara told a hilarious story of Bob on the freeway in the truck passing a semi in first gear. He was sheepish, and I think they abandoned the truck in Albuquerque and flew home after the visit with us. Still I was impressed; he was engaged and insisting on a semblance of a normal life at that time. We drove up to see Dennis Hopper and toured the mountains. Bob liked New Mexico, though Truchas was too remote for him. He let me think he might be interested in a place close to Santa Fe but didn't commit to anything.

A couple years earlier, Tommy Masters and I had put fifty dollars each down on two lots in a new subdivision south of Santa Fe. I bought Tommy out by trading my share of the land in Truchas, dreaming that I would build a couple passive solar homes and sell them. I had this notion with absolutely no bankroll. I did manage to get a building contractor's license and started a construction company called Maya. Work was pretty steady but I needed a good chunk of money to drill the well and pipe the two acres for water and put in the waste management systems for the houses.

In an offer I couldn't refuse, the dope dealers offered to front me one hundred kilos of pretty good marijuana and said I could have anything I made over two hundred dollars a kilo. Linda, then five months pregnant, was initially hesitant but game. So I loaded the one hundred kilos of pot into a waterproof crate that I framed together for the top of the Travco. I strapped a tarp over it and we drove the interstates from Santa Fe to Woodstock with that load on the top of the bus. It now seems pretty funny, but at the time, it really was the road to our future, a home for my budding family and a platform for me to build a life that would support them.

The trip passed uneventfully. We traveled during the day and saw the wilds of America. At one point we stopped in Kansas to rest for the night and woke up in the morning with about fifty National Guard vehicles camped out around us. I did sweat a bit about that one, but nothing happened; America was a different place, sleepy and quiet and pot was sort of out of the picture for the average person in 1972. Woodstock was home to some old friends, Rick Danko and other Band members, and Norma Cross, who had been around as part of our crowd since the days in the Village. Bob Dylan always liked Norma and kept up a relationship with her until about 1992. I left Linda with Norma, who owned and operated the Squash Blossom restaurant, and proceeded to get rid of our load. There were always outlets for pot in those days, and the East Coast would smoke or bake those kilos in no time. After reaching out to a few people, I was put in touch with a friend of a friend who paid me two hundred dollars a pound for the pot, which meant I was getting five hundred dollars a kilo, more than double what I owed. That was a much-needed financial boost. I could instantly see the future. Linda and I spent the remaining time with Rick Danko and I checked in with Maggie Denver, who had made a new life there.

Bob and Sara were no longer living in Woodstock; they had a place in the Village and a house on Long Island for the summer. Linda stayed in Woodstock for a few more days as I went down to see them. Bob related horror stories about his loss of privacy and how frustrating his fame had become, a kind of prison that closed in around him and made him fear for his own safety and that of his family. He naturally resented all that. I could hardly explain my situation, scrambling for money to build a house, so I did not say much. I went back to Woodstock and Linda drove home with fifty thousand dollars in the cash box. I paid off the dealers, and that one and only dope deal set us up well enough to pay for the water and the infrastructure for our first two houses on a five-acre piece of land south of Santa Fe, on which we were making one-hundred-dollar-a-month payments. I was a long way from Bob's reality and I felt in some ways I was better off.

Linda was never comfortable with my pot habit or our relation to Ralph and Larry, the dealers. But the movie idea appealed to me. I worked the script for *All for the Good* into something I hoped was funny, a slapstick pot odyssey. John Law, Ted Markland and Michael Greene were my actors, while Tommy Masters worked the camera. We picked a scene from the script and shot a couple hours of film that we edited down to ten minutes of thirty-five mm. With that teaser, we hoped to get funding for the rest of the project. I wasted a lot of time taking that film to L.A., looking for a backer. We needed a lot more than twenty thousand dollars to make the feature and nothing came of that effort. I always had the notion there was an easier way to make money, something that would keep me in the loop of my old life. The dope dealers knew it was a risky proposition, so by all accounts the debt was a write-off. I could sense they were happier pretending to be Hollywood producers than actually producing anything worth watching.

I had work in Lindrith that fall, remodeling a house for Michael Gold, another transplant from Los Angeles who made a small fortune as an entrepreneur. Linda and I pitched a tent on a bony rock outcropping and would hike up there to sleep at night. Michael Greene came out and spent time there, and he and his wife, Pat Donovan, would buy land. Dennis owned a

unique piece of land called Valley of the Gods—beautiful and
so remote, right on the Continental Divide in Apache country.
There were Indian artifacts everywhere in that country.

By November Linda said she wanted to be closer to a hospital for the baby's birth. We rented an adobe house in the plaza
close to the Santuario de Chimayó. I went back to New York
looking for work for the following spring and found none, so
went home knowing money would be tight with our baby soon
to arrive. On the last day of November about ten p.m., Linda
started having contractions; it was snowing and her doctor was
in Los Alamos, about one hour away. She had watched Lisa
Law give birth to her daughter, Sunday Peaches, a couple weeks
before and that night decided to have Aerie at home. So the two
of us watched the snow fall, watched a candle drip wax into a
flag and I tried to help her be comfortable with the contractions. By ten thirty the next morning Linda was so tired, I wondered if we should go to the hospital. Aerie's head was showing,
and she struggled up on her knees and gave the push that deliv-
ered Aerie Viktoria into the world. Our friends Joan and Stewart Pappe came over that afternoon and Stewart took great
photos of Linda, Aerie and myself. It was one of the greatest
moments of my life.

Fortune smiled, and the well and waterlines and septic system were ready on our Villa Linda property by January. We
bought a trailer and hooked it up on our land and moved in. I
started work on our home. I went to work on our first custom-
designed passive solar home in the summer of 1973, a design
we would call the Lima Bean. It was built of adobe bricks, and

we drove up into the mountains and harvested the Douglas fir poles, some eighteen inches in diameter, that would be the house roof beams. Traveling to Juarez, we brought back red clay tile for the floor and the geometric, colorful mosaics called talavera for the counters and bathroom. We commissioned local tinsmiths to make the filigree tin light fixtures that were common in old Spanish homes.

In the summer of '73, Bob dropped in out of the blue. Linda and I were in the trailer; he was traveling in a van with a couple I'd never met. He wanted to play a tape of his new stuff. We did not own any kind of music player, but my Martin guitar was in the corner. Bob picked it up and played and sang to us for about an hour. We caught up on our recent history. He mentioned the new songs he had been chewing on, a couple of which he ran by me. He was planning to record them for the *Planet Waves* album. We discussed them; I had not heard much of his recent music. This was all new and had more bite, though nothing political.

Later that fall he called and invited us up to Denver to stay on his nickel and see the performance with The Band. It was around the time of the album *Before the Flood*, which he recorded with them. The Denver Coliseum was a massive venue. Aerie was thirteen months old and slept in Bob's limo, watched by the driver, so Linda and I could be backstage. Bob and The Band ripped thirty thousand people out of their seats and up onto their feet. Powerful music and a collaboration that had

matured to musical perfection left us all speechless. This was
Bob's first American tour in eight years and the time away only
seemed to make his stage presence stronger and more intense.
At his hotel after the show, Bob told me to buy him a piece of
property not far from Santa Fe—anything I thought was the
right spot for him. He gave me his accountant's number and
told me to call if I found something.

We kept our eyes open for property for Bob, though I was
pretty busy then. Linda and Norma Cross found an eighty-acre
piece of land that was the site of the San Marcos Pueblo. The
site had been abandoned in 1680, when the natives moved down
this long arroyo to establish the Santa Domingo Pueblo on the
Rio Grande, that pueblo is still in existence. The original move
was to protest enslavement by the Spanish. The San Marcos Indians were turquoise miners and traded with the Pueblo Indians at Chaco Canyon, where there was a huge turquoise mine
about a mile from the back of this piece of property. Several
springs were on the property, and it had a great building site
and a long southern view. It was about three miles from the
town of Cerrillos, where our musician friends lived. Baird Banner was in the process of building a small but excellent recording studio on his property—he was the drummer in Eliza
Gilkyson's band. Norma Cross, my old friend from the Village,
Woodstock and early hippie days in New Mexico, was living
with one of the singer-songwriters in the group, Dennis Over-
man. With a vibrant music community nearby and the rather
amazing archeological history of the place, I thought Bob
might like to have a house there. I gave him the rundown on

the property; he said buy it and call Naomi Schwartzman, his personal accountant, with the details. The eighty acres was sixty thousand dollars.

Linda, Aerie and I drove to Guatemala and spent two months in a bungalow on Lake Atitlán that winter. Aerie was two, and Linda had immersed herself in Native American history and the migration patterns of people in the Americas. She spent her mornings in a village learning to weave and getting the lowdown on how the locals were being treated. Guatemala looked perfect: Esso stations, endless green rainforest, quaint Indian villages. Panajachel was an expat community on a huge, clean lake. We were in the picturesque heart of Maya Country. We slowly got the political picture. When driving one day, we watched a military vehicle hit an Indian walking on the side of the road, kill him and keep driving. And later, one of the Spanish doctors chewed Linda out for bringing in an Indian mother and baby with chronic diarrhea to his clinic about thirty miles from her village. He told her in clear terms that it was pointless to help those people. It was hard to get the locals to talk about what was happening, but there was something ominous in that beautiful place.

We drove north toward Mexico and the relief was palpable. It was 1974 and we were often on unpaved roads that trip. We found a road from Oaxaca to Puerto Escondido and drove up the coast to Acapulco, dropping my seventy-five-year-old mother, Goldie, at the airport; she had flown down to Guatemala City to share the trip with us. We headed north up through Guerrero, Michoacán and Colima. The trip was amazing and we brought home tiles and great tinwork for Bob's house.

We came home and I began work on Bob's place. I designed a sort of Y-shaped adobe; the house faced south and had spectacular views. I really had no idea what Bob wanted, but I knew we had a similar taste and that he trusted me. He gave me a budget of twenty thousand dollars for the whole investment. He had a family, by then five kids, and I assumed he wanted a place that was flexible enough to serve him alone and to deal with the family on vacation. I understood his need for privacy and security and it wasn't the first time I defined how and where those protections would be put in place. The house was set a quarter mile back into the property on a peninsula of land that overlooked a long canyon. I built the house in a traditional Pueblo style: adobe, brick floor, wood vigas and Mexican tile bathrooms. The downstairs rooms opened out onto a veranda that had a hundred-mile view south down the San Marcos arroyo. Sunsets were spectacular from the upstairs.

The house was finished by Thanksgiving.

Bob had moved his family to Los Angeles and, at my suggestion, bought land on the coast in Malibu. He wanted me to see the land he purchased and Sara invited us for Thanksgiving dinner at a beautiful two hundred-year-old hacienda she had in the hills up toward Santa Barbara. This was separate from the main compound they purchased on the coast; Bob purchased the hacienda as a private retreat for Sara. They were going through a difficult time. Bob did not say anything to me but Sara confided in Linda after playing several songs from Bob's new album, *Blood on the Tracks*. Linda was taken aback by the painful honesty in those songs, and wondered why Bob would put his life so openly on the line. At one point while they were listening and talking, Bob literally walked into the glass door of their bedroom where Linda and Sara were, blinded by his agitation over them talking pretty obviously about Sara's and his relationship. Linda found the songs to be very profound, not knowing what else to say. Visibly annoyed, Bob asked, "How could anyone listen to that?!"

Sara and Linda cemented their friendship during that visit; she became a sounding board for Sara during a very difficult time. It was an awkward spot to be in for her. Linda had no history with Bob and she and Sara had similar interests at the time: mythology, medicinal plants and a mystical feminism that allowed them to communicate.

Linda referred Sara to Pat Donovan, Michael Greene's wife, who would become a loyal, quiet confidante for Sara in L.A. I stayed out of it. In the years since I had left, Bob had taken charge of his life, had definite ideas about his privacy and was committed to protecting that for his family's sake as well as his own. Bob has always worked hard to sculpt his own history.

Sara was isolated in general, for the spotlight was always on Bob, but moving to Los Angeles had opened up a completely different social world. Her kids were old enough and she had enough money to hire help with them. Her beauty in her midthirties was undiminished; she was, if anything, more attractive. Sara wanted a personal identity beyond that of wife and mother.

Alone, in the dead of winter in 1974, Bob took a train ride to New Mexico to see the San Marcos house. He made it clear to me on the telephone that he did not want to see anyone, including Linda. I picked him up at the Santa Fe station and drove him out to the property. He spent two nights in the house and took the train back to L.A. The house was unfurnished, empty, and the winter meant it was closed up. He did not like it, said it reminded him of a hotel. I was sorry about that; he never got what we saw in that piece of property or took enough interest to figure it out. I felt pretty defensive about the choice and responsible for his investment. I mean, I really did not want to disappoint him.

Sara and Linda stayed in regular contact for the next few years. Bob was maneuvering, his music was back and he seemed to be exploring creative options that L.A. offered. He wrote a musical film, *Renaldo and Clara*, and put together a band for a tour in '75 called the Rolling Thunder Review. He called Norma, not me, and told her to arrange to have her, Dennis Hopper and us come to the show at the Red Rock Stadium on May 23. He said there would be rooms for us at the Stanley in Estes Park.

During that time I was designing, building and selling houses to make a living. We were living in our original house, the projects I had kept me working, I did well enough financially, but the sales did not create a sustainable income past my working. I wanted property that would generate income on its own, so I decided to sell our original house and use the proceeds to buy a piece of commercial property. I needed an investment that could earn more than I owed on the building loans I was acquiring. I also bought ten acres in San Marcos and an acre in Hyde Park Estates, which I wanted to be our permanent home. The money was enough to buy the land, but it left us temporarily with no place to live.

The Rolling Thunder Review was a curious show. Bob had gathered quite an entourage and he was filming for a TV show, to be called *Hard Rain* or something. At the hotel, he kept a tight wrap on who was let in: I was and Linda was not. My four-year-old daughter, Aerie, would remember that as one of a long list of exclusions in her mind, exclusions that made me part of Bob's world and left my family out. Actually, to me he was as supportive as he could be. In Colorado, I asked Bob if we could rent the San Marcos house for a couple years, thinking if I lived there I could finish the details that would soften the new-construction feel and the place might be of some use to him. He said yes.

We moved in the summer of '75 and lived there until just before Jacob was born in 1979. We loved that house. I pitched a tipi on one of the bluffs, built a corral for Linda's horse, she planted herb and vegetable gardens and I manicured a lawn the horse would be led up to mow. I built a wood-heated, redwood hot tub lined with copper and perched it below the house so you walked off the lawn into the deck and tub area. I had built the house for privacy and I loved that we were unobserved; we could sunbathe, wander the hills and the quiet was punctuated only by coyotes and birds and the odd fox that wandered through the yard. Regularly Linda packed Aerie up on her back and hiked the hills, bringing back old stone tools, turquoise, even a skull she found in the arroyo.

Our connection with the Cerrillos music community continued. Eliza Gilkyson, a prolific singer-songwriter and daughter of folk musician Terry Gilkyson, and Kathy Hammerlee, who was dating Baird Banner, had kids Aerie's age and Linda often hosted them over at the house. Except for Norma, the musicians in Tusker were closer to her age than mine and their partners were her social group. Producing their shows was a way to keep Linda entertained and my hand in a world I knew and missed. Dennis Hopper came down for weekend poker games that I set up with the locals from our old group—Stewart Pappe, Tony Price and a few contractors or friends from town. Dennis was struggling to keep Mable's house, but had cleaned up drug-wise. Still, those were difficult years for him financially. Dennis would always take home a couple hundred dollars from those games. I mean, you would have given him the money just to see him perform and hear his stories. Linda would make herself scarce for those nights but he would stay over and he and Linda would catch up.

Dennis was ever the genius, reciting a Rudyard Kipling long poem at the drop of a hat. He loved to remind me that we lived without a net, true outlaws, despite finding our ways both in family and life as working professionals. I continued to play Go with a Los Alamos scientist and found time to play chess in the

afternoons at the coffeehouse in the La Fonda with Greg Mc-
Farland, another contractor in town. Maya Construction had
an office in town and my secretary was a smart nineteen year
old. Not much to complain about.

In Estes Park before the show, Bob Neuwirth had introduced me to T-Bone Burnett, David Soles and David Mansfield, members of Bob's band. They were contemplating a debut
album as the Alpha Band after the Rolling Thunder Tour later
that summer. I had a job remodeling a great property in Tesuque
outside Santa Fe, called Shidoni, into a nightclub. T-Bone decided
to come to Santa Fe after the tour for rehearsals and to debut
the band there. The summer of '76 was pretty lively and my life
was full.

Then things fell apart.

The significance of 1976 probably escaped me at that time, but
looking back, I see that I had achieved what I wanted leaving
New York ten years earlier: I had a partner, a beautiful daughter and a business that was a success. I designed and built houses
that were appreciated by their new owners. I had a few ideas
that I tried to act on. I was trying to expand exponentially, I
needed to get away from doing the physical work on houses
myself; it simply could not support my family or me. I expended
a lot of effort, money and energy trying to get a contract to build
low-income houses for several of the Indian pueblos. I submit-
ted designs and a proposal for homes that were oriented to solar
gain, kept the soft round Pueblo look, used imported tile and

certain stylistic details that kept the feel of Taos Pueblo architecture, yet incorporated prefabricated modules that would make
them profitable to produce and assemble in three designs. I
favored floor plans that were like my houses, open big rooms, a
simple beginning with the obvious potential for add-on as families grew or prospered, bomb-proof insulation to hold heat and
make living in them cheaper and full exposure to the winter
sun. Though I spent a lot of time and money on that proposal,
I could not get the contract. I was a small-time player, trying
to be bigger, and though the door appeared open, in retrospect,
there was no way in.

Those in power in New Mexico tend to be a tight-knit group
and I was still an outsider. Hard lesson though that was, I
pulled back and decided I needed to focus on what I could do
(and own), so as to increase my income. Santa Fe as I knew it
was an artists town and in the old days the rents were affordable
and great spaces were available, regardless of the medium you
wanted to operate in. I liked that energy. I had a ten-acre commercial piece of property; I was developing it as artist living/
work studios. I envisioned well-lit, high-ceilinged open work-
spaces with affordable, small, loftlike living areas. I wanted to
keep the rent below six hundred dollars a month. I was interested in steel as a building material and had some training in
metal construction, so I could build the artist studios with an
industrial, yet pleasing, aesthetic.

Santa Fe was known for Native American and Western art
but there were significant artists working in town from within
our group. Tony Price, an old friend, was simply a genius. One

of Dennis Hopper's first investments in New Mexico was a piece of his work, five or six musical instruments that Tony had fashioned from sterilized pieces of equipment he'd sourced from the Los Alamos National Laboratory. The equipment had been contaminated by radiation during the construction of the first nuclear weapons. His work for years would be to bend the huge supply of usable nuclear waste into art and he collected vast amounts in a warehouse at the edge of town. Kachina masks, totems and musical instruments were his vocabulary and the precious metal and fine-machined parts came together in an explosion of expression.

In Santa Fe I was politically and musically engaged at a low level, through a vocabulary I understood, producing benefit concerts for local musicians. Eliza Gilkyson was an off-hand protégée—not one I felt ultimately responsible for, but certainly one I believed in as an artist and wanted to showcase as a poet and musician. I was happy to produce a demo for the group she was in, called Tusker, and to underwrite the monthly shows at the La Fonda. The proceeds went to local causes. I took the demo to L.A. to sell, but it was tough; Eliza was the real talent in the band. At that moment, she was committed to the group, because she was not ready to step out without the social support. Her kids, Cisco and Delia, were Aerie's age— under ten years old—and the rigors of becoming something in the music world meant that the needs of your family were secondary.

The Tusker group was tight and the social commitment to our kids' educational development was paramount. We sup-

ported local educators in their creations of learning environments, doing benefits for the places our children would spend
time. Those early attempts at meaningful education in our little
social group were important to me. Personally, my schooling
had not been very helpful to me and I wanted something better
for our kids. I tried to make money to support the social causes
that Linda embraced. There were benefits to stop a gold mine
that threatened the Cerrillos Hills; the gold there had achieved
a higher market price that made extraction profitable. Linda
had roamed the hills so extensively and written poetry and
stories she researched. She had a great connection to the geography and through her, I learned about the prehistory of the
turquoise mines and their connection to the decorative masks
of the Aztecs and Toltecs through the trade route of Chaco
Canyon. Over the years, Linda and I had visited those outposts
of prehistory and to be living peaceably on the San Marcos arroyo pleased and inspired her.

One of the band members, a fine poet named Dennis Over-
man, was partnered with Norma Cross. Norma was a constant
in my life since Bleecker Street in the early sixties and she was
an enduring intimate of Bob's. For decades the two of them
would spend a few days together in any given year. Fate had
twined our time together in New York, Woodstock and even in
New Mexico. She was a friend to me and over the years became
one of Linda's closest friends. They shared a love for weaving.
Norma spent countless hours carding and knitting. Her textiles
and designs were beautiful and sensuous. She had an impeccable aesthetic where design was concerned. She could reweave a

priceless Navajo rug for the Museum of New Mexico or design a draping, hand-spun, hand-woven cashmere silk dress.

My Go partner, Rolf Khan, was about ten years older than I. Few people even played Go, so partners who were just interested in the game were noticeable. I played all the years I lived in New Mexico with a Los Alamos physicist and with Rolf Khan. I knew Rolf from San Francisco in the early days; he was married to Barbara Dane, a well-respected musician. He started a folk music club in Berkeley where he showcased Mississippi John Hurt, Lightnin' Hopkins and the Chambers Brothers, people not popular at the time but known in our circle as progenitors of our musical interests. He recorded a few albums and became the first person I know to discipline himself in the art of kung fu.

Our weekly Go games were an important source of intellectual stimulation. Go was not like chess, which I also continued to play. Chess is considered the merchants' game and Go is considered the warriors' game—a four thousand-year-old exercise in territorial control. With simple rules: Each position must maintain two possible exits or it is no longer viable. A well-matched game ends up looking like the yin-yang symbol and effectively handicaps evolve so the players are always challenged and well-matched, regardless of skill. Given our mutual history, his Jewishness, interest in music and in Go, these long sessions with Rolf were a refuge for me. I trusted him.

My reconnection with Bob was important in some ways, for it validated that I had, and might continue to have, a role to play

in his personal evolution. But by then our situations were very
different; there was little common ground left for us. For Bob,
it felt you have to be physically useful to him, and he demands a
loyalty that excludes all other possibility. I was not that desperate
then, and pragmatically I needed to generate a certain amount
of business to keep my life going and protect my family. I was
still doing that on my own terms. I was grateful for the opportunity to design and build the San Marcos house and non-
plussed by his lack of appreciation.

I was finding more work in the context of Santa Fe's ex-
panding popularity as a hip place, and then, like every focus of
popular interest, it became overblown and competitive as bigger financial players entered into the local field. To compete,
you needed a bigger bankroll. Property prices increased and
financing for projects went to those with more substantial financial backing than I, or else to contractors more willing to
schmooze, drink and hang out. None of that was my strong
suit. Moving into the San Marcos house gave me a momentary
respite. The rent was very reasonable and it allowed me to operate on the simple principle of buy and sell without putting
Linda and Aerie through yearly moves.

T-Bone Burnett, Steven Soles and David Mansfield's decision to debut their collaboration as the Alpha Band at Shidoni
in Tesuque, with my help, reconnected me to L.A. and my old
world and gave me a lasting sense of continuity. I liked them
and their music. Though, it must be said, this connection was
always an alluring siren, destined to cause difficulty at home.
It's hard to explain the relativist ethic that makes a man want

his partner to be faithful and still allow for his own position to remain unencumbered. Marriage could mean everything and nothing to me. And there is a fatal flaw in that argument.

Early in 1976 I had flown to Mexico to meet Bob, Sara, Tommy Masters, his wife Gloria, and Dennis Hopper in Yelapa. Sara met Dennis Hopper for the first time there. Sara and Bob still were having trouble, which did not resolve itself after his release of *Blood on the Tracks*. Linda and Sara had a friendship; I don't think Sara could talk to anyone in L.A. or in the old group, or even the new group, because Bob has a strange sort of mafia-like control of everyone around him. In the end, I think it's been self-defeating. But it's his thing. Likely because of Linda's relationship, her age and her innocence, Sara trusted her and would call and report what was going on in the years of their breakup. She came out a couple times to see us, once on a mission to see and talk to Dennis. I got the report of that meeting secondhand; Dennis, like everyone else, was not stepping into that minefield. Poor Sara.

In the end, I think she ended up with a bundle but I can only imagine the price she paid. In that time, Bob did one of the stupider things he accomplished in life by talking candidly on the telephone to Lisa Law, by then Tom's ex-wife. Lisa, ever the record keeper of history, relayed the telephone call to our very close friends; apparently Bob said some of the dumbest stuff possible on the phone, which I have zero interest in repeating. When I found out I just shook my head, not only at what

Bob may have said but also at Lisa for repeating it. I think
Norma Cross called Bob and told him about it. I knew from
Linda how he was acting but stood back. After losing interest
in the San Marcos house, he did not maintain any real contact
with me.

As Bob and Sara's divorce progressed, Bob's business man-
agers were pressuring us to do something with the house. I
offered to buy it, but asked that Bob consider holding the
mortgage. Bob's accountant said no way. Bob had about two
hundred thousand dollars in the house and property. It was a
spectacular eighty-acre piece I could have easily built one house
on and paid off the mortgage if he had been willing to hold the
note for two years, but that was not an option, according to the
accountant. It became clear that I couldn't swing the mortgage
with the bank—I already had two building loans out: the artist
studios on Airport Road and a beautiful house for speculation I
was building in Hyde Park Estates above Santa Fe. With these
projects unfinished, the bank refused to stretch to another
mortgage.

Linda was newly pregnant with Jacob. It killed her leaving
the San Marcos place and in many ways, she never truly got
over losing that house and land. But when Bob's accountants
wanted to raise the rent and put the house up for sale on the
open market, she decided she wanted to move to the Hyde Park
house. She did not want to put up with showing the house to
strangers and we felt our own interests were better served by
putting all of our energy into completing cosmetic details on
our Hyde Park investment. Plus, she was insistent that after six

years of building houses and leaving them, she wanted to have our baby in our own home. We did that. In the end, Bob's house sat on the market and empty for almost two years, but eventually he did get more than I wanted to pay for it.

That spring of 1979, Linda went to work for Southwest Outward Bound, bookkeeping for her friend, the director Harry Freshman. By then Linda was accomplished as a river rafter and her own excursions into the outdoors became more independent. Pregnancy had not slowed her down much, but Harry nixed her going down the Grand Canyon that summer before Jacob was born, after he pulled her out of the water in a complicated set of rapids in the Rio Grande Gorge.

It was after a similar river trip that the whole group, including kids, wives and John Phillip Law, who was in town, trooped into the El Paragua restaurant in Española. It wasn't exactly the place you expected to run into Richard Avedon the photographer, but there he was. Linda and Kathy had arranged a back table for about twenty of us and Avedon was blown away by our raw, brown athletic beauty when we walked in; he came to the table and asked if he could visit the house the next day and photograph us. It turned out John knew him and they recognized one another at the table. That photo survives in a dozen houses as a moment memorized for us.

In appreciation for her work at Outward Bound, Harry Freshman offered Linda two seats on a river trip down the Grand Canyon; it was to be a fund-raiser for Outward Bound. She gave her seats to John Law and me, and we spent three weeks camping, hiking and paddling eighteen-foot rafts down the two hundred miles of the canyon. Linda and Aerie met us at the Havasupai takeout. She was eight months pregnant with Jacob and thirty-one years old. I have to say that trip was one of the high points of my life.

Jacob was born at home in late August. Kathy Miller, Linda's rafting buddy, was called and came over for support. Jacob arrived at sunrise, the light on the Jemez Mountains making them glow red when he gave his first cry. Linda pulled herself up to count fingers and toes. I put him on her chest. The golden light of day crept toward us across the Rio Grande Valley as we embraced the newest addition to our family. Jacob came easily and was a perfect eight-pound-plus kid. He was nursing like a pro one hour after coming into the world. The house filled up with light as the sun crossed the sky. By the afternoon, Jacob was basking in the sun-draped room in the hollow of a huge beanbag that Linda had covered with an old mink coat. Aerie, six years old, hovered, not sure the new guy was all that welcome. In the end she was kind and a good sport, but reluctant to relinquish her only-child status.

The day after Jacob was born we drove up to the road to Santa Fe Baldy. We buried Jake's placenta high on the mountainside, at about eleven thousand feet. Linda was already searching for the mountaineer in him.

We knew we would not be long in the Hyde Park house—a great sadness, really. I finished the Airport Road project and the place was rented.

I flew to Hawaii in November with John Law to see a small Japanese hotel he wanted to buy in Kamuela, a town on the Big

Island of Hawaii. John wanted me to remodel the place and to live there and run it for him. I liked Hawaii and thought five or six years there while the kids were little with a steady job that looked like a family-run deal would be okay. Both Linda and I were tired of building and selling. The real-estate market was in a glut in Santa Fe, so the Hyde Park house, like Bob's property, did not sell immediately. By the time it eventually sold, we had eaten through half of our profits.

We arrived in Kamuela in April 1980. John was negotiating the purchase of the hotel from L.A., and I was supposed to finish the deal after we arrived. We moved into the hotel as a temporary home. A local businessman and real-estate developer found out the place was for sale and pressured Mr. Moon Samashima into dropping John's offer in favor of his own. It was a somewhat shady transaction, but John was not there to push back and I had very little leverage with the locals. The loss of that opportunity was devastating. Linda and I found a house that we bought and began to remodel. But there was no security in Hawaii, and the building trades were pretty locked up. I couldn't find work and little by little our savings evaporated.

I was sick over and over, eventually figuring out I needed a huge amount of dental work. Nothing went well. In January 1982, while Aerie stayed with me because she was in school, Linda went back to New Mexico to handle repairs and deal with renter issues on the Airport Road property. When she returned she had decided we should separate, that I needed to go back to New Mexico and try to reestablish myself in that market and that she would wrap up our scene in Kamuela and sell the house we had remodeled.

It was a painful time.

Eventually I took a job helping out the stage crew for Peace Sunday, the We Have a Dream concert on June 6, 1982, at the Rose Bowl in Pasadena, California. I was running out of money after moving back from Hawaii and it was a good gig to open myself back up to the scene in Los Angeles. The huge show promoted nuclear disarmament and was attended by over eighty-five thousand people. There was an all-star list of performers: Graham Nash, Bonnie Raitt, Donovan, Crosby, Stills and Nash, Steven Stills, Taj Mahal, Stevie Wonder, Joan Baez, Stevie Nicks, Linda Ronstadt, Nicolette Larson, Bette Midler, Jackson Browne, Tom Petty and Bob.

I hadn't talked to Bob in a few years and though I knew he was playing the show, I didn't reach out or try to communicate with him beforehand. Bob and Joan Baez were scheduled to perform three songs in between the sets of Stevie Wonder and Stevie Nicks, on a small stage that extended out from the main stage. Behind them was a big, blue piece of fabric that was blocking the view of the main stage where Stevie Wonder's equipment was. During Joan's set, I was a part of the small group of guys swapping out all the gear and instruments. As we were pushing everything around, I heard Bob announced and saw him walk onstage. He was only a few feet from me but through the blue fabric he couldn't see me.

As we were tying up the loose ends onstage I noticed the fabric was bending down and about to collapse, so I ran over and propped it up and just then, Bob turned around to adjust his guitar and noticed me standing right behind him onstage in front of the eighty-five thousand people. Bob yelled out, "Victor!" Joan was in the middle of her seven-song set and about to introduce the song they were going to play, so it was not the time for me to talk to Bob. Well, Bob walked over and said it was great to see me and started to have a conversation. Then Joan turned around and noticed me and waved and said hi. I was completely embarrassed standing there, holding this truss onstage, keeping it from falling down, and Bob wasn't paying attention to the massive crowd behind him. He was looking at me. Then Joan grabbed Bob by the hair and pulled him back to the microphone. It was pretty funny and a picture of Joan grabbing Bob was splashed all over the magazines. It was a bizarre moment, and the first time we had connected after several years of not talking.

Linda returned to New Mexico in the fall of 1982, telling me Jacob was starting to call everyone "Dad" and she did not want that. I mistakenly took that as a possible reestablishment of our relationship. She said no. So that was the end of that. I was living in one of the units at Airport Road. I bought a two-bedroom trailer and set it up so the kids would be comfortable when she let them visit. I thought of Bob and Sara and realized a lot about divorce and just how low you could go. I found work, but had no ambition to really do big projects. Our separation took a year to finalize. In that year after one of our argu-

ments about money, Aerie was thrown from a donkey; Linda
had allowed her to ride with a neighbor's kid and she'd frac-
tured her femur in four places. I was so angry I could not see
straight.

Aerie recovered but spent two months in leg traction in the
kids' section of Saint Vincent Hospital. Linda was there day
and night. I could not bear to see my daughter like that, and I
did not trust myself to talk to Linda. I called daily and split for
L.A. to look for work. I am not proud of that moment, but
facing my own emotional attachments and expressing grief is
not my strong suit. My tongue was bitter and sharp, cruel and
callous. Linda and I could barely utter a civil word for months,
the guilt and recrimination was so thick. Divorce is a miserable
failure on everyone's part.

In the end, I kept the Airport Road property, and we settled
on how I could support the kids. She asked for very little,
really, and valued the time I would spend with them. Finally
we worked at keeping me a part of the picture. She never cared
much about money and was pretty good at giving it away, but
had some devoted friends. Linda made a living in that time by
managing construction projects for a wealthy girlfriend, Mela
Leavell. She bought a house in partnership with Mela in one of
the old Spanish neighborhoods; she remodeled that house and
managed to put herself through nursing school. That, she said,
was the aftershock of Aerie being in the hospital, which left
Linda with a determination to not be powerless in the face of
health authority again.

We lived separate lives. I have to say that I felt like I had been hit in the head and that I had been off balance for years. I retreated into myself, just tried to get by.

~

End of Tape Six

It's incredible to relive these stories, to wander in my father's footsteps, but also incredibly taxing. It's a mixed bag of sad nostalgia with stories I've heard before and the excitement of new ones. I didn't realize how close my mother and Dennis Hopper had been, or the depth of Dennis's working relationship with my father. My father had always played down his acting role in *The Last Movie*. "I was just an extra," he'd say. He joked about being killed twice and bummed that each time his look-alike dummy hit the ground, its face was pointed away from the camera. This meant that when he took the same position as the dummy, you couldn't even see his face and thus couldn't tell that it was him! Because he panned the movie and never glorified his role, I never watched it. But in the past few weeks I found the complete film on YouTube, streaming for free. I'm bizarrely proud of my father for acting in what's widely considered the worst movie in cinematic history and, to add another feather to his cap, he's one of the first actors to be shot and killed in the movie, while nearly getting stepped on by a horse. That's quite some feat.

Some of the history in the New Mexico chapter completely baffles me. Drug running several hundred pounds of marijuana across state lines to earn money to buy a house? Are you kidding me? I've asked my mother a few times about this and each time she shakes her head in embarrassment and points out that she was only twenty-one and that it was a very different time in her life. She goes go on to state that "nobody lives a full life without red marks on their scorecard."

To me, the reckless, adventurous young girl that I've just heard my father discuss and my mother are two irreconcilable people. And yet they are the same. Learning about their lives back then and knowing my mother now seems like I'm learning about someone completely different. Her life has moved on immeasurably from those crazy days in the heady seventies. That young girl that I've just heard my father talk about called me the other day with a story that further illustrates her departure from adolescence.

Moments into our talk, I could tell she'd had a long day. I heard it in the tone and exhaustion in her voice, from what exactly was anybody's guess. In true form, she skipped divulging anything about herself and asked how I was and what my day was like. I explained what I was up to but knew something more was brewing in our conversation. When I ask her how her day was, my mother sighed and said in a simple and matter of fact way, "It was pretty weird." I asked her to elaborate, and she went on to explain that while she was at work, Dolores the secretary received a panicked call from a woman en route to the medical clinic.

The woman on the phone stated that her husband was acting oddly and she didn't know what to do. My mother was informed of their impending arrival and the nature of the call fueled her intuition that the situation approaching was dire and grim. She asked Joyce, a caring, no-bullshit Hispanic nurse, to double-check that the oxygen tank wasn't empty. As Joyce went to check, Linda walked out front to watch an SUV drive into the gate of the clinic compound. When it stopped she noticed the man in the passenger seat: He was blue, foaming from the mouth, unconscious, not breathing and, by all accounts, dead.

My 120-pound mother yanked this 220-pound man onto the gravel and checked his pulse—nothing to be found. She started CPR and eventually Joyce came running out into the parking lot with the automatic emergency defibrillator.

When the AED was properly attached, the analyzing function began with a robotic voice stating, "Analyzing now, stand clear." After a moment it announced, "Shock advised, stand clear." Linda gave the approval and Joyce hit the shock button. The man's chest arced up in the air while being electrocuted and released when the shock had finished. No breath, no pulse, so they shocked him again.

As their collective faith started to wane, the gentleman started to breathe. The three women standing over him were in disbelief, but just as their spirits lifted, they were brought back down as the man stopped breathing again. Life was dancing at his fingertips and he couldn't hold on to it. The AED kicked into action for the third time, analyzing and stating, in its robotic tone, "Shock advised." The three women were not going to give up; life had peeked out behind the man's pale blue skin and lifeless expression. They shocked him a third time and slowly, with much difficulty, he started to breathe and kept breathing.

A flight-for-life medical helicopter was dispatched from Santa Fe to receive the man for faster transport along the way. With the helicopter, his transport time would be cut down from fifty minutes to twenty. On the phone with my mom, I could hear how shattered her nerves were. She was deflated and still in shock, but for some reason she wasn't sharing the same excitement about the event as I was. I was thrilled! She'd saved somebody.

And that's what that young wild girl in the Travco is doing these days, full of redeeming social value. From the outside it seems like a lifetime away.

CHAPTER 7

～

I Need a Job

Bob Dylan posturing for Victor, behind the lens of the camera.
(Courtesy: Victor Maymudes)

Tape Seven

In 1987, I found myself in dire straits financially.

I lost the commercial building I owned to the bank. Some of the most respected rock-carving artists in New Mexico were tenants of mine. As I handed the keys over, it was heartbreaking. I had secured the building with a variable-rate loan and that year the local housing market crashed, dropping the value of my property. At the same time interest rates were rising, which was the final nail in the coffin. After I missed several mortgage payments, the bank foreclosed on the property, leaving me distraught and on my way to being homeless.

I was running out of money rapidly and needed income. I gave Bob a call in my desperation. He answered and I simply said, "Bob, I need a job." He instantly replied, "You're hired! Come out next week, and we'll talk about money." His willingness to help me and his no-questions-asked approach was a blessing. I don't think he ever really knew how much he saved me from complete ruin.

I drove out to Los Angeles a week later and met Bob on the coast in Malibu. He told me, "I'm going on tour, but I've got everybody I need already and I don't really have a place for you. But I'll pay you and you'll come with us and we'll see what happens." I was thinking, Great. I've got nothing, so this is the best deal in town.

The day before we were supposed to be flying to Athens, Bob called me up and told me to drive out to the house and we would ride to the airport together. I said okay, assuming he had someone picking us up—like a limousine, car or a friend. I arrived at Bob's place, parked and walked inside. The people there told me he was walking around the property and he would be ready shortly. I sat down and started hanging out. The time just kept rolling by and I was still sitting there, reading books, taking a moment to smoke a joint. With less than an hour to go till the flight, Bob was nowhere to be found. Bob's estate was about forty miles away from the airport, so it would take an hour driving fast to make it there. It was now forty minutes until departure, already an impossible feat.

He finally came casually walking through the door. He looked at me and, without even so much as a hello, said, "Victor, we'll go in your car. Suzy Pullen will drive your car back here." I didn't know Suzy Pullen, it was the first time I ever saw her. He told me she was his wardrobe lady from Australia. I was thinking to myself, I'm going to give this lady my van? I don't even know her! I introduced myself. She spoke with such a thick Australian accent I could barely understand her. "Well," I said, "okay, let's go." What else could I do?

My van outside was a full-size Chevy conversion van. It was made for traveling; there were two seats in the front, two in the middle and a bench seat in the back, which could fold down to a bed. It was an older model and fairly beat-up from the years of use. It wasn't fancy or fast, and definitely not safe while driving at speed. I told him and Suzy I was going to really have to make an effort to get there; that we didn't have enough time as it was to make the flight. Bob looked me hard in the eyes and said, "We'll do the best we can . . ."

I drove those forty miles on two wheels. Down the middle of the Pacific Coast Highway! It would be an unbelievable feat to get there on time and I was determined not to fail. The rest of the group was already waiting for us at the airport. Gary Shafner, the tour manager in charge at that time, was wondering where we were and already had assumed we were going to miss the flight.

Bob sat sideways in the front passenger seat. He didn't look

up once, just kept flipping through a big handful of photo-
graphs, snapshots that he had taken with his camera from some
other place in time. I couldn't precisely see the photos; I caught
a glimpse of a few and think they were portraits. He was
looking at each one closely and then throwing it out of the
window, one by one, the whole distance I drove. Just casually
tossing them out. I watched through my rearview mirror as
each photo caught the wind with a loud, ripping sound before
dancing and floating in the slipstream. I imagined the photos
telling a story. If someone was lucky enough to have been in the
exact right place and time they would have had a personalized,
stop-motion film displaying the depths of a moment in Dylan's
life that he so wanted to leave behind. The visual poetry struck
a chord with me, and I was sure we were going to get pulled
over for littering the whole ride.

This all happened while I was running red lights, driving
on the shoulder of the road, passing cars by entering oncoming
traffic and generally driving like a maniac in my huge, blue
van. Not to mention Suzy Pullen screaming and hanging on like
she's going to die any second, screaming at me to slow down
while hitting me on the back of the head. Bob was completely
relaxed in this chaos, deep inside his mind. I was putting the
pedal to the metal as I was trained to do. Suzy was practically
having a heart attack. I couldn't understand her when she was
speaking normally, let alone when she was having a meltdown.

We rushed up to the curb at Los Angeles International Airport, jumped out and I handed Suzy the keys. As we walked
into the airport, Gary Shafner and his group immediately took

our bags from us and checked everything in. Gary was yelling, "Come on, we got five minutes to get on the plane!" Bob turned to me and said, "We got a lot of time," as if we had all the time in the world.

That flight took us straight to Cairo, Egypt, and then on to Israel for our first show on the Temples in Flames Tour. The show was scheduled at Park Hayarkon in Tel Aviv on September 5, 1987. Bob and Tom Petty had agreed to split the tour and they had cobilling. As for the shows, Tom Petty would go on first for a few songs, then Bob would do his set, and then Tom would come back out and close the show.

Roger McGuinn did a solo opening act to warm everybody up. It was unbelievable that Roger could get out in front of the audience that was expecting rock 'n' roll legends with only his guitar and captivate people. He was amazing on and offstage. A real sweetheart and charmer of a guy, I think he's a much better entertainer than he gets credit for.

From what I understood, Tom Petty and his group had arrived a week earlier. At this time I didn't know him or his crew. They were all new people in my life. When we arrived in Israel, Bob came to me and asked me not to associate with the Tom Petty group. Since I was the new guy and didn't really have a job, I just agreed and went about my business.

I was standing backstage watching the first show. Tom had four more songs before the night was over, and Bob was performing with him, when an Israeli general approached me and said there was a curfew and that he was going to pull the plug promptly at ten p.m. I looked at my watch and it was a quarter to ten; it seemed there was going to be just enough time to end the show and not have to worry about the general's threat. Despite it not being my job (I was not the appointed tour manager) to deal with this situation, I told the general we understood and that the show should end right on time. He walked away and Tom kept playing. At ten p.m., Tom was still playing and the general approached me again and said, "All right, that's it. I'm shutting you down." I shot back with, "Wait a minute, we're almost finished. Let's just make it the last couple of minutes and everyone will be happy." The general responded sternly, looking me right in the eyes: "We're bombing Jordan right now, this instant, and we're afraid of retaliation. This concert is too good of a target to let sit on this beach."

Well, doing what I do best, which is adapt to situations quickly and figure out solutions, I jumped into a response that was continuous without interruptions or pauses. I was pulling things from the air to talk about, making sure the general's attention didn't move away from me. While I was talking to him, I saw soldiers with machine guns walking up to the stage on both sides. There were ten or so soldiers surrounding the stage and another twenty behind, but I was undeterred. I waved my hands in the air and talking erratically about the political landscape of the region. I was going on and on, buying time. My random monologue had to be about ten minutes long, which is a lot to generate on the spur of the moment. The whole time the entire security force was waiting for the go-ahead from the general, since it was now past curfew. I heard Bob and Tom stop playing and thank the audience, and that instant I wrapped up my diatribe. "Hey, man, great talking with you." I shook the general's hand, but he just looked at me bewildered and walked away. Nobody in production knew what was about to happen, nor did Bob or Tom. That moment just had a funny way of resolving itself, as do most things on tour, because you're constantly living in the moment. Constantly dealing with unforeseen challenges.

The next night we played a show in Jerusalem. After the show I arranged a private tour of the Old City for Bob and me with the head of the hostage negotiation team for the Israel Defense Forces (IDF), and an agent with the Israel Ministry of Tourism. The IDF guy showed up with an Uzi strapped to his back and a pistol attached to his leg. We started our tour at midnight on foot; the IDF soldier opted for midnight specifically so we would have less chance of drawing attention to ourselves.

There was a sharp contrast between the look and function of what both men brought with them on this trek into the inner city: one with a copy of the Old Testament, one with a submachine gun. I felt deep parallels between the two. The irony was not lost on me. I believed neither man was deadlier than the other. If the Uzi were removed from the boundaries of time, as was the Bible, even Lady Justice wouldn't be able to tell them apart. The symbiosis of the tools used in the great con of man was on clear display as we walked into the center of the holiest place on Earth.

Both men told us the histories of ancient Jerusalem, both were very smart and articulate. I asked the soldier many questions, and he opened up about his personal life and described his academic studies: He was actually a doctor. I could see the Jekyll and Hyde paradox he lived in right away: a trained killer who had learned advanced anatomy to be a more efficient killer and the medic who had a deep appreciation for life and a desperate need to preserve it at all costs.

We came to an area that was associated with the Hebrew University; it was a large chamber with rock walls, floors and ceilings. It was four in the morning and there wasn't a single person on the streets. However, the lights were on in the large chamber, so many lights that it looked like daylight inside. From where we were standing, we could hear tremendous arguing. What sounded like people on the edge of a fight, severe anger and screaming. Our guides informed us they were not fighting, they were discussing. Bob and I asked, "What could they possibly be discussing like this at four in the morning?" The soldier responded, "The interpretation of the word."

Bob and I were taken aback by this, but since day one the Jews have been arguing this topic. Since the dawn of time, the meaning of a word is never the literal, it's always the interpretation. Bob is magically one of those people who can bend the interpretation for the rest of us without even knowing it, without realizing this is an ancient thing. Bob and I would run the same argument as the Jews inside on the edge of fighting, heavy debates over the interpretation and meaning of a word. So with that response from the soldier, Bob and I looked at each other, shrugged in a collective "Yeah—that makes sense" and walked off.

For the next few concerts, we kept our tours separate from Tom's, despite playing the same shows. We didn't move at the same time, we didn't use the same equipment; we didn't use the same boats or planes to travel. It was very odd to me; the relationship didn't exist behind the curtain like it did onstage. Onstage they would sing a couple songs a night together and from the audience's point of view they were friends, but their relationship was far from developing to what it is today.

A few shows later we were in Germany, and I was hanging around backstage looking for something to do. Since I wasn't the tour manager and didn't have a firm role, I was trying to listen to everything and attach myself to any and all decisions and functions on the road. While I was backstage at the first German show I saw an interesting-looking guy hanging out with Heinz, the West Germany concert producer. I walked up to him and asked him who his buddy was, and Heinz said it was his East German counterpart, which I couldn't believe, but Heinz insisted that he was the concert promoter for all the shows in East Berlin. I was fascinated by the life and hardships of the people over the Berlin Wall, so I asked to be introduced. Heinz grabbed the guy and we started talking. One thing led to another and he mentioned he would have loved to have had the show in East Berlin but things didn't work out. I asked him why not and he said they couldn't afford the tour. I immediately encouraged him to talk to the guys on the road, specifically Elliot Roberts, who was on the road with us. Elliot formed Lookout Management with David Geffen and was the guy who could make things happen.

From my little encounter, it was as if Bob said to pursue the idea and from that Elliot and Bob talked, then Bob and Tom talked and by the next day the entire tour agreed to do the show. It was to be one of the first Western rock shows ever in East Berlin, and it materialized out of thin air. In the few days prior, they released forty thousand tickets and planned the show in an outdoor park. The forty thousand tickets sold in two minutes. When that happened the promoter contacted our group and asked if they could sell another thirty thousand since the show was already sold out. We agreed. For us their money was worthless, so it didn't matter financially how many people came. We were willing to entertain them all. The next day, one day before the show, they said that the extra thirty thousand sold in an hour and half and that they would like to sell more, which we agreed to. They ended up selling one hundred twenty thousand tickets in three days.

When the show started, you couldn't see the edge of the crowd. They had put up a fence but they didn't have a fence big enough for one hundred twenty thousand people, so it didn't matter who had tickets by the time the show started. It was a sea of faces.

When Bob and Tom took the stage it started to drizzle a little bit and it was a fabulous moment in history, as the whole audience swayed together with the rhythm. It ended up a historic concert, one that added to the civil unrest of the nation, which within a couple years culminated in the destruction of the Berlin Wall.

Jim Callahan was head of security on the tour; he had just jumped ship from working security for the Rolling Stones, and specifically Keith Richards. This was back when Keith was at his depths with drugs and irreverent behavior, which could have contributed to Jim's decision to leave the Stones and tour with Bob.

A few days after the East Berlin show we pulled up in the bus to the Johanneshovs Isstadion venue in Stockholm, Sweden. Everyone started to unload and exit the buses to stretch and get some fresh air. Most of the crew were gathering near the front of the bus on the sidewalk. Jim was trying to win over my confidence in him and called me over to the other side of the sidewalk from where the busses were parked. I walked over and stood next to him and he said, "Watch this," as he pointed to Bob's bus. "Bob is going to come off the bus and he's going to go the other way from the crowd." I took it like a bet, so I was interested to see if he was going to be right. Sure enough, Bob walked off the bus, looked at the group and immediately walked the other way. Jim was showing me that he was studying Bob, calculating his movements. As a security guard he was very in tune with what was happening on the road. He took the role seriously and was good at it.

For Bob, on the other hand, I would have said of course he's going to go the other way. If anything, just for some personal space; just five minutes alone when you're on tour is a big deal.

Bob *has* to sneak away to get some time alone; he's always under the eye of someone. Someone is always trying to talk to him or look at him, and he feels it. There's an expression, having eyes in the back of your head. Well, Bob, just like all of us, can feel when people are staring at him. I believe he's even more sensitive to that stuff than most people. But it was still interesting to see Jim studying Bob and predicting his movements; it's the right type of forward thinking you want to see in your head of security.

Doing security on tour is a delicate job to do right. It's easy to mess up, for instance, if someone charges at Bob and the security guard grabs the person and, in the heat of the moment, punches, kicks or is too aggressive. The security guard's actions can become a big deal or even make the local news, and that's a red mark on Bob's scorecard, not the security guard's. Nobody knows the security guard, but everyone knows Bob. Little things like that can explode into major news stories, little mistakes that sometimes nobody is even to blame for can balloon into major news events, make Bob look bad and potentially cost money.

All the times I had to lay a hand on people, I was very careful. I tried to be diplomatic, and I tried to keep talking. I tried to reason with people, to encourage them to expose themselves; like a therapist, I would manipulate the dialogue until the person stated their motivations.

In one situation I remember from the road, Bob was backstage having a drink after a show and this lady ran up to give him a hug. She spread her arms out wide and rushed up to Bob way too fast, so he reacted and stepped to the side; she adjusted to Bob moving over and thrust to the side to grab him and she missed, hitting Bob hard and knocking him to the ground. It was unbelievable. Bob isn't a big guy and she hit him by accident just the right way to completely knock him to the ground. I ran over and grabbed her as she was still trying to go after Bob. She was struggling to get at him, even when he was on the ground, which elevated the situation. So I pushed her away. I'm a big guy and I really pushed hard. The problem in these situations is nobody really knows what to do. There's no school that teaches you how to handle aggressive people on tour. It's a world of its own and you have to figure it out in the moment, you have to react. And if you overdo it, you could be fired or sued. This crazed lady threatened to sue and called the police, but luckily for me she vented her steam and the police were sympathetic to me. Still, that little moment could have ended my career.

I believe my value to Bob and the tour was that I knew how to react in the moment. What I brought to the table was my ability to make an instant decision—what to do or how to handle it, whether it was a financial decision or something as simple as manipulating the taxi driver. That's where I had my greatest strength, where others would freeze up and fail to make a decision, their thoughts going in too many directions, and you could see it in their eyes. In many circumstances I would take power away from people who had more power than I did, simply because when shit hit the fan, I could react. I would yell at them and control the situation in and around Bob.

When I started back with Bob in the eighties, I asked him

why he didn't have his own bus. His response to me was, "They wouldn't let me. Nobody has tried to figure that out for me." It could have been a mixed bag of issues regarding Bob not having his own tour bus. The shows in the eighties were not huge shows; they were not making significant amounts of money. Also, getting Bob his own bus would require a lot of work by him. He would need to inspect it, specify what he wanted, make decisions on color and so on. These are details that would have required someone like Jeff Kramer, Bob's current manager, to help with. But Jeff wasn't into buses, so when I showed up I asked these questions. It didn't make much sense to me that Bob was still traveling in the band bus with no actual bed. No privacy. No place to write.

I told Bob I'd look into it. I researched and found out where the other guys like Willie Nelson, Tom Petty and such were buying their personal buses. I researched where the used buses were being sold, where to fix them and where to remodel them.

Along the way I informed Bob what I was finding. I wanted to take him on the path with me, so he felt connected to his new bus, if and when we found it. When a used one popped up, it was an old MCI bus, about twenty years old. I was sent pictures of it half-buried in the snow in Portland, Oregon. The sellers wanted sixty thousand dollars for it, which was a great deal at the time; it had new tires, new rims and a rebuilt motor, but nothing in the inside—totally gutted.

Bob was interested and we decided to purchase this bus and I would have the inside remodeled to my specifications. Bob and I have always shared a similar style, so making decisions on the interior of the bus was easy for me. I knew what he would like without having to ask him. I admit I've missed the mark in the past, but on most occasions Bob would appreciate my design decisions.

As it turned out, the owners of the bus were originally building the bus out for a drug dealer. It was a shady organization, but they had a full mechanic's garage along with the ability to do upholstery. The reason the bus's interior was gutted was the guys at the shop were in the process of creating secret compartments where large amounts of drugs could be stored. Their audacious plans were to create enough space for hundreds and hundreds of pounds of drugs in the main cabin of the bus. Then they were going to build out benches and seats like a real tour bus. The guys in the shop were only contracted to do the buildout, they didn't know much about the actual group or guy that owned the bus. Since I was a pot smoker and clearly wasn't a threat, we bonded over the bus and they told me everything about it. What the plans were, where the bus had come from, everything. It was actually this insight that made me think the bus was a good buy; I knew the whole history of it.

I made arrangements with Bob's accountants and we purchased the bus. We also hired the same guys who were going to build out the bus for the drug dealer to build out the bus for me. I had full control and was very meticulous about what I wanted. The entire interior had to be natural fibers, I demanded it—only wools, cottons and silks, nothing made from plastics. I also had the guys rework the three different electrical systems and put in two TVs: one in Bob's room in the back and

one in the common area in the front of the bus. I put in a size-
able bathroom (for a bus), a small kitchen and four bunk beds,
two on each side near the back, right before Bob's room.

Down the road when the bus was in full use, I added a custom trailer for Bob's motorcycles and several bicycles. I also
hung a full-size punching bag between the bikes so when the
bikes were removed, Bob could get inside and exercise.

The very first time I showed the trailer to Bob, he was on
the start of a West Coast tour. I was out late and arrived back at
the hotel later than everyone else, so Bob and the gang had already checked out the trailer without me. When I arrived, Jeff
Kramer ran up to me and started flipping out. He said that Bob
was hysterical, that trailer was a piece of shit and didn't work
and it wasn't what he wanted. Kramer kept going, saying I was
in a lot of trouble with Bob and he was giving me fair warning
to watch out. I walked two more feet and heard Bob yell at me
from across the parking lot.

"Victor!" I walked over to him. "What the fuck is this
trailer? What am I going to do with this? How is this going to
work? You send this home right now! This is not what I wanted!
You're an asshole for wasting my money." On and on, Bob just
hammered me on the trailer.

Before I gave up I asked him if he wanted to see the bikes
inside. He sarcastically said, "Yeah, show me the bikes." Then
he stalked off and got on the bus. Well, I opened up the back
door of the trailer, which opened like a ramp from the top
edge—not a typical door where it splits in the middle, this one
folded the entire back side down to create a huge ramp with

easy access into the trailer. In two minutes I had all the bikes out and the punching bag up, and it looked great.

I knocked on the side of the bus and asked Bob to come check it out. He came storming out, huffing and puffing, and instantly couldn't believe how wonderful it was. He was blown away. The issue had been that he and the other guys couldn't see how to lower the back gate and make the ramp. They thought the only door in was the small door on the side of the trailer. If that had been the case, then yes, it would have been a huge mistake. It would have been painful to remove any of the bikes and very time consuming. But with the ramp exposed it was a whole little environment that Bob could use. He jumped on a bike and rode around; when he came back I could tell he loved it. Not that he could really say that out loud, but I knew he was excited about it.

There were numerous occasions like this where he would tear me a new one before giving something a chance and I would just have to take it and wait him out. Eventually he would see what I was trying to do and really liked whatever it was.

~

End of Tape Seven

I've been rummaging through the plastic boxes my sister dropped off and came across a document titled "The American Tour, 1989: A Journal." To my surprise, it's actually the original copy of a book idea my father had that he was going to call "The

Journey of the Invisible Bus." It's a twenty-six-page account of life on the road during the summer and fall North American tours, printed on white paper and coil-bound with a title page and clear vinyl back cover. The original idea was for the book to be a journal, narrated from the perspective of Bob's tour bus. I'm not sure if my father intended for the bus to be personified in some way, but this slim document is all that exists. It captures the day-to-day life on the road driving from gig to gig; the travels of a modern troubadour on a Never-Ending Tour.

CHAPTER 8

~

The Journey of the
Invisible Bus

Bob's first tour bus, which Victor found, bought, and remodeled.
(Courtesy: Victor Maymudes)

Our plane arrived around two p.m. on June 29, 1989, in Chicago for the start of the North American summer tour. It was the tail end of a long trip from Athens, Greece. Jet lag had already set in and everyone was exhausted. We were very grateful when customs stamped our passports and passed our pile of bags through without opening them. Richard Fernandez met us with the band bus, which we boarded for the four-hour trip to Peoria, Illinois. As we pulled into the parking lot of the Jumer's Castle Lodge, Bob's personal bus was waiting for us. I had asked Tommy Masters to pick up the bus in Sacramento, California, drive south to Malibu to pick up Brutus, Bob's two-hundred-pound bullmastiff, and drive it out to meet us in Peoria.

This was a big surprise for Bob, as he wasn't expecting his personal bus to be on this leg of the tour. I wanted to surprise him, since the remodeling and upholstery recently had been finished and the bus was finally ready for its big debut as Bob's first personal bus.

When we disembarked from the band bus and tried to board the personal bus, Brutus caused a scene solely by being an overwhelming sight. Too many fans and random people were interested in seeing the dog, making Bob feel uncomfortable and forcing him to head straight for his hotel room rather than see the newly crafted bus.

After the luggage had been checked in and sorted to the crew rooms at the hotel, Bob called me up to his suite. He was very upset that Tommy, the bus and Brutus had showed up. He felt bringing his own bus on tour was premature. He was worried about alienating the band, with whom he had shared a bus up until this point. But rather than sending it back to Malibu, he agreed to a ten-day trial period at my request.

It's hard to gauge what Bob will appreciate or be annoyed by. He doesn't like causing a scene and prefers to be as anonymous as possible. I understood his reaction to the bus, Brutus and Tommy, but I didn't agree with it; the ten-day trial was a fair compromise.

We had a day off the next day, and after some much-needed sleep to fight off the severe jet lag, Bob came around to his bus and took his bikes out for a spin with his friend Larry. He also spent some quality time with Brutus, who was extremely happy to see him.

Bob may have had a good afternoon with the bikes and seeing Brutus, but he wasn't going to be swayed easily and remained on the band bus the next day for the 157-mile ride to Arlington Heights, Illinois. Once again, Tommy and Brutus would drive an empty bus to meet us at the Woodland Hilton, a square, flat, uninteresting box located in a newly developed commercial area. Bob and I took the Florida Coach bus to the show at the Civic Center; the Steve Earle band opened the show and everything went as scheduled.

The following morning, Bob and I finally boarded his new bus. Tommy drove us to the Arlington Park Racetrack and we spent some time riding the bikes, exploring the stable area and relaxing on the grass by the fence while viewing some horse races.

Hanging out on the grass, Bob and I talked about the bus. He was still slightly hung up about it and asked for it to be parked a few miles away from the Poplar Creek Music Theater, which was the venue for the night's show. After a few hours he changed his mind and Tommy drove the bus into the venue. He parked it just short of the entertainer's pavilion. The show was fantastic and afterwards Bob boarded his bus with Tommy and drove eighty-seven miles to Milwaukee, Wisconsin. The bus was starting to win him over.

On the morning of July 3, Bob took Brutus for a walk, and in the afternoon, Bob and Mitch, his bodyguard, rode the bikes along the waterfront from the Pfister Hotel, where we were staying. After the gig that night, Bob went to see Edgar Winter's show. While he did that Tommy and I stayed on the bus and smoked a couple joints to relax and de-stress from the workday, relieved Bob was starting to accept the bus and that Tommy wasn't halfway to Albuquerque. When Bob returned, he, I, Tommy and Brutus started the three hundred sixty-mile trek to Troy, Michigan. It was bumper-to-bumper traffic getting out to the freeway, but once on the interstate it was smooth sailing. Bob and I lay down to sleep and Tommy drove through the night with Brutus providing much-needed company and the occasional release of wretched gas.

We had the next day off so Bob went with some of the crew to see *Batman* at a local theater. Back at the hotel we ran into Paula Abdul and her crew. They were playing the venue that night. She and Bob said hi but kept it brief.

Carolyn Dennis, Bob's second wife, and their three-year-old daughter, Desiree Dylan, arrived on Saturday the eighth of July. Having the extra bus on tour opened up more possibilities for personal guests. Bob seemed very happy and comfortable with his family traveling together; it would have been a much different dynamic on the band bus. That night, Bob was playing at the Deer Creek Music Center in Noblesville, which is on the outskirts of Indianapolis. The bus was parked outside the pavilion in a pleasant park by the lake. We all stayed on the bus till it was time for the show, which went off fantastically. Afterward we jumped onto the bus and headed three hundred and ten miles to Akron, Ohio, and checked into another square, sterile Hilton Hotel.

~

Bob's marriage to Carolyn and their daughter, Desiree, were completely unknown to the public until Howard Sounes's 2001 biography *Down the Highway: The Life of Bob Dylan.* If my father's tour diary had been published in 1989 when it was written, it would have been the first mention of Carolyn and Bob's secret marriage, and Bob's sixth child, Desiree.

~

The Sunday night show was at the Blossom Music Festival on Steels Corners Road in Cuyahoga Falls, Ohio. The turnout was immense. After the show, Bob, Carolyn, Desiree, Brutus and I were driven by Tommy three hundred sixty miles to Harrisburg, Pennsylvania. Once in Harrisburg we ran into a detour. Our directions were coming in over the phone from the clerk at the desk of the hotel. He talked us down to the railroad tracks at the end of a narrow, dead-end street, lined with trees and cars on both sides. It was pitch-black and located in a rough part of town. Tommy backed us out and we found the hotel at about five a.m. The Hershey Hotel is a historic landmark built in the 1920s: It's four stories tall and sits on the biggest hill in town. There are grand staircases and a ballroom reminiscent of another era. The rooms overlook the beautiful grounds of the hotel. During the day Bob, Carolyn, Desiree and I played tennis, swam in the pool and even managed to ride some horses from their riding stable. The hotel was so fantastic that after that evening's show we stayed another night in Hershey. From a distance, Bob's family looks like any other. They're happy and enjoying their time together. I get the feeling Bob enjoys playing the role of father on the road.

On the twelfth we drove eighty-three miles to Allentown. When we arrived, we parked the bus across the street from the pavilion at the Allentown Fairgrounds. Desiree played with her fire engine in the parking lot while Brutus kept an eye on her through the window. We managed to remain invisible; nobody seemed to recognize us. After the show we drove three hundred and fifteen miles to Mansfield, Massachusetts, stopping along the way to shop at a 76 truck stop.

The thirteenth provided Bob some entertainment when he was launched three feet in the air while lying on his bed on the bus. The suspension was starting to fail and was making the back of the bus extremely rigid. The show that night went off without a hitch and instead of driving to the next venue in Portland, Maine, we drove to Cohasset, Massachusetts, a quiet little town on the bay where Trish Mulligan lived. She was Bob's nutritionist on tour. That night we stayed right at the water's edge.

On the fifteenth we spent the day in Cohasset, riding bikes and relaxing. Later that afternoon we boarded the bus for Portland, Maine. The venue that evening was the Old Orchard Beach Seashore Performing Arts Center in Old Orchard,

Maine. We stopped and checked into what seemed like a small, secluded hotel on the beach. The evening plan was to drive across town for the show. What we didn't know was that the venue was just a half mile away. We spent the better part of the day on the beach relaxing. On our walk back to the hotel we passed an open-air restaurant and we overheard people saying, "That must be Dylan's bus." There was even a cover band performing Dylan songs. Bob didn't mention anything about it. The show happened as scheduled and afterwards we departed on the two hundred and seventy miles of road to Bristol, Connecticut. I could feel Bob's performance getting better as the shows were marked off the calendar.

Tuesday, July 18, was our day off. We had driven two hundred and thirty miles to get to Columbia, Maryland. Bob and Brutus checked into the Turf Valley Inn, which resembled a military installation. There was a bizarre repeating occurrence of people walking through Bob's sliding-glass door into his room. It happened several times during the day. Despite the bleakness of the architecture, the hotel surrounded a beautifully maintained golf course. Bob and I were asked several times not to use our bikes on the golf course, so we waited till nighttime and took a wonderful ride on the grass. The next day we were happy to leave—the entire time we were at the hotel it felt as if we were being watched; even the other guests looked like CIA agents.

On the morning of the twentieth, we checked into an old hotel on the boardwalk about thirty miles south of Atlantic City. After some rest we drove the hard way to Atlantic City. The venue was Bally's Grand Hotel Pavilion; it was on the corner of

Boston and Pacific. The stage and grandstands were in the middle of the street. The police didn't want us to park our bus next to the stage. They were being cautious due to a large and rowdy crowd starting to file in. The police chief tried to walk onto the bus unannounced but was greeted by Brutus, who was lying on the couch. Brutus said hello in a deep and powerful bark, causing the chief to jump about six feet out of his shoes. He walked off the bus and said we could stay if we wanted to. Brutus the negotiator performed excellently. Soon after, the crowds became too much for us to bear, so we moved the bus to an empty lot by the ocean two blocks away and stayed there undisturbed until the show. Bob took Brutus for a walk and managed to go unnoticed. It was a rather strange crowd of mostly older fans. They loved the show, and we hit the road.

Thursday, July 27, was another day off. We arrived at the Westin William Penn Hotel in Pittsburgh at seven a.m.; there was an unusual number of local police at the hotel before we arrived and once they noticed the bus, which was immediately upon pulling into the parking lot, they refused to let us park or even stop longer than it took to talk to them. After being asked to leave, we discovered that a crew member of another band had been murdered in the hotel a week before. Apparently there had been a fight between members of the stage crew, which led to one being bludgeoned to death. The victim managed to crawl his way to the hotel lobby, where he took his last breath. We took that as a bad sign and decided to stay across town at the Best Western. I called and received permission from the Board of Education to park the bus in a schoolyard across the street. We called a local vet to come and check on Brutus as we prepared to head to Canada. The vet found Brutus in good health and spirits, but took a blood sample as a precautionary measure. Midway through the day it started to rain and raged through the night.

July 31, we pulled into the Four Seasons parking lot in Toronto and checked in. Once I had the keys to all the rooms, I jumped back on the bus, which we needed to move to a better parking spot with easier access. As we drove around the several buildings we managed to get lost and in doing so noticed a strange car following us. We alerted security, who pulled the car over and found an overenthusiastic fan wanting to know where we were staying. He was given a warning and escorted from the premises. Tommy then found a perfect spot to park nearby, next to a bank. As Bob and I were gathering our things to disembark the bus, the police instantly surrounded us with their guns drawn. Completely baffled, Bob, Tommy and I just held our hands in the air and looked at each other searchingly. Brutus didn't seem to mind the sudden siege of police; he tended to pick his battles carefully. It turned out the bank's alarm system was set off by accident and the situation was resolved fairly quickly.

In the afternoon I sent the bus to the MCI garage to have the suspension looked at; it was still feeling like a rough ride despite traveling on smoother roads. The guys at the garage couldn't fix it or figure out the root cause of the problem, so at five p.m. we were back on the bus for the twenty-seven miles to the venue. Bob was playing the Festival de Lanaudière in Joliette, Québec. The doors opened at seven thirty p.m. and Steve Earle was onstage at eight thirty p.m. The show went smoothly. Later, Bob, Tommy, Brutus, and I were on our way to a private airport, which was located about an hour and a half away. We followed someone who thought they knew where the airport was but ended up getting us lost, so we asked a passing car for directions and they suggested we follow them, which quickly ended up with us getting lost again. Five hours later we found the airport. Bob's brother David was meeting us there and he and Bob were flying to Minneapolis.

The second of August was a day spent being searched by U.S. Customs officers at the Sault Ste. Marie border crossing. The officers spent the better half of the day strip-searching Tommy and Trish and going through the entire bus with a fine-tooth comb. After their personal searches, they were allowed to take Brutus to the grass, where they watched the bus be torn apart. I didn't feel the need to mention this to Bob, it would have been a useless event to be worried about. After many hours, they were released. They drove a few miles away and stopped next to a lake to put the bus interior back together.

Wednesday, August 3. Tommy and Trish arrived in Minneapolis midmorning and went to Bob's, where they stayed until four in the afternoon. On the way to the venue they stopped to pick up my daughter and me at the airport. I flew Aerie in from Los Angeles to join me on the road for a few days. I put her on the band bus, and I rejoined Bob, Tommy and Brutus. The venue was the River's Edge Music Fest on Harriet Island, in St. Paul, Minnesota. The show had a large turnout; roughly twenty-five thousand fans watched the show. Afterward Bob and Aerie rode the support bus while Tommy and I followed in the band bus to Madison, Wisconsin, two hundred and sixty miles away.

August 4. Our hotel was the Edgewater Hotel located on Wisconsin Avenue. This hotel seemed like a particular favorite for Brutus because of the large amounts of grass that he had free rein to roll around in. As I sat and watched him, the results came back from his heartworm blood test: He was positive and needed treatment. His American tour would have to be cut short, so we made plans for him to fly home, unattended, for treatment in Malibu. Later that evening we drove to the venue, the Dane County Coliseum in Madison. The weather was ugly; tornadoes were reported to be touching down all around us. Midway through Bob's set, thunder and lightning knocked out the power. To keep the spirit alive, the drummer broke into an impromptu solo that led into an acoustic version of "Shelter from the Storm," with Bob playing the cowbell. The crowd loved it. Afterwards we boarded the bus and headed to Mears, Michigan, three hundred and sixty miles away

August 6, Tommy, Brutus and I rode in the hotel van to the vet to see if Brutus was physically fit to make the flight home to Malibu. Kirby, Bob's security guard at home, flew someone to meet us with a big crate for Brutus to travel in. The attendant, Brutus and the crate went on to the airport in the van. Tommy and I went back to the hotel and took the bus to the Greyhound terminal to have it worked on. They too couldn't figure out the problem and sent us on our way.

August 7, we checked into a Day's Inn in St. Louis, Missouri, and made arrangements for the bus to be fixed at Bosell Truck Repair. They installed a new rear end, which took two days to complete.

August 8. Back on the bus.

August 11 was our day off. It was raining heavily all day long, but that didn't stop Bob and me from riding our bikes. Along our wet ride we stopped by a few lakes and said hello to the local ducks.

August 13, Bob's bus was riding much smoother after receiving its new rear end. We arrived before the others and I checked everyone into their hotel rooms. Bob rode his personal bus to the Carowinds Amusement Park in Charlotte that night. Ramblin' Jack Elliott came by after the show to say hello to Bob and myself. It was good to see an old friend.

August 22 and 23, while Bob and the band played Bonner Springs, Kansas, and Oklahoma City, Oklahoma, Tommy and I took the bus and looked at properties for him in Gulf Shores.

August 25, the venue was the UNO Lakefront Arena in New Orleans and the show was fantastic. Bob rode with us for the first time since Nashville, where the repairs were completed. It was a three hundred and fifty-mile trek to Houston, Texas. It was a night we dubbed "the Night of the Great Bus Race." Steve Earl's buses left ahead of us for the same destination. Our band left shortly after, followed by the support bus and, last but not least, were Bob, Tommy and me. One by one, we started to pass the other buses, never looking back and cruising at eighty-five miles an hour the whole way. Bob woke up while we were in the middle of our bus race to Houston and laughed about winning our lead spot. Once we landed in Houston I looked for another La Quinta Motel, which was quickly becoming my favorite chain. Bob jumped on the bus for the evening ride to the venue as Tommy was in midconversation with "Woody the truck driver," who gave us another route to use. Following Woody's route, we ended up on the wrong side of Houston just one hour before showtime. Bob and I were talking and Tommy got back on the phone with someone else to get him going in the right direction. While making a sharp turn, he nicked a curb, which shot a pot of coffee in the air and all over Bob. We're now lost in six-p.m. rush-hour traffic, nowhere near the venue, and Bob is burned and soaked in day-old coffee. Things were not going as planned. Finally, someone on the phone got us back to the beltway and to the right side of town. We found the venue in time and after the show Suzy Pullen and Bob boarded and we drove 242 miles to Dallas, Texas.

October 1, 1998, after a twenty-one-day rest, it was time to kick off the fall tour. These short breaks and back-to-back tours would become known as the Never-Ending Tour, which is a term Bob never really identified with because of a fundamental difference in the way he viewed touring. Bob considers himself a simple man who performs a trade. Like a plumber, carpenter or stone mason. As with those trades one does not stop for a period of time only to pick it up again at a later date. So Bob sees himself as a musician, that's his trade, and musicians play concerts. That's the simplicity behind the Never-Ending Tour. It's a fundamental part of who Bob is as a person. And it was the same for his roadies and myself.

That fall tour began as many would in the years to come. Tommy and I drove out to Bob's house to fetch the bus and Jumbo, Bob's other dog and Brutus's twin two hundred-pound bullmastiff. It was his turn to go on tour. Unlike Brutus, Jumbo didn't have the same fascination with the bus and would frequently choose to stay at any given location simply based on his level of comfort at the time of departure. For any dog of lesser size, dealing with its stubborn attitude would be as simple as lifting it up and placing it on the bus. But, to Jumbo's benefit, it was nearly impossible to lift him or push him. Your only hope was to coax him onboard with the illusion that he might be more comfortable somewhere on the bus. We left Bob's house and set out on our journey across the United States to meet Bob in New York. Without warning, the bus broke down again, this time in the middle of the Mojave Desert. I let Jumbo off so he could relieve himself, although I wasn't entirely sure if I could coax him back on. But the consequences of not letting him off were much worse than figuring out how to get him back on board.

After many frustrating phone calls, we found a local mechanic to drive out and look at it. The mechanic showed up, looked at the bus, shrugged his shoulders, said he couldn't do anything and drove off. Instantly back to square one, still annoyed and very hot. I think the only reason Jumbo walked back on the bus was the AC was on, otherwise he would have been another problem.

A few more phone calls and we found another mechanic, this one went by the handle "Mojave Bill." Just from his name he seemed like the right guy for the job. He drove one hundred miles from his station to fix the bus. Upon arrival he explained to us that the problem was a loose fuel line that led from the fuel tank to the generator, sucking air pockets into the engine. He fixed it on the spot and sent us on our way. Tommy and I couldn't believe it, Mojave Bill saved the day and the rest of our drive to New York City was fairly uneventful.

On the ninth Tommy brought the bus into the city and found a park along the Hudson River, on Seventy-eighth Street. Bob, Mitch, Rick and myself grabbed the bikes and went for a ride. Afterward Bob and Jumbo spent some time together and Bob was very pleased with the way he was behaving.

Our first four shows were held consecutively at the Beacon Theater in New York and the crowd loved them. After the fourth show on the thirteenth everyone jumped on Bob's bus ready to hit the road for the ninety-mile trip to Philadelphia, but were dismayed when Tommy, in an attempt to kick-start the bus, caused it to belch a massive cloud of thick, black smoke. Instantly there was a huge oil leak where the turbo tied into the engine. I got everyone out of the bus and sent them on in the support van. Tommy stayed with the bus and called another mechanic to come fix it. I left with Bob and the band and headed for St. David's Inn, a hotel about thirty minutes from the Tower Theater in Upper Darby, Pennsylvania, which was the venue set for our next show in two nights. There was a day off for me to figure out what to do with the bus. To add to the chaos, it started to rain.

On Wednesday the eighteenth, I rented a brand-new forty-five-foot MCI bus, which, when it arrived, Bob hopped on and inspected. It met his approval so Trish and Suzy jumped on; the bodyguards took the support van while Tommy and I took the personal bus. We all arrived at the venue and Bob had a good show, in spite of the rain.

Friday the twentieth, our rented bus was late arriving with a new driver. The weather was miserable and, to make matters worse, Tommy backed the personal bus over Bob's bike. Nobody was laughing. We took the bus to the venue at the Mid-Hudson Civic Center and after the show we made the 158-mile trip to Scarborough, Rhode Island, and managed to get lost for two hours right before finding the hotel. Not a good day.

Saturday, the twenty-eighth, we checked into the Howard Johnson's Inn at two a.m. Shortly thereafter the fire alarm went off and everyone ran out of their rooms into the streets. The firemen came, but when they couldn't find the fire everyone returned to their rooms. Later in the day it was time for Jumbo to get on the bus, but he refused. Everyone pushed, shoved and sheer numbers and strength finally forced him on.

The second of November we checked into the Stouffer Hotel at three a.m. and got some rest. Bob walked to the venue in the evening at the Palace Theater on Euclid Avenue. Finally, it had stopped raining. After a good show we drove 130 miles to Kittanning, Pennsylvania. Bob and I were playing Go and there was a relaxed atmosphere. We stopped for fuel and the bus wouldn't start. Bob moved to the support bus and our Go game was put on hold. He was winning, so I didn't mind ending the game early.

Ninth day off. Arriving in Atlanta, we had to park the bus in a pretty shady neighborhood, several blocks from the hotel on Peachtree Street. Prostitutes plied their trade and dope deals were going down in the shadows.

On the tenth, Bob went to the venue at the Fox Theatre on the bus. The theater was out of another era, it had a painted sky and clouds on the ceiling, and the show was memorable. A girl from the audience got up on the stage and started to strip. Bob let her do her thing to the cheers of the audience. The atmosphere was high and the show was really good. We drove 646 miles to Sunrise, Florida, afterwards.

On the fourteenth, Bob took Jumbo for a walk with his sparring partner, a boxer who was giving Bob lessons. Jumbo was lying in the shade watching them work out. When they were done, they started to walk across the street on their way back to the bus. They forgot that Jumbo was with them. Jumbo woke up from a nap, saw Bob across the street and made a fast run to catch up with him. The only car in sight on the street slammed into him. It was devastating for Bob to watch. The car hit him really hard. Jumbo rolled on the pavement several times and stood up, shaken, and ran off into the trees. Bob, fearing the worst, sensed that Jumbo was running into the trees to die. I was in the bus looking out the window when I saw Jumbo running full tilt towards me. He came flying into the bus. Jumbo had run into trees and straight through them for five blocks in our direction. He was in the bus for a full ten minutes before Bob and his sparring partner returned. He recovered from his experience without any lasting effects.

On the fifteenth, Bob and I rode the bikes to the venue and Tommy drove the bus, parking it behind the gate. After the show we drove out of town a short ways and stopped the bus so Bob could get out and say good-bye to Rick, Mitch and Suzy, who were following in the van. Bob got out in his bare feet to hand Suzy his stage clothes and say good-bye. He stepped on an ant hill and got bit pretty bad. We drove all night through an intense storm to Gulf Shores, Alabama. Visibility was almost zero and the bus just stopped running. It was the same night the tornadoes did the damage in Alabama that was on all of the news the next day. The bus started up again and we continued to drive into the heart of the storm.

On the twenty-second, it was nine a.m. when we arrived at Bob's. The roads were ice packed, but we didn't experience any problems. We dropped Bob at the farm, then Tommy and I tried to drive straight through to Santa Fe, New Mexico. The weather was subzero and the heater froze. I was driving through the Raton Pass in New Mexico when the bus stopped. We determined that there was a bad oil leak and I started to walk for help. Tommy got the bus started again and picked me up on the highway. We drove into Las Vegas, New Mexico, about sixty miles east of Santa Fe, where Mark Masters, Tommy's son, picked up Tommy and me and we stayed with the bus for the night. The next day we made it home to Santa Fe.

~

It seems my father only documented those two tours, perhaps with the intent of writing a book starring Bob's personal bus.

It's interesting for me to understand the monotony of touring, the day-in, day-out repetitive nature of it. The Never-Ending Tour was a simple way of life for them. I think the consistency is what made it possible, their mantra: Play a show, ride the bus to another hotel, play another show. After three or four shows, take a day off. Rinse and repeat.

For over two decades now, Bob has been on the same path with only minimal breaks. I heard my father explain it to someone once: "It's much healthier for Bob to be active than inactive. It's much better for his mind and physical ability to be in demand and under the pressure of a captive audience to perform."

The "Journey of the Invisible Bus" reminds me of my own experiences on Bob's bus. Over the years it was always awe-inspiring to see it roll up to my mom's house. My father would stop by on occasion with the bus when it wasn't needed on tour and I'd get to show my friends around, watch TV and sometimes take it on a short outing with my father driving. The single, longest period of time I spent on the bus was on a section of the Never-Ending Tour, a small West Coast run that my father invited me on.

I arrived at the airport in Eugene, Oregon, around midday on April 30, 1992, where my father came to pick me up and sign the necessary release forms for the airline. At thirteen years old I was a minor, so only a parent or guardian could pick me up. Once outside the airport there was an unmarked white passenger van with a driver waiting for us. My father and I jumped in and headed for the hotel. When we arrived at the La Quinta Inn, my father immediately took me on to one of the tour buses and showed me where I was going to be sleeping for the next few days. It turned out to be Bob's personal bus and my bed was one of the two spare bunk beds located in the middle.

Once I was situated and had put my bags away, I was ready to explore the hotel. As I walked off the bus, Bob rode up on a bicycle and greeted me. The conversation was fairly simple; Bob said, "Hello, Jacob, remember me from the dark alley?" I responded with a "Yes." Bob continued, "Sorry about that," and I shrugged it off as if it were completely in the past. What Bob was apologizing for was a tense discussion he and I had a few years prior. "Tense discussion" is the best simple description I can give it. It wasn't really a discussion but it was certainly tense, as I remember it . . .

My father was picking Bob up at Universal Studios after his rehearsal; since my sister and I were in town, he brought us with him in his blue conversion van. As we drove onto the back lot, my father asked my sister and me to be quiet and well-mannered. Well, "quiet and well-mannered" isn't the easiest thing for a seven year old to be.

My father parked the van and said he needed to run into the studio to tell Bob he was here. He walked in and a few minutes later walked out of the back door of the sound stage with someone wearing a gray hoodie and a towel who looked like he hadn't shaved in weeks. I was severely confused because this wasn't Bob Dylan, not that I really knew what he looked like. I just expected the famous guy my father worked for to be more fantastic looking: black jeans, black shirt, black shades. But certinaly not this normal-looking guy; he looked like everyone else. So I had to ask once he had jumped in the front passenger seat of the van.

"Are you Bob Dylan?" I inquired. In a soft voice he said, "Yes." But I just couldn't believe it, he couldn't be. Maybe he didn't hear me correctly, so just to make sure, I asked again, "Are you the *real* Bob Dylan?" I was seven. Bob didn't respond. Thinking he didn't hear me that time I asked once again for good measure, "Are you really Bob Dylan?" After a long day in the studio, he just didn't have the wherewithal to deal with an obnoxious kid. I completely understand that now. As an adult I've been in the exact situation and now can relate to his response, which was to ask my father to do something.

In a fleeting moment of parenting amnesia, my father asked my sister and me to exit the van and to wait for him to return after he dropped Bob off at home. Bob's house was in Malibu and Universal Studios is in Universal City, which is forty miles away and fifty minutes traveling time by shitty blue van.

I instantly knew I was wrong and had been too overzealous about my celebrity encounter. But the damage was done, and I was out on the curb. For the next three hours, my sister and I managed to entertain ourselves by eating fifteen dollars' worth of snacks from the vending machine. Once our bellies were full of junk, we explored every square inch of the back lot and ended the night playing hide-and-seek between the soundstages.

After several hours, my father returned to pick us up. I wouldn't say he won any parenting awards that night, but the outcome was fine as far as I was concerned. My mother, on the other hand, couldn't believe he left a seven year old and a fourteen year old in a dark parking lot alone for several hours in the middle of the night. This event would become a major topic of contention between them for many years to come.

Bob's apology for basically kicking me out of my father's van was a welcome peace offering. Not that I held any grudges whatsoever. But since I was going to be sleeping on his personal tour bus for the week, it would have been churlish of me to pretend that that moment in the dark parking lot had never happened.

Meeting Bob out of the way, I was free to run around and explore. After a couple hours in the hotel parking lot, we departed for their third show on the short run of the West Coast tour. I was flush with excitement; this was my first invitation to be on the tour.

This trip was also a rare amount of time that I would get to spend with my father. From about 1986 to 1994 my father was on the road with Bob nonstop, doing almost two hundred shows a year. I was about seven years old when he started and fifteen when he stopped; for some of my most important years for growth and maturity, my father wasn't around. It was common to only see him once, usually sometime over the winter holidays. Even speaking to him on the phone was fairly rare, especially when he was on a world tour. I tried to understand the circumstances, but it was still painful not having my father around as a kid growing up.

The show that night was at the Silva Concert Hall in the Hult Center for Performing Arts. Since it was the first show I was attending, my father asked for me to stay close to the stage and pay attention to when things were ending and to be in the right spot when Bob was walking offstage to leave. I didn't do too much exploring that night, just followed direction, and after the show I boarded the buses with my dad, Bob and the crew for the three hundred thirteen-mile ride to Redding, California.

The concept of a satellite TV on a bus was completely alien to me; it might have been my favorite part of the whole tour. That might come as a shock to most people, but for me at thirteen years old, the music and the stardom were lost on me. Granted, I freaked out years prior while being a tad starstruck in the parking lot of Universal. But it was different now; Bob seemed friendly and like a normal guy. All the roadies were friendly and just went about their business, and I was free to explore.

I spent the first couple hours on the road watching movies in the dining area of the bus and watching the world roll by outside. When we arrived at the venue everyone went to work, as did I, exploring. My father gave me my own personalized all-access pass: my golden passport. That single artist pass would remove all barriers, unlock all doors and be the foundation for a week of fun. I was curious about everything and wanted to meet and talk to every single person about his or her role at whatever venue or location we might be at. I walked out to the front of that night's venue and out to the parking lot, I tried counting all the people in line for the show. There were hundreds and hundreds and hundreds.

A woman in line, probably in her early forties, noticed my

backstage pass. She beckoned me to come over. She was seeing the show with her husband, who was standing next to her. I walked up and said hello and she asked who I was and what I was doing on tour. My response was pretty vague, but apparently enough for her to assume that I had direct access to Bob. When she realized this, she asked me a favor as she detached a diamond earring from her left ear. It was a sizable earring, it looked expensive, but I really didn't know the value of such a thing. She placed it in my hand and asked that I deliver a message to Bob. I didn't agree but I also didn't reject her, she was so passionate with her message that she wanted me to convey. She asked if I could mention her gratitude and love for him as she placed the earring in my hand. I knew instantly that her kindness and honesty was a no-fly zone for me.

I felt protective towards Bob. I knew that presenting him with this gift would confuse him regardless of its intention. I nodded to the woman and said I'd do my best and put her earring in my pocket. I walked away and jumped back into my campaign of intrigue and wonder. By the end of the show, I had talked to nearly all of the security guards, the lighting tech, the sound tech and anyone else who looked like an interesting character. My father instructed me to be near the stage at the end of the show so I could follow him and Bob onto the bus after a possible encore. The encore was always the first thing to get chopped from Bob's act if Victor felt their departure from the venue was going to be impeded by fans. With that in mind, I had to be on the side of the stage at the last song or before. That night, Bob ended the main act with "Highway 61 Revisited" and to my surprise he walked offstage next to me and said hello. He waited a few minutes with the other musicians and my father and then went back onstage to stun the mostly college-age crowd with "Absolutely Sweet Marie" and my favorites, "All Along the Watchtower" and "Blowin' in the Wind." The legend was at work, and he killed it that night.

After the last song, the band walked off the stage, and my father led Bob with a flashlight directly onto the waiting bus with Tommy Masters at the wheel. Within minutes of the song ending, Bob and the crew were back on the road. You could still hear people clapping as we pulled away. I was impressed with my father; the flow of things really seemed like a well-oiled machine.

We drove two hundred miles that night to Santa Rosa, California. The show the next day was located at the Sonoma County Fairgrounds. When we arrived at the Doubletree Hotel at four a.m., I remember being annoyed when I was woken up to go inside. I was sleeping really well in one of the bunk beds on Bob's bus.

In the afternoon we went to the show, and I recall finally paying attention to the lyrics of "Idiot Wind" and completely cracking up over it. I was blown away by the song's caustic and public narrative. "You're an idiot, babe. It's a wonder that you still know how to breathe." It's hard to say to whom he's referring, and it could be an amalgam of people. Doubtful. But I'd certainly hate to be the focal point of that lyric. It's known that the *Blood on the Tracks* album is mostly born from the tension and malice of Bob's divorce with Sara. But still, he's not throwing rocks with those lyrics, he's throwing boulders. I have been on the receiving end of Bob's temper before; it's easy to get there and not a place you want to stay.

I was digging through the plastic bins that my sister brought over. In an unmarked beige folder in one of the paperwork bins I found a handwritten letter that appears to be by Bob. It's extraordinary and reads like "Masters of War." It's addressed to some journalists who are on the receiving end of Bob's wrath. Although, I have to admit, it's also one of the most poetic beratings I've ever encountered. It starts with questioning their brazenness and lack of forethought:

> Greetings Gentlemen,
>
> Does your house not have glass windows? Do you journalists not have addresses and mothers? Do your family members not have names? Having a prefabricated laugh at the expense of my own dear mother without provocation of cause is not my idea of gratitude for the interview which took up 10 or more pages in your puerile smoke screen periodical masquerading as songwriting litany!

The letter continues to dismantle the magazine and the author and questions whether Jackson Browne, Burt Bacharach and James Taylor would have gotten the same treatment. At one point he calls the text "trumped up witty ejaculations." The letter swings to a powerful end with a closing phrase in Latin, "Extinctus Amabitur Idem." The rough translation is "the same hated man will be loved after he's dead." So I assume Bob is saying: "I'll like you when you're dead." Powerful, epic and poetic.

This letter has been hidden in my father's desk drawer for over two decades, and it's never been viewed by anyone in that time—another testament to the level of protection my father bestowed on Bob. I can only assume that this letter was never intended to be mailed. If it had been, it would have already been auctioned. Bob and Victor were smarter than that. They mastered the art of staying out of the spotlight and avoiding public embarrassment. Sending this letter to a journalist would have ended up with it being featured in *Rolling Stone* magazine. What's obvious about it is that Bob was venting on paper. If my father were still alive, this letter would still be hidden and Bob would still be protected. Make no mistake about that.

That concert in Santa Rosa ended in a typical fashion, and we headed out for the tour's next stop in San Francisco. The tour was scheduled for two back-to-back shows at the Warfield Theater on Market Street. It's a beautiful theater that holds around 2,300 people. It was built in 1922, which meant that there were going to be plenty of random old places and things to explore while the show was going on.

As the crew was setting up, I started watching *Full Metal Jacket*, the intense 1987 war film by Stanley Kubrick. It was my father's favorite film on the road, he and a bunch of other roadies were quoting it all the time, so I finally decided I needed to get in on the joke. I was about thirty minutes into the movie when Bob Dylan, Tony Garnier, John Jackson, Winston Watson and Bucky Baxter walked in. Instantly I was worried that I was in the wrong spot and needed to leave; my father constantly made sure I was aware of my surroundings and stayed clear of the guys working. I figured watching a movie in Bob's private room in the back of his bus was a pretty safe spot to hang while the show was getting ready to start, but apparently it wasn't.

As I got up to leave Bob looked at me and said, "You're okay, hang out." I couldn't have felt cooler. I did, however, turn the movie sound down to a minimum so I could hear what they were discussing. The band came in that night to plan the set list; I was surprised by this. I had missed this moment in the days leading up to San Francisco but this was a nightly ritual. To keep the show fresh and exciting, not only for audiences but for them as well, the guys would get together and map out the songs for the show. Bob led the conversation and took suggestions. The guys settled on playing "Rainy Day Woman," "Lenny Bruce," "Union Sundown," "Just Like a Woman," "Stuck Inside of Mobile," "I Don't Believe You," "Shelter from the Storm," "Love Minus Zero," "No Limit," "Little Moses," "Gates of Eden," "Mr. Tambourine Man," "Cat's in the Well," "Idiot Wind," "The Times They Are a-Changin'," "Maggie's Farm," "Absolutely Sweet Marie," "All Along the Watchtower" and "Blowin' in the Wind."

When their list was complete I almost blurted out "Subterranean Homesick Blues"—it's my absolute favorite song by

Bob—but I managed to hold my tongue. When they wrapped up they apologized for interrupting my movie, which caught me off guard since I felt like apologizing for interrupting their meeting.

After those two shows my trip had come to an end, and I had to head home to Santa Fe for school. I still have fond memories of that time on the road, and it was great to see my dad in action. From that moment onwards, Bob was always much more welcoming to me.

CHAPTER 9

~

The Never-Ending Tour
1992–93

Victor carrying Bob Dylan's guitars to the Panathenaic Stadium in Athens, Greece, during the start of the second year of the Never-Ending Tour. June 28, 1989. *(Courtesy: Maymudes Family Archive)*

Tape Eight

I helped create this lifestyle of working that became the Never-Ending Tour. We made it happen by working with promoters. Bob was ready to make touring a full-time job and I was pushing for that. We did it by giving the promoters back their deposit if the show lost money. This allowed us to build partnerships throughout the country in tiny markets. We didn't have to drive back and forth all over the place because we could do smaller shows along the way to bigger shows. If we couldn't fill the room we wanted, we moved the show to a smaller venue. We were flexible and went out of our way to make friends with the promoters. Our goal was five shows a week, sometimes six. As time went on we worked our way up to bigger venues. When the Never-Ending Tour started a lot of the shows weren't making money. Now the same shows are financially very successful and it's because we allowed a whole new generation of young people access to Bob's music during the late eighties and early nineties. Those young kids became a whole new following for him and fueled a surge in his career.

There's a lot of stress associated with being Bob Dylan, walking in those shoes on the Never-Ending Tour. Playing five shows a week, week after week. Doing the shows right, you have to be there emotionally singing the songs. Well, night after night he wants to do it but the gas tank runs low. His emotional gas tank is drained, in the sense that there's an ebb and flow to how emotionally tied he can be at any given moment onstage. All the songs he sings he's attached to, so after a while the emotional charge that it takes to sing them can beat him up. It's a hard thing for him to feel honest to himself and still feel like he gave the audience his best shot. In some cases people drive hundreds of miles to the shows, and Bob is aware of this; he has a broad sense of the communities that he's drawing from.

Sometimes he would call me in and say he was drained and tired. I would acknowledge that I couldn't do what he did, that not many people could, and then I would move the dialogue to the car full of kids that was driving a hundred miles to see the show. Seven kids all crammed into a little car and they all have tickets; I witnessed this time and time again. Bob would start to dwell on this and pump up with stamina, the air would get into his body and he would stride out onto the stage like a bullfighter. He would look the audience straight in the face and do the best show he could.

When the environment was more aggressive and intense, Bob would be more into it. There was a show in Wisconsin and huge storms raged around us all day as we were setting up. As Bob started singing, lightning struck the venue and knocked out the power. The packed venue descended into darkness, pitch-black except for a few emergency lights. And then silence. Some of the band evacuated the stage. Bob remained; contractually he's obligated to, but he's also committed to ensuring the show continues. So Bob just walked over to the drums and began pounding away. Seeing this, Al Santos, the production manager, put his entire team to work; it was some of the best work I'd ever seen him do. I had Tommy get all the buses ready to go in case something happened that made leaving the best option. To my surprise Al Santos was in the process of connecting to the emergency generator that was running the exit signs.

One by one the band members came back onstage and began playing whatever percussive instrument they could find. Even the cowbell was taking a beating to keep everyone entertained.

Twenty minutes later, Al was able to get one guitar and one amp online and Bob started playing guitar. Then another five minutes went by and Al had another guitar up. When the whole stage was rewired Bob played "Shelter from the Storm" and blew everybody's mind. The audience felt electrified after the show, they couldn't believe what they had witnessed.

Storms and lightning were just the tip of the oddball iceberg; everything imaginable would happen on tour. Tommy was driving the bus one night on an East Coast tour and out of nowhere there was this loud bang! We were traveling around eighty miles an hour when it happened and it woke everyone up. Bob shot up out of his bed thinking the bus had crashed. When we pulled over, the bus was covered in blue-greenish goo. When we really looked at it, it was shit. It was actual human shit. The only explanation was it came from the sky, and I really thought about all possibilities. It covered the entire bus! I got on the phone and called everyone I could in an effort to get to the bottom of its origins. I called the FAA, they said it was impossible. I called the sheriffs, they didn't know. Still to this day, I have no idea how it could have happened, other than military planes unloading their toilets midair. In the end, no government agency took credit for it and I dropped the whole matter out of fear that the media would run a story with the headline "Bob Dylan Got Shit On."

Many other bizarre things happened on tour. We were driving near the Okefenokee wildlife refuge in southern Georgia and we saw a lone turtle crossing the two-lane road. Tommy did what he could to avoid it without disturbing the bus passengers, but a minute later there's another one and another one. Then instantly, thousands of turtles on the road! Every square inch of the road was covered with turtles. Our fascination was instantly trumped by the horrifying reality of being forced to drive over them. We were going too fast to stop quickly enough and when we did, there were too many to do anything about it. We couldn't just stay there for hours, as we were on a tight schedule to begin with. It was awful, one hundred percent. Made me sick to my stomach.

Bob walked out of his room after hearing pops, one after another. I was already emotionally unglued and didn't want to explain what was happening to him. He took one look out the front window, went completely pale in the face, turned around and went back to his room and didn't say a word to us for the next thirty or so hours.

~

Some of my father's best stories were little random vignettes. He had thousands of them, many more than I've heard on the audiotapes, which is unfortunate since my recollection of them isn't clear enough to write them down. If my father were still alive today, this chapter, much like the tour, would be endless.

~

On October 16, 1992, we had scheduled the thirtieth anniversary show of Bob's first album at Madison Square Garden in New York City. The show had an A-list roster of artists performing classic Dylan songs, with Bob scheduled to play three songs to end the evening. The house band was Booker T. Jones on organ, Steve Cropper on guitar, Donald "Duck" Dunn on bass and joining them were drummers Anton Fig and Jim Keltner. G. E. Smith served as the musical director.

Neil Young called the concert "Bobfest" at the beginning of his "All Along the Watchtower" cover. Sinéad O'Connor spent the whole evening running around barefoot and wild. The Band, Johnny Cash, Tracy Chapman, the Clancy Brothers, Eric Clapton, Shawn Colvin, Steve Cropper, George Harrison, Richie Havens, John Cougar Mellencamp, Willie Nelson, Tom Petty and the Heartbreakers, Lou Reed and Eddie Vedder were just a few of the music legends stopping by to play some tunes.

As I understood, the show was originally a benefit concert, that's why all the heavy hitters signed up. George Harrison, for instance, would only have done it if it *was* a benefit show. Half-way into the preproduction, the office called me and said it's now a for-profit show. They didn't give me an explanation, but it didn't have any effect on me anyway. My crew was going to get paid the same rate regardless of whether it was a benefit or not.

Jeff Kramer was going to record the concert, film it and Bob was set to own all the intellectual property rights involved. Since everyone was already on board for free, it ended up being a financial windfall for Bob, but it pissed off a lot of the performers that night. George Harrison was so angry about it being a for-profit show, he made T-shirts with dollar signs on them and sent them to me and Bob.

In another attempt to squeeze as much profit as possible out of the show, Jeff Kramer had the horrible idea of streaming it via pay-per-view. In 1992, hardly anyone had the technology to buy pay-per-view! It was a complete failure; it was an idea before its time.

George Harrison was staying at the same hotel as Bob and me, and I took control of his logistics: what room he was in, how he was getting to and from the venue and so on. On that trip he got in trouble with Olivia, his wife. She tracked the last number he had dialed on the hotel phone to a limousine company that I had arranged for him to use to send a limo for a girl that he was involved with. When Olivia blew up over that, I found myself in the middle of their confrontation.

The day of the show Bob told me not to talk to anybody. Actually, he shouted, "Don't talk to anybody!" He was really beating me up about it because he knew I was close with most, if not all, the people performing. So it was going to be a big party for me, a big reunion so to speak, with all my friends around in one spot. It felt like it was my thirtieth anniversary concert; I was having a great time. Bob, however, was under a lot of pressure—it was him on display, he was the center of the bull's-eye that night.

It was a big deal for him and I worked very hard to keep him comfortable. I would bring people to see him one at a time. I thought that was best for him under the circumstances. In doing that, I believe I was the most liberal of the people working for Bob. Jeff Kramer would have sealed him up and sheltered

244 Another Side of Bob Dylan

him from being human if he had the chance. I tried to get him to talk to more people and tried very hard to get him to relax, to be himself and to be comfortable.

People like Elliot Mintz, the media consultant and publicist whose clients have included the John Lennon estate, Yoko Ono, Christie Brinkley, Crosby, Stills and Nash, Diana Ross, Don Johnson, and Melanie Griffith—they thought they knew what's best for Bob, but they just didn't understand him like I did. I'd known Bob a long time; we had grown up together.

Elliot Mintz provided the security for our big shows or public events; he would get Bob a small army of guys carrying guns to protect him. At a big Universal Amphitheater show where we were giving away a bunch of Gibson guitars signed by Bob, Elliot brought a bunch of armed security guards to protect him backstage after the show where there was a big reception planned.

Jesse Dylan, Bob's oldest son, had become unglued and was screaming at me for letting too many people get close to him. Jesse didn't realize two thirds of the people close to his father were carrying guns! Bob didn't stop to tell him that he was surrounded by plainclothes security, so Jesse just kept on losing it. Eventually I had to pull him aside and explain that I was paying for these people to be around Bob and even though it looked like a lot of random people, I actually had it set up so Bob could talk to one person at a time, so that he wouldn't be rushed and overwhelmed. He was having a good time backstage and it was because of the controlled environment. I thought the guns were way over the top, but Mintz requested that.

That whole evening I was only a few feet away, but I made sure I wasn't overly manipulating the situation. I did the same thing for George Harrison and Tom Petty when George Harrison received the Billboard Century Award in 1992 from Tom Petty. They called me and asked if I would run the security backstage. I advised the security team, I gave the whole team explicit instructions. I was in control of it all, right down to the press photographers swarming around trying to take candid photos of Tom and George. I hired a guy dressed in plain clothes whose sole job was to bump into people taking pictures. He would wait around watching the photographers and right when they were going to get that revealing shot, he would nudge them or knock their arms. If a photographer did happen to make a nuisance to the point that either Tom or George acknowledged them, even with a slight look, they were gone.

～

End of Tape Eight

CHAPTER 10

~

Uncovering the Past

Tom Petty's birthday party in London, late 1980s. *(Courtesy: Victor Maymudes)*

Tape Nine

𝄢 **We showed** up in Krakow, Poland, on July 17, 1994.
Fans greeted us as we pulled into the backstage area of the
Cracovia football stadium holding up signs that read "We waited
30 years!" As we arrived it started to rain harder and harder, to
the point that we were setting up the show in a deluge, rain

coming in diagonally and horizontally. The stage production team told me I should cancel the show. Despite the pounding rain, the stadium was *full* of people. Before the show even started there was an inch of water on the stage.

I went and talked to Bob, who said, "I don't really feel like doing the show. I don't feel like I'm in the music."

I had to fight for the fans suffering through the torrential weather.

"Look, Bob, there's ten thousand people out there. They've been standing in the rain for a couple hours." We had already delayed the show by an hour at this point. "Think about it for a minute."

Part of the reason behind my fight for putting on the show was the fact that Krakow, Poland, has been treated like the toilet bowl of the world throughout history. These people got shit on by everybody. The Red Russians, the White Russians, the Germans, the Austrians, you name it. World War I was here, at their doorstep. The Nazis invaded them in 1939, arresting their university professors and academics, putting them in jail for being smart! The Jews were murdered, sent through the Krakow train station to Auschwitz, which is about forty miles out of town. Even after the Nazis, they were under Soviet control. These people were fucked over and over and over. It was our first time there, in a deluge; fans were waiting for us and the production department was begging me to cancel the show. I couldn't do it. It had to be Bob's choice. Luckily, I didn't have to say anything more. Bob thought about it for a bit, then jumped up and said, "Let's do the show." Bob and I were on the same page. Al Santos, the stage manager, yelled out, "No! Don't do it. It's dangerous." But Bob had already made up his mind.

A few minutes before the show, there was two inches of water onstage. All that electronic equipment—electric guitars, amps, soundboards, all sitting in water. The audio and power cables from the stage were running out to Ed Wynne at the sound booth in the middle of the seating. They were completely under mud. He was standing at the soundboard petrified to touch it. You could feel the buzz coming off of it and see the heat misting the condensation on the cables. You could feel the electricity in the air; it was as if lightning could strike at any moment. Bob took one look and started walking out to the stage, full stride. I passed Al, turned to him and said we're going on. He yelled, "What?!" I kept walking. I didn't even look around. He had to run through the rain to the stage to get the lights on because Bob was coming to do the show.

Bob walked onstage to a roaring crowd; they didn't care that they were cold and wet. Wind was blowing so hard Bob was leaning forty-five degrees forward, his hair blowing straight out. Bob looked like Leutze's *George Washington Crossing the Delaware*, standing on the bow of the boat in that famous painting. Holding the guitar like a sword to the side. Battling the forces of nature. Inches of water everywhere. Bob was ready to go to battle for these people. As he played "All Along the Watchtower," lightning lit up the night sky and stretched far above the town. It was as if the gods were listening, setting off a light show. Bob didn't miss a beat.

He did the whole show like this; we didn't do an intermission, so it was an hour and forty minutes just like this. Near the end of the main set with about three or four songs to go, we switched our electric guitars for acoustics. This was one of those "safety third" moments. Once he got to the encore, he came offstage. Everything was at its breaking point. The level of danger had reached its maximum before somebody was going to get hurt or killed. I told Bob we couldn't do the encore. He shouted back, "What's wrong?!"

I said, "You're standing in three inches of water."

"What's wrong with that?" Bob asked.

I repeated, "The amps and all the equipment . . .", but he cut me off with, "Pick it up!"

I pleaded, "I can't, the guys won't fucking touch it. Look at the crew."

I pointed to the guys all wrapped up in plastic, taking any shelter they could. It was like a war zone for the crew. Only then did he realize that I was begging him not to do it. Al Santos was pulling his hair out. The tour accountant Marty Feldman was already hysterical that I let the show go on in the first place. Well, the show up till this point was fabulous. The audience was ecstatic. They didn't care if it never stopped raining and neither did Bob. The show went down in history. Bootlegs from his set in 1994 are online now. You can hear the rain hitting the mics.

Another important milestone in Bob's life happened in 1994: He stopped drinking. He just stopped on a dime. He didn't talk as much once he stopped and he didn't laugh as loud either. It was a big deal for him and really showed his commitment to changing his behavior. He was capable of dealing with a broader range of personalities when he was drinking and after stopping, his tolerance for certain types of behavior diminished. Bob lost a bit of his self-esteem when he sobered up too, became a little more introverted and less social. That is common for heavy drinkers when they sober up, because they don't have that false wall of protection that alcohol provides. Drinkers lean on the buzz to be funny and outgoing. That charisma feels lost to them when they sober up, as it was in Bob's case.

End of Tape Nine

Sitting at my desk listening to these tapes is bittersweet every step of the way. There's a multitude of reasons for that, but I'm bringing it up now specifically due to the fragmented stories I constantly come across. I've heard my father say "We'll come back to that later" or "Let me dwell on that and I'll remember more" a hundred times. Every time I hear it I know the story is now lost in the ether. It's disheartening for me and I instantly have a knee-jerk reaction upon hearing those words. As an example, I've spliced together a few of the fragments.

Excerpts from Various Tapes

The Traveling Wilburys recorded themselves in Dave Stewart's studio. Dave Stewart, from the Eurythmics, built a studio near Balboa in Los Angeles. For the second album they rented a German's castle in Hollywood, which was unbelievable. The only stipulation was they couldn't film or take pictures of the paintings on the wall. It felt like the owner was insinuating that nobody should know the paintings were even on the wall. Huge works of art, thirty-foot paintings and tapestries, obviously from some Jew's home in Europe, maybe not, but that's what it felt like to me.

Early on the guys agreed that they wouldn't involve anybody, no lawyers, no agents, no record label execs—just the band: Bob Dylan, George Harrison, Jeff Lynne, Roy Orbison and Tom Petty. The only two guys allowed to be involved who were not playing music were Alan Weidel, known as "Bugs," Tom Petty's guitar tech and close friend, and me. That's all. I have to admit, it wasn't a bad group of guys to be with. Listening to the music, hanging out, the food was great. The swimming pool was fabulous; it was like living in a dream for me. If you're into the music and into those personalities and into supporting music . . . because for me, it was not only entertaining, it was the voice of my social and political feelings. Coming from a left-wing activist family, music satisfied my need to be a part of the struggle. To be in the forefront, to be marching with César Chávez or with Martin Luther King.

During those days, the guys were all invited to a party at the Playboy Mansion. Bob asked if I could drive him over to where everyone was meeting, at the house they had rented for their recordings. When I arrived, all the guys were ready to go: Tom Petty, Roy Orbison, George Harrison and Jeff Lynne, and Bob said, "How about we all take Victor's van to the party?" I'm instantly against it. After all, it was a very beat-up van. But the band thought it was funny. So they all jumped in, and we smoked joints and I drove us into Beverly Hills. When we got there, I pulled into the parking lot amid a sea of limos. The very best, all of them. Not a single normal car and then there was my rusted, dented, paint-chipped blue van. It looked as if the caterers had just showed up late to the party. And when the doors swung open the supergroup of the decade got out. I opened the door and bolted inside, I couldn't handle it. I spent the night hiding from Hugh Hefner; he would get on my case about smoking pot anytime I saw him.

One day Bob asked me to go to Sony/Columbia Records and pick up some tapes. He didn't say much, just told me where to go and when. I got there and the guys at the vault started loading up my van with boxes and they didn't stop. Box after box after box and I realized what was being put into my van. It was all the masters, all of them. Bob's entire career was being loaded into my van. Tons of music, some of which has never been released. Boxes of unreleased music.

Bob and I were in Woodstock one afternoon when Brian Jones called. He asked if he could stop by and hang out, so we invited him up. On the phone he sounded really bummed out; you could hear it in the cadence of his voice. His words were drawn out and the pauses between questions were oddly long. When he arrived he told us that the other guys in the Rolling Stones rehearsed without him—that he really felt the group slipping away from him. It was his band and they were slowly and passively pushing him out, and we felt bad for him. We liked him; he was a smart guy and could hang easily with our group.

David Crosby called me one day and said he wanted to write a book about activism and rock 'n' roll, focusing on the parallels between them. He said he wanted to talk to Bob about being in the book. I thought it was a great idea; anything promoting social awareness and political activism is a good thing. I went ahead and connected them to talk about it.

A few months go by, and David calls me again. Right off the bat he says, "Victor, where's Bob? I want to punch him in the mouth." I respond with, "Well, right this instant I have no idea where Bob is. What's going on?" David explains that he just received a phone call from Jeff Kramer saying that Bob was no longer interested in helping with David's activism book. David was furious because he had already put the pieces together with a publisher and made the deal and now Bob was backing out. To make matters worse, Bob didn't back out in person, he had Jeff do it for him, which is what really upset David. So with David pissed off I take this opportunity to interject my opinion on the matter. I told him that Bob was never really an activist in the first place, that he was asking the wrong guy. David loses it and yells back, "What do you mean?! He was in Selma, Alabama! He sang and marched and was beaten by the cops!" Before I could respond, he said "forget it" and hung up.

The thing about Bob being in Selma is that Theodore Bikel bought him a ticket to fly down there, and yes, Bob was there. But from what I know, that was the only real time that he was a part of a march like that and engaged with the people. Never again did he do that. He made appearances at the big demonstrations, but he wasn't really a part of it. It really wasn't his thing.

~

End of Tapes

The audiotapes I have focus on the time my father spent with Dylan, but there are gaps among them. For instance, my father didn't record any stories regarding late 1994, after the Japan tour, and 1995. This was around the time he retired from touring and I remember him telling me how tired he was of going on the domestic tours. The abundant Denny's food, the low-cost American family diner, had finally gotten to him. He intimated that he might go on European tours, but was staying away from anything in the United States for a while. It seemed like a logical step to me so I never really gave it any thought. Now that I've taken on writing about that time, I wish I knew more about that era.

In late 1994 I was fifteen years old. I had recently dropped out of high school and was attending writing classes at a nearby community college in my home town of Santa Fe, New Mexico. My mother was away that year for six weeks; she went to the Himalayas to build a memorial for her late fiancé Greg Gordon, who had died there the previous year while climbing Mt. Pumori. I was supposed to be in the care of my father, but due to a last-minute change in his schedule he wasn't available, and I was left to fend for myself. Making it to high school on my own and figuring out creative ways to eat was pretty easy for me, and I begged my mother to leave me unattended for that length of time. I knew it was pushing the limits of what most parents would do, but I couldn't resist the autonomy of being alone at fifteen for six weeks. Before my mother had even left, I had planned a lifestyle that was more similar to *Ferris Bueller's Day Off* for forty-four days than anything respectable.

My father was in Los Angeles, California, at the time and we talked a fair amount on the phone, but it was never related to his work life. It was more of a typical father-son conversation: *How's school,* et cetera. Offhand, I can't remember why he didn't stay with me in Santa Fe or why I didn't fly out to stay with him.

This leads to my lack of information regarding what he was doing during this time period. So to help fill in the gaps, I've decided to search the Internet for stories about him that I can reference, or maybe find someone to interview for a little more detail into this time. It's always been an amusing thing for me to do, searching for stories online about my father. It's not something I did twelve years ago, but I've grown accustomed to doing it now, especially since I've taken on the project of finishing his memoirs.

The sheer number of Bob Dylan books available actually blows my mind; he must be one of the most written-about celebrities in the world. Most of them have some anecdotes about my father, though not many, and usually along the lines of, "He was tall and didn't speak much."

I've recently come across a book I hadn't looked at before. It was published in 2011, fairly recently. It has a short paragraph regarding my father that, upon reading it, pulled my heart into my stomach. It's something I've never been aware of. It says the reason my father stopped touring in 1994 was due to a statutory rape allegation against him—that the mother of a seventeen-year-old girl accused him of having a sexual relationship with her daughter, which led to Victor being arrested. The paragraph continues to say he was in jail for a day or so and then the charges were dropped. There was never a conviction, no declaration of guilt, the charges were merely dropped. According to this book the damage was done as far as Bob was concerned, and, fearing negative publicity, he personally asked Victor not to accompany him on tour for a while. This was at the advice of Jeff Kramer. Bob made it official and Victor was off the road for the time being.

However, Bob didn't fire Victor. Not in the slightest conceivable way; he kept Victor on payroll at his full salary. However, he instructed him to look after the side projects that he and Victor had undertaken in recent years: remodeling Bob's daughter's apartment in Santa Monica and buying small plots of land in Glorieta, New Mexico, and Los Barriles in Baja California. Their intention was to build small houses on them for investments. The largest of the projects was the acquisition of a massive building on 18th street and Broadway in Santa Monica, California, that housed a synagogue, the corporate offices for Bob Burns's restaurants and some damaged retail space that had potential to be built out into a coffee shop or office space.

I can't believe what I just read. It can't be right, how could I not have known about this? It's been twenty years! It's making me sick to my stomach just thinking about it. I can't even fathom how my sister would feel about reading this or just knowing that it's out in the world. Was my father lying to me all those years? I'm heartbroken; I decided to write this book to learn about my father's interesting life, not to unearth skeletons in his closet.

I have to check out this story; I hope it's wrong. It has to be wrong. On Saturday, the twenty-first of September 2013, I call my mother to see what she knows. If she has been hiding it from me, I know she'll come clean if I confront her.

I am able to reach her on the phone; we talk for thirty minutes about it, but she has no clue regarding the incident—even denies it happening since it was so confusing. I'm somewhat relieved; the fact that she's never heard of it gives me hope that the author made up the story, vilifying my father to have an antagonist in his Dylan bio book.

I think I need a break; I'm going to sleep on it and figure out a plan for this in the morning.

I am woken up by my mother calling. She took it upon herself to investigate the sex-with-a-minor story. She says she called Tommy Masters, Bob's personal bus driver for decades and Victor's closest friend on the tour outside of Bob. The story is true from what Tommy said to my mother. Victor had been accused, arrested and he posted bail and subsequently the charges were dropped. Tommy went on to say that while in jail Victor made one call for help—he called Bob. Bob called his lawyers, who came to Victor's defense; they paid his bail and worked on Victor's behalf. Shortly after, the charges were dropped and the incident was swept under the rug. Tommy didn't know the details of Victor's relationship with the girl, or if there had even been one. He said Bob handled it with the utmost secrecy.

I have a knot in my stomach because I can believe that it happened and at the same time I can believe he was innocent. The lack of information is driving me nuts, and not having my father around to set the story straight, for good or bad, is infuriating. I'm quite aware that my father's lust for sex was only outstripped by his appetite for smoking marijuana. He had many younger girlfriends, but all were within an acceptable range. Even when he passed away, his then-girlfriend was twenty-eight years old. He was sixty-five when he died. My sister took particular offense to his younger girlfriends, and for good reason. She was also twenty-eight at the time.

I personally had little issue with him dating the twenty-eight year old; she seemed nice and definitely loved him. I thought, Good for him. He's old but he still has it. This story regarding a minor is a different beast. It makes me want to puke, and for the first time I regret even attempting to finish his memoirs. I want to throw my computer out the window right now and walk away from this project. I was lied to, and that's what matters to me. Did he have consensual sex with a minor? I don't know. The only person who would know is probably Bob. It's entirely possible Victor was victimized by an overzealous Dylan fan, at least that's how Tommy Masters feels about it; he's been tricked before by people claiming to be his friend just for a chance encounter with the rock star. Who knows? I wish I did . . .

I don't know why I've been so naive in thinking that I wouldn't find any skeletons in my dad's closet. Honestly, the thought never even crossed my mind; I figured his known laundry list of vices was bad enough and I'd already come to accept him with them. The chronic weed smoking and the story of him smuggling two hundred pounds of marijuana on top of the Travco van was the top of the list, I assumed. These are the types of dips in moral turpitude that I've come to accept and brush off. I say things to myself like, Well, it was the sixties, or, He was a roadie in a rock 'n' roll band, as a method of talking myself into being amused and not upset by his delinquent behavior.

It just doesn't work for me in this case. I don't care if what he might have done was legal a little more than two hundred miles away in Nevada, where the age of consent is lower. If he did it, it's morally unacceptable. Even if he didn't do it, I feel betrayed by him for lying to me either way. I feel tricked and I'm forced into a position where I have to decide if I should tell my sister about it. She loves him dearly and misses him like none other. The last thing I want to do is tarnish her admiration for her father. She even named her firstborn Viktor in homage to her father that she lost so abruptly years ago.

This revelation has removed all the enjoyment I've had learning about my father. I'm thrust into a painful situation that I know I'll have to deal with publicly, and I'm still unprepared to deal with it internally. I don't know what to say about it; I'm so upset. I know that no matter what, I still love my father.

This event does, however, speak volumes about his relationship with Bob. There must have been many other people he could have reached out to for help, but he chose Bob, and Bob helped him. From the limited details I have, it was entirely Bob's involvement that kept me from knowing about it and kept it out of the press at the time.

In addition, with that type of accusation, one would expect to be fired from a job for an act that was a razor-thin edge from being national news. If it went to court it would have certainly been a scandal of some sort for Bob to handle, but the remedy would be easy: cut all ties with Victor and publicly fire him from his role as tour manager. But that's not what happened. Victor kept his job—changed roles and transitioned into a business developer of sorts for Bob, and their friendship remained strong.

The space between these words may seem small, but the amount of time they represent is worth noting. These last dozen or so paragraphs have taken days, weeks and months to write. I've pondered the outcome of writing about this event in my father's life over and over again and the conclusion I've come to is that despite his lifelong efforts not to become a public figure, he became one when authors wrote about him in Dylan biographies. As a public figure, your dirty laundry is hung out for the world to see and there's little to nothing you can do about it. My intention with this book is to be honest. I've never run from the truth, I've lived my life attuned to an open book. That's not a joke I'm trying to make, it's a way of life that has become the cornerstone of the respect I give myself. I don't do things that

I'm not willing to let everyone in my circle know about and through this ideology, I've accumulated some of the most wonderful friends a man could ever ask for.

If my plan is to publish my father's unwritten memoirs, then it's his memoirs on my terms. The good, the bad and the ugly, it's who my father was. He was an extraordinary man, a man I loved unconditionally. He was caring, strong and an admirable leader. He was smart, articulate, funny and full of great stories.

Now that I've given myself some space to process this event in 1994, I've realized the profound impact it had on me without ever being aware of it. My relationship with my father was good but lacked any real quality time spent together. I resented him for always being away, that is, up until 1994. When he stopped touring on the Never-Ending Tour, I finally got to know him. He was finally in one place and available to me. Our relationship flourished in the seven years before his death. We became more than father and son, we became friends.

In those years I moved in with him at his house in Pacific Palisades, and we traveled abroad numerous times. He came to my rave productions in Colorado and gave me insight into how to handle security and the talent that I was flying in from around the world. He met all of my friends and by all accounts was a real father. He put in the time and made up for not being around for eight-plus years.

He wasn't perfect by any stretch of the imagination. But that doesn't mean he wasn't still my father. I loved him and I miss him like crazy. I'm sitting at my mother's rental house as I write these words, the house that overlooks the canyon and our burned family home. It's December 25, the anniversary of Anatoli Boukreev's death and a mere week from the one-year anniversary of the house burning down, the catalyst to this book.

This year has been incredibly painful. I've learned more about my family than I would have liked to have known. I've finally processed the death of my father and can now talk about it publicly without breaking down in tears, and I feel good about this book. It's real, it's brutally honest and I think my father is worthy of a biography; his life was incredible. A few years before passing, he told me, "I could die tomorrow and it would be okay. I've lived an amazing life. I did it all."

If I had to pick one thing to call his legacy, it actually wouldn't be his time with Bob. Maybe I'm a little annoyed some of that time wasn't spent with me, or maybe I give more weight to things that are a little more tactile. I consider his true claim to fame the coffee shops he built. The Unicorn in the fifties and the 18th Street Coffee House in the nineties, particularly the 18th Street Coffee House. It's his design and concept entirely and it's still exactly how he left it today. I spent a lot of time there writing this book; it's a fabulous place, and these days it's packed with writers. It's the premier writer's cafe in Santa Monica.

CHAPTER 11

~

Stalemate

My girlfriend and I discuss our plans for the day next to Bob Dylan's 18th Street Coffee House in Santa Monica. We're leaning against the wall of Bob's private boxing gym that's accessible through the walk-in cooler inside the cafe. April 27, 2014. *(Courtesy: Jacob Maymudes)*

B ob's coffee shop on 18th Street and Broadway in Santa Monica is a beautiful amalgam of recycled red brick, exposed wood beams, rusted metal and an eclectic mix of artwork. It's brightly lit from its southern-facing French glass doors that run the whole front-facing wall to the street and down the entire west-facing side that opens to a large patio, slightly reminiscent of a patio found in the Tuscany region of Italy. There's a small fountain attached to the north wall of the patio that sets the ambiance for the ten or so cast-iron tables and chairs. Old jazz swings through the air, carrying along subtle notes of coffee and freshly baked pastries. The inside is occupied by six round tables, some wood and some with ceramic tiles, sitting on a checkered black-and-white–tiled floor. The chairs are rose in color with black cushions that match the large bench seats adorning the four larger tables attached to the wall on the east- and west-side walls. The east is also the home of a large, twelve-foot painting by M. O. Malley that depicts a questionably friendlier vision of slavery life on a cotton plantation. It fits in with the other sparse pieces of black and white artwork of classic boxing athletes. The boxing memorabilia is a statement to Bob Dylan's personal taste, not only in style but hobby as well. The coffee shop isn't advertised as owned by Bob, and it never has been. It's not so much a secret but a philosophy that Victor and Bob shared: Bob's fame isn't worthy of selling by itself, it's not an asset to be exploited. If the coffee shop is worthy of being a hit spot, then the coffee shop will become a hit spot was the shared philosophy.

Behind the large counter, partial kitchen, pastry case and small storage area is a full-size, walk-in cooler door. A place that would most likely be the storage area for a commercial kitchen, but the magic of Bob's coffee shop isn't necessarily the coffee shop itself but the combination of three very important aspects of Bob's life. Through the full-size, walk-in cooler door is a full-size boxing gym, complete with a regulation boxing

ring, speed bags, punching bags, changing area and small reception area. This is Bob's personal gym that is used by him
and a variety of A-list celebrities and well-known boxing aficionados. When I was the only employee of the cafe in the late
nineties, I had regular encounters with Quentin Tarantino and
Ray "Boom Boom" Mancini. Quentin used the gym to drop
some weight after directing his breakout hit *Pulp Fiction* and
Boom Boom was in and out as Bob's sparring partner.

I found Boom Boom to be a very interesting sparring partner for Bob considering his pedigree—World Boxing Association lightweight champion from 1982 to 1984 and son of veteran
boxer Lenny "Boom Boom" Mancini. Ray has had thirty-four
career fights, twenty nine wins and five losses. His most notorious fight was at Caesars Palace on November 13, 1982, against
a twenty-three-year-old South Korean boxer named Duk Koo
Kim. Ray, then twenty-one, went fourteen rounds dominating
Kim for the win, a win that would transition to tragedy within
four days when Duk Koo Kim died from brain trauma sustained during the fight. Ray "Boom Boom" Mancini fell into a
deep depression in the aftermath of Kim's death and within
three years retired from boxing at the age of twenty-four.

I met Ray with my father at the coffee shop and spoke to him
on occasion; he was a nice man, soft spoken. He enjoyed training with Bob and spending time in the ring. My father was impressed by his legacy and always referred to him in high regard.

Above the boxing gym is a large storage area that, from time
to time, has been used as an office for the cafe. It's bizarrely
decorated with leopard print carpet, which counters any other

style choice in the entire compound. With the carpet in the storage area as the only exception, every other aspect of style, architecture, layout and vibe was my father's creation. Pulling from his own legacy of iconic coffee shops, Victor employed a "build it and they will come" mentality.

He found the building while on the hunt for investment property and convinced Bob of the idea of having his own cafe to foster late-night musicians and a place to work out. Bob agreed and gave his accountants the approval Victor needed to proceed. The building was damaged in earthquakes in the eighties and was left largely unused except for a synagogue that occupied the eastern half of the building. Because of its damage and not being centrally located, the building was a steal, so it was ripe for investment. Once Victor purchased the property, he single-handedly took on the construction of the cafe. He kept as much of the original exposed red brick as possible and purchased more recycled red brick to match when he built out the patio. The roof and French glass door walls had to be completely built from scratch, which is what I'm most proud of.

When I was eighteen, I took a job working for my father nailing the plywood down for the roof of the cafe. For weeks and weeks, I worked hand in hand with my dad building the roof and setting the seven large wood beams that run the width of the cafe. Due to the building's earthquake damage, my father spared no expense when building out the cafe. He fixed the foundation and went above and beyond all the legal city code requirements associated with earthquake retrofits. The cafe is built to last and I know this firsthand.

It's as nice, and as cool, as I imagine the Unicorn was in the late fifties, although there was one major difference: when Victor opened the Unicorn there was already a social group in desperate need of a place to congregate. His "build it and they will come" idea hinged on the same prospect. When all the finishing touches were completed and the cafe was ready for its first customer, the door swung wide open to a population drenched in corporate coffee from the likes of Starbucks, Coffee Bean and Peet's. I took the job as the cafe's first barista and literally didn't have anything to do all day other than facilitate my own addiction to cappuccinos. I would ride my skateboard around the block for hours waiting for somebody to stop in and order something. Anything would have made me happy, even a single glass of water was more than I served in the first few months running the cafe. Every moment I had I questioned my father's lack of advertising, and he would shoot back, "They will come. You'll see, when the word gets out. They will come." So in the meantime, the days rolled by as I slept on the counter of a vacant coffee shop.

The most exciting moments of any given day were when Victor and Bob would play chess sitting at one of the booths. They looked just like they did in the photos from four decades prior. It was exciting to see them play, although watching a chess game is strikingly similar to watching paint dry. My fascination had less to do with the physical act of playing chess and more to do with the folklore aspect of these two men playing chess. People from all corners of the globe have asked to play chess with my father just because he's shown in those old photos as Bob's chess partner. Kinky Friedman, the songwriter, novelist, politician and columnist, was one of the better-known personalities to proposition my father to a game of chess solely based on the decades-old photos. My father thought it was silly that someone would track him down just because he played chess with Bob, so he usually denied anyone who asked. Kinky was one of the few to have his offer accepted.

Victor and Bob's chess matches were silent for the most part; they appeared to communicate mostly on a physical level and if they did speak it was quiet and nearly inaudible.

When my boredom with the coffee shop reached its apex, I moved back to Colorado to continue my brief career as a rave promoter. It was something I enjoyed doing, more for the organizational aspect than the music or culture. In hindsight, I'm surprised how much my teenage years mirrored my father's early years. We both promoted and created environments for our social groups to hang out and enjoy the music of our generation. I completely acknowledge, however, that the folk music of the sixties spoke a message that resonated for decades to come and the techno and house music of my generation, well . . . my point is obvious.

My departure from the coffee shop left an opening for my sister, who was twenty-five, to fill in as the first official manager. She was given the keys and security codes and full control to make the coffee shop a success. It was a dream job for her, one that she cherished, and one that would ultimately be the cause of an irreparable rift between my father and his friend of nearly four decades. Aerie was not only given full control, she was also given little to no oversight. It was a bold move for anyone paying the bills, entrusting a young novice restaurateur to find the path to success with only a bizarrely existential mantra as the advertising platform, "Build it and they will come."

About a year after opening, Aerie had transformed the cafe into a lovely place to spend time, write or connect with a friend. It was wonderful except for the simple fact that it was still empty and bleeding money with every cappuccino given to the members of the private and exclusive hidden gym. Was it my sister's fault that the coffee shop on paper was a financial failure? Absolutely, of course it was. Was it Bob and Victor's lack of oversight and management that fueled Aerie's lack of experience and her inability to curb the downward financial spiral of the cafe? Absolutely. If you're going to believe in magic as your pathway to success, then you'd better be ready to pave that road with dollar bills.

When the end-of-the-year profit-and-loss statement was calculated, the accountants were only seeing one color: red. Bob went into a furious rage that precipitated an explosive and violent firing of Aerie, which Bob personally attended to in full view of my father. My father fought back in defense of Aerie's unjust treatment, not out of denial of the facts but because of Bob's sheer abandonment of respect for her. Her removal from management of the cafe may have been warranted, but the way it was done was unforgiveable.

The clash between Aerie and Bob was so intense that my father, bewildered, quit that instant. He walked out of the cafe and never returned; it may have been the last time he and his friend of four decades ever spoke to each other, at least without the presence of a team of lawyers. When he described the situation to me, he explained that he was so angry he wanted to hit Bob and the most rational thing he could do was walk away. In the months that followed, Victor sued for retirement funds. Bob probably felt the financial losses of the cafe was reason enough to resist giving anything to Victor. Eventually they settled out of court through a mutual hoisting of a white flag, an agreement that Tommy Masters helped solidify by inadvertently becoming the mediator. Bob gave Victor his retirement fund and the two cemented their separation as friends.

I'd hear my father say repeatedly, "All he had to do was apologize to Aerie and all of this would be different." I imagine that Bob feels the same way about receiving an apology regarding how the cafe was managed. I believe over time a truce would have manifested; I may be naive to think that, but I've had my own explosive ends to sacred friendships and over time repaired damage that for years seemed irreparable. Time can smooth out the jagged history between two opposing sides; that negative energy is a bag of bricks that's being carried and longs to be set down. Eventually it's just too much to carry and, even if the damage is not repaired, it can be forgiven. Unfortunately, time has one method for setting permanence: death.

CHAPTER 12

~

Tsumego

Victor points to the future in Los Barriles, BCS,
Mexico, 1995. *(Courtesy: Aerie Maymudes)*

After the dust had settled between my father and Bob
Dylan, he needed another source of income. He had
never been very forward thinking financially. He didn't have a
savings account, 401K or stocks and didn't own any real estate.

So once again, he was in dire straits. For many years his friends and colleagues suggested that he write his memoirs; it seemed like a logical step considering his well-traveled life and intimate relationship with Bob Dylan. However, my father never felt the need to do such a thing. It's something he never actually wanted to do. Victor spent his whole adult life protecting Bob, guarding him from reporters, photographers and the likes of Dylan biographers. For him to write his own book was in direct conflict to the role he played in Bob's inner circle; Victor was the gatekeeper to accessing Bob. Writing a book exposing his friend would make him one of "them," an outsider.

My father would joke and say, "I'm going to write the tell-all book! All the others only got ten percent right, but I know the whole story." I always felt that he wasn't serious. He would repeatedly bring up the arrangement Bob and he made about a possible memoir: "We agreed, whoever would die first, the other would write the book and fill it with lies!" It was a funny concept; he said they had this talk many times over the years. It was always brought up jokingly, but brought up nonetheless.

The reason I knew my father wasn't actually serious about writing his memoirs was this repeated statement, and neither of them had died. Therefore, the deal wasn't activated. Now, I know this was a joke between them and not a contract signed in blood. But there's a little bit of truth in every joke. And I do find it very interesting that within three years of my father's death, Bob wrote and published *Chronicles*, part one of his memoirs, and didn't mention Victor once in the entire book—despite the fact that every Dylan biographer in every Dylan book has at least touched on their friendship. I have to assume that the omission was intentional.

As my father's finances dwindled in 1995, he was pushed more and more toward the idea of writing a book. His internal struggle with this mounted, but ultimately he decided it was time. He did consider several job options, one of which was for Universal Music, but he explained to me that he just couldn't take on a desk job this late in his life. He was sixty-four, a year away from collecting Social Security. He was ready to retire, not join the workforce. He knew taking a corporate job was an uphill battle he was going to lose; anyone who spent a better part of a lifetime as a roadie in a rock band would find it rather difficult to sit in a chair all day, making calls and answering emails.

During a phone call, my mother broke it down for him and she leaned on the fact that he was flat-out broke and needed to do something before he was out on the street. He conceded to his fate as a writer and agreed to meet my mother's literary agent in New York, Kathleen Anderson.

Kathleen didn't need much to realize the potential book that Victor was capable of writing. In the weeks that followed, he flew out to New York and met her in person. His charisma and charm won her over and she signed him for representation. The next step was helping him write his book proposal. She set the guidelines, requesting three chapters and a chapter outline. Victor acknowledged that he would need help with the written word—that the stories were all there, but getting it on paper wasn't his forte.

Upon his return to Los Angeles he recruited the help of several friends who were writers. Victor would record his stories on a microcassette and the writers would transcribe what they heard. Having transcribed, they would massage the words into proper literary vernacular. He would set the tone and structure of the book and the writers, with his help, would fill in the subtle details.

He decided that his book would primarily be about Bob. He wouldn't focus on his personal history at all and split the book in half, the first being his time in the sixties when he met Bob, and the second half about the eighties and nineties when he returned as tour manager. He would leave out his time in New Mexico working for Dennis Hopper, building houses and purchasing properties for Bob.

The closest thing to a personal history was written into the first chapter of his book proposal; it started by juxtaposing historical events with the era he was growing up in. Statements like: "I was born the year the jukebox was invented," which is entertaining to read but much too vague to be factually true. He never mentioned which jukebox, of which there were many; statements like this one filled the first chapter and it read like an abridged folk music history lesson, not necessarily like a biography about him or Bob.

Victor officially started working on his book proposal in 2000 and settled on hiring an author in Brazil to help with the writing. He had conceived a chapter list and a synopsis for each chapter that was entertaining and seemed like a wild enough ride without overexposing his friend Bob. Many months would pass as Victor worked on the book. He would invite friends over for long drives around Los Angeles while he reminisced, shared old stories and smoked joint after joint. These rides were recorded to microcassette, the passenger's duty being to make sure the recording device was always on and always had tape available. The stories would ramble on in a nonlinear fashion, bouncing from the 1960s one second onto building the coffee shop in Santa Monica the next. The friends along for the ride would ask questions but would seldom keep Victor on track with one story. My father was an amazing storyteller; he perfected this ability early on in life, and by his midsixties he could keep an audience entertained for hours as his memory toured the world.

Email after email, fax after fax, he worked out the kinks of his book proposal which, when completed, was bought by George Witte at St. Martin's Press on July 24, 2000. The eighty-five thousand-word manuscript was due December 1, 2000. Victor agreed to the five-month schedule and immediately proceeded to fill out the rest of his concept for the book.

He continued in the same fashion, driving around with friends, jogging his memory and emailing back and forth with his writer in Brazil. As the months peeled away not much actual writing was completed. I believe this was due to the fact that Victor wasn't sending the audiotapes to Brazil; they were staying with him in the Pacific Palisades. This bottleneck in the process led to the manuscript being months late and required an extension from George Witte, but it would ultimately play a vital role in the creation of this book. It's solely because these audiotapes never left my father's hands that they're sitting in my desk now in Los Angeles and not in Brazil, and, most importantly, not in ashes in New Mexico.

By that January, George was waiting patiently for the book. He was ready to see something. Victor had more than enough audio but still little traction had been made. Over the holidays Victor had a falling out with his ghostwriter and was searching for a replacement, and this was drastically slowing the process. I was calling my father daily at this point; I was becoming increasingly excited about the process. It was one of these excited phone calls a few weeks into January that would prove to be life altering and change the course of the book, my personality and the history of our family.

Thursday, January 25, 2001, was my typical morning that started with an egg over medium, toast and some veggie bacon. It was slightly overcast in Oakland, California. I was cooking in the kitchen of my house that was nestled on the side of a small mountain on the far-east part of the city, a few hundred feet from an old strip mine that left a scar in the side of the mountain that was visible from every point in the city, even as far away as San Francisco. It was a stand-alone structure with three bedrooms; I shared the house with two friends, Eli and Larry, who attended Ex'pression Center for New Media with me, a newly opened digital arts school located in Emeryville, a few miles north. I was four months into studying filmmaking and 3D animation and was very much enthralled with the prospect of becoming a filmmaker—to the point that I made my father the subject of a planned documentary. I was very engaged and excited by his process of writing his memoirs. I wanted to help any way I could and felt his life and process of writing it down was worthy of film.

My father, however, hated this idea.

For him, the idea of writing his memoirs was already akin to pulling teeth. Granted, he was now excited about it, but that excitement was specifically manifested for the project. It wasn't automatic. Being on camera was even more of a stretch for him. He was notorious for jumping out of the way when still photos or films were being made. There's a shot in the D. A. Pennebaker film *No Direction Home* where you can see Victor physically jump out of the way when the camera pans around inside of a tour bus. That was his modus operandi: stay out of the limelight. He wasn't a friend to Bob to become famous; he was there solely to help him and help foster his genius. He understood Bob better than anyone ever understood Bob.

He took the same approach to avoiding the limelight with me. On occasion I would show up at his house in the Pacific Palisades for a weekend visit with my video camera, and he would be jumping and dodging anytime I pointed the camera in his direction. He would laugh about it, but at the same time was adamant that he didn't wish to be filmed.

The upcoming weekend, I planned another trip down to Los Angeles and this time I would bring Jeff Baldauf, a friend and fellow filmmaker. We were planning to step up our production value and bring lights and a proper sound package to film with. In preparation for this weekend I was calling my father daily, prepping him for our arrival. He wasn't buying it;

every time I mentioned filming him he would shoot down the idea. He was absolutely welcoming for our visit, but there was a line in the sand when it came to filming him. He just kept saying no.

Around noon I picked up the phone and dialed Josh Hassell, my father's assistant, who also rented the garage as a bedroom from my father. He had become an integral part of my family over the previous decade. I met him for the first time in Baja, Mexico, in the winter of 1993. I was on a trip with Gregory Gordon, who had been childhood friends with Josh. Gregory Gordon was the son of Greg Gordon, the doctor my mother was to marry but who had died mountain climbing in the Himalayas that October. His memorial service had been only a few weeks before we arrived in Baja. Gregory and I picked Baja as the place for our retreat from the troubling recent events that we had just endured. Josh had offered to host us at his parents' house in Los Barriles, knowing full well that we desperately needed to decompress from the emotional chaos that we had left at home.

That trip to Baja forged a friendship between Josh and me, and ultimately my family, which still remains strong to this day. After that winter he moved into my mother's house and helped her build the rock house for a couple of years, doing stone work and various other construction tasks. During the same time he helped remodel a house my mother had purchased, which was right next to Greg Gordon's house in Santa Fe. Despite him being nine years older than me, we became close friends.

That Thursday afternoon, I was calling Josh to discuss my

plans for the weekend. I was hoping to get his assistance in cornering my father for an interview. When the phone rang I was surprised to hear my father's voice. But something wasn't right. My father wasn't speaking clearly; he was forming complete words but the sentences were confusing and bizarre. "Six, nine bread under wing flight one now style," he said. I was baffled. "Dad?" I said. He responded with more confusing words, "Elegant, somebody nothing six, nice nine. Nine." My voice started to crack. "Dad, what's happening? Are you okay?" He understood me and responded to my questions. I knew that from the timing of his responses, there was a flow to our conversation, but the responses were heartbreaking. I told him to hang on and that I was going to call right back.

I hung up the phone and immediately dialed my mother. I was frantic, and when she picked up the phone I described my father's problems speaking and urged her to call him. She agreed and said to wait for her to call me back. I hung up as my heart sank to the floor and I waited.

One minute passed and my phone rang. "He's having a stroke, Jacob, you need to get an ambulance to him. I told him to go lie down and wait for help. Hurry, Jacob."

Alarm bells rang in my head, panic and every possible option whipped through my mind. My father, who had been perfectly healthy the day before, was in desperate need of help. I was in Oakland and he was in Pacific Palisades, a little less than four hundred miles away. My options were limited. I dialed 911, and when the operator answered, I frantically explained that I needed an ambulance to go to my dad's house.

When the dispatcher heard the address, she declined to help. The dispatcher said that she was at the Bay Area call center and had no method of contacting the emergency services in Southern California. I begged her to help and she repeated they couldn't do anything. I hung up and called information next. I asked the operator how I could get an ambulance to a house in another city. The operator didn't know the answer. She mentioned I could try calling the local police department, to which I agreed. I asked for the Pacific Palisades police department. She responded that there wasn't one and I panicked. I was melting down. She asked if there was another nearby city. I suggested Santa Monica, which I knew had a dedicated police department. The operator connected me.

I ran into another roadblock, but at least the Santa Monica police had answers to my questions. They gave me the direct line to the emergency dispatch for Los Angeles; what I didn't know is that Pacific Palisades is just a neighborhood of Los Angeles. It's not an actual city; it doesn't have its own call center, police or fire department. Once I was on the phone with the Los Angeles County emergency dispatch my quest for help was answered and they promptly sent an ALS (advanced life support) unit to my father's address. I hung up and called my mother. I notified her that an ambulance was en route. She responded by telling me I had to get the next flight to Los Angeles. She also said she was trying to contact my sister but she wasn't picking up her phone. I hung up and called my father back; he answered quickly but with the same confusing garbled words. I was destroyed; I didn't know what to say. I told him to hang tight and that an ambulance was on the way.

Of my very few regrets in my life, this moment is one that hurts the most. I hung up without telling my father I loved him. What I didn't know at the time was this would become the last moment my father was capable of understanding me and in twelve hours, he would be gone forever.

It turned out to be sheer coincidence that I had misdialed Josh's phone number entirely and called my father's home line instead. Josh was across town and wasn't planning to return the whole night. If I hadn't called by accident, my father could have passed away without any of his family members knowing. Josh would have found him the next day.

I made my way to the airport and on the way I called the Los Angeles County emergency dispatch. They informed me they had my father and were making their way to the UCLA Medical Center in Santa Monica and that he was still conscious.

My sister was unreachable because she forgot her cell phone at home that day. This simple lapse of memory was very unlike her; this was the first time she'd been without her phone in recent memory. It's possible she was too flustered as she ran out the door to Santa Barbara Community College—it was her first day of the spring semester of an architecture class that she wanted to take. When she arrived back at her apartment, her roommates informed her that there were numerous messages for her on the house answering machine and that her cell phone had been ringing nonstop. The messages were from our uncle and our mother, stating that our father was heading to the hospital and that she needed to make her way there at once.

Aerie immediately turned around, got in her car and headed south to the hospital. It was an hour and a half drive and she arrived at three p.m. She met our Aunt Zicel and Uncle August in the emergency room and saw her father for the first time on life support. He wasn't speaking. He was lying still, breathing, heavily connected to several machines. The doctors had intubated him with a foot-long plastic catheter that was pushed down his trachea to support his breathing. The doctors showed Aerie the CT scan of his brain and she could clearly see two large black areas, the size of two medium tomatoes. They were located in the right-side occipital area near his brain stem. The doctors went on to say that even if they had caught it earlier there was nothing they could do, that his condition was terminal.

Aerie spent the next three hours on her own with our father. She passed the time lying next to him, holding his hand and telling him stories about her first day at school. She remembers falling asleep and while dreaming, hearing him snoring. In her dream she imagined she was at his house and he was sleeping in his bedroom snoring while she was in the living room. When she awoke, it took a moment for her to realize the painful dichotomy between her dream and the immediate reality.

I arrived at LAX around five thirty p.m. and found a taxi waiting on the curb. I was in full-blown shock, barely able to speak. Navigating my way through the airport and arranging a taxi was a struggle for me. I wanted people to know the pain I was in but couldn't for the life of me explain why or what was happening. I spoke quietly and was very direct; any small talk was promptly ignored. I asked the cabdriver to take me to the emergency room at the UCLA Santa Monica Hospital. When I arrived, I found my sister at my father's side. I broke down and cried with her.

The sight of him on life support was damaging to my psyche, but not for the traditional reasons. My father told me on many occasions that he would never under any circumstance want to be left on life support, especially in the event of severe brain damage. It's the type of thing your parents could say to you and you just nod in agreement, hoping to move on to the next subject. Every time he brought up the idea of having to deal with this, I immediately disregarded it as an improbability.

This improbability was my painful reality; I was thrust into a world I wasn't prepared for. Just four months prior I was celebrating my twenty-first birthday with my father. The choices I was used to making were simple and typically had little or no consequence. Which course to study, what to eat, how do I ask the girl I like out on a date. The moment I walked into the hospital, I was faced with my father's living will, the hardest decision I've ever had to make, the removal of his life support. I was running on fumes, tired, emotionally wrecked, but if there's one personality trait I've inherited from the man that was lying in front of me, it was how to perform under pressure. I watched him do it on tour, making split-second decisions with major consequences.

I informed the attending doctors that I was going to remove

his life support. Then, to their confusion, I started to remove everything myself. The doctors said I had to let them do it; I politely declined their offer. My sister stood blocking them and I started to pull the foot-long plastic tube from my father's chest. He gagged and choked and when all the ventilators and nose oxygen tubes had been removed, he found his rhythm and started to breathe on his own. He was fighting to stay alive.

It's a complicated memory I have regarding this moment. I feel like I contributed to my father's death, for by impulsively removing his life support I may have destroyed any real chance of recovery he might have had, as little chance as that was. The doctors made it very clear that there was no hope. But I can't help thinking about the possibilities. Did I make the right choice? I like to think this was the right and only choice. But was it?

Once my father was breathing on his own his condition appeared to be fairly stable. We took this moment of stability to transfer him to a private room in the hospital and out of the busy emergency room. Doctors and nurses were still on hand, but this freed us up to grieve and to invite extended family and close friends to say good-bye.

My mother arrived shortly after Victor was transferred. I didn't realize this at the time, but the reason my mother was so readily available on the phone to talk to my father and to fly immediately out to Los Angeles from Santa Fe is that she was at the tail end of a year off from work as the medical officer for the Peace Corps in Ukraine and Cambodia to write her book about Anatoli Boukreev, her late fiancé.

I can see now that the book she was writing has strikingly

painful parallels to my own story about my father. Her book, *Above the Clouds,* was compiled and edited from collected diaries that Anatoli wrote while climbing Mt. McKinley, K2, Makalu, Manaslu and Everest, including his diary entries on the infamous 1996 Everest disaster. He's known in the elite circle of mountain climbers as one of the greatest adventurers of our time.

Where I have audiotapes to chronicle my father's adventures with Bob Dylan, my mother had journal entries written while Anatoli was in the death zone of the world's most dangerous mountains. The two couldn't have lived more different lives, yet were connected by one amazing woman. Their memoirs were written the same way, from a trail of pieces left to fascinate those interested in their particular professions and crafted into a story by someone who loves and misses them dearly.

My mother arrived at the hospital at nine p.m., and she quickly examined the CT scan and looked over all the diagnostic paperwork. She followed up and discussed the situation with the nurses and doctors on staff. She didn't expect to find anything positive in the situation, but she looked anyway.

It was easy to see his prognosis was grim. She joined us grieving and encouraged us to call his friends and invite them to stop by. Alan Weidel, known as "Bugs," stopped by first. He and Victor had been friends from the first time Bob Dylan and Tom Petty toured together.

A steady stream of people came and went as the hours passed: Katherine Tierney, an ex-girlfriend of mine, Josh Hassell, Steve and Diana Ungerleider, the mother of my best friend, Aaron. It was touching to have the support of our closest friends. By midnight all of the visitors had left and it was just the family members. By one a.m. we collectively requested that Victor receive some pain medication from the doctor, as all of us acknowledged that if Victor was given the opportunity to take some drugs in this ordeal, he probably would have happily requested them. The doctor was sympathetic to our request and returned at around one thirty a.m. Victor was breathing uneasily and his condition seemed to be deteriorating. By now the bleeding in his brain must have been incredibly severe. We knew the moment he was going to transition into death was near.

The doctor connected the IV with the pain medication and before she initiated the morphine drip, Victor took his last breath.

There was a dynamic change in the room as his life left his body. It had been twelve hours since I had spoken to him on the phone and now my father was gone forever.

In the days that followed, my mother, sister and I attended to his personal belongings. We called his friends in far-off places and made arrangements for his memorial service. We decided the most fitting place to host all his friends was McCabe's guitar shop on Pico Boulevard in Santa Monica, California. It's a musical instrument store that opened in 1958 and my father had purchased many of Bob's guitars there. It has two large rooms with an upstairs for musical instruction classes. The front room is mainly a showroom for the various types of instruments available. The back room is more spacious and is used frequently as a live music venue that holds about seventy-five people.

We picked a Saturday three weeks after Victor passed away as the date of our memorial service. The room was packed and many people told stories and reminisced about their friend Victor. Tom Petty came with his girlfriend, as did Tom's tour manager, Richard Fernandez, along with other lifelong Petty roadies Mark Carpenter and Bugs. Jackson Browne and his girlfriend came and showed support, and my father's best friends Michael Greene and John Phillip Law, iconic actors from the sixties, led the service and kept everyone in high spirits. It was a great night of music and laughing.

Without asking, several people offered to play: Bob Neuwirth sang a song, as did my girlfriend Cate Coslor, who led a sing-along to "Amazing Grace." She sang it with such conviction and passion that during her high notes only Tom Petty and Jackson Browne could be heard matching her octaves. At the end of the night Jackson Browne congratulated her on singing the hard version.

When it was all said and done there wasn't any sign of Bob Dylan. He was invited, but to my knowledge didn't show up. But there was talk of a mysterious character in a hoodie and glasses that came in late and left early. My sister noticed this person from the stage, but didn't manage to greet him. Now, it should be said that there were many bizarre characters in my dad's life, and who's to say who this person was. But, if it was Bob . . . my family thanks you for coming. My father always loved you.